Information Architecture

for the World Wide Web

Information Architecture
for the World Wide Web

Louis Rosenfeld and Peter Morville

O'REILLY™

Cambridge · Köln · Paris · Sebastopol · Tokyo

Information Architecture for the World Wide Web
by Louis Rosenfeld and Peter Morville

Copyright © 1998 O'Reilly & Associates, Inc. All rights reserved.
Printed in the United States of America.

Published by O'Reilly & Associates, Inc., 101 Morris Street, Sebastopol, CA 95472.

Editor: Linda Mui

Production Editor: Jane Ellin

Printing History:

> February 1998:   First Edition

Table of Contents

Foreword

In 1987, I wrote a small report using the Guide hypertext system. Guide was the first commercial hypertext product for personal computers, predating the Web by five years. I tried to make the hypertext document as easy to use as I could, and it was very small, as most hypertexts were in the early days. But even in this small information space of fewer than 50 pages, users reported severe disorientation problems. Around 1990, fairly large hypertexts with thousands of pages became available on CD-ROM, and usability studies by myself and others again found disorientation to be a serious issue.

Fast-forward to the end of the century. A large web site like *www.sun.com* can easily contain 25,000 pages or more. Furthermore, designing in this environment is much harder than on a CD-ROM, where the finished product is static and under strict control of a single program manager.

It is a sobering experience to observe usability studies of Web users. If you give people a specific problem to solve on the Web, they will only rarely succeed in arriving at the correct solution. Instead, users often end up very close to the solution without knowing it, and with poor information architecture, "being close" is completely worthless.

In five years of lecturing about Web design at events in thirteen countries on four continents, I have met hundreds of customers who have almost all made the same mistakes in their Web projects. Worse, I have made these mistakes myself. I finally came to realize that the reason for these mistakes is that the Web intrinsically leads you down the wrong path if you approach it without knowing its special characteristics. The natural way most people run Web projects leads to mistakes at all levels:

- Business model: treating the Web as a marketing brochure and not as a fundamental shift that is changing the way we conduct business in the network economy.

- Project management: outsourcing to multiple agencies without coordination.

- Information architecture: structuring the site like the company's own org chart instead of reflecting the users' view of the service.

- Page layout: using heavy graphics because they look gorgeous on the art director's high-end color monitor where they are downloaded over a direct line to the server.

- Content authoring: writers don't realize the need to cut their copy in half for online readers. Neither do they modularize the text into multiple hypertext nodes.

- Linking: banning external links in an attempt to imprison the user on your own site.

A web site must grow from a carefully planned information architecture for users to be successful in finding pages and accomplishing tasks. Confused users, lost users, and dissatisfied users can quickly turn into no users.

Companies that are new to the Web are destined to make all the same mistakes as everybody else, unless they learn from those of us who have been in the trenches for some time and seen these problems again and again. If Rosenfeld and Morville were Web Marines, their uniforms would be filled with medals for the battles they have fought and often won. Please listen to their war stories instead of getting wounded yourself.

Jakob Nielsen
Atherton, California
January 1998

Preface

Although information architecture may seem to be a high-handed and daunting term, it's really nothing new or mysterious. Think about it: why did the Ten Commandments come to us as two huge stone tablets? Perhaps Moses preferred a trifold design, or a portable wallet-size version, only to be overruled by his Project Manager. In any case, *someone* decided how to present the information to that audience of potential users milling about at the foot of Mount Sinai.

From clay-tablet scribes to medieval monks to the folks who organize your daily newspaper, information architects have contributed in subtle but important ways to our world. Information architects have balanced the whims of authority with those of unforgiving users of every stripe, while forcibly fitting their efforts into the constraints of the available information technologies. In many cases, information architects have been responsible for major advancements in those technologies.

The World Wide Web is the latest advancement in information technology, and, as with the previous innovations, certain principles carry over and others must be completely reexamined and overhauled. Because the Web integrates so many technologies and content types into a single interface, it challenges designers of web sites and intranets greatly.

Our Perspective

We believe that truly successful web sites, especially large and complex ones, demand the expertise of professionals from many different disciplines. Besides information architects, great sites also require the skills of programmers, graphic designers, technical specialists, marketers, copywriters, project managers, and others. This book concentrates on the skills needed for information architecture; although we discuss these other disciplines when we can, we are *not* graphic designers, programmers, or anything but information architects, so everything we say about those areas should be taken with a very large grain of salt.

As information architects, two major factors influence us:

- Our professional backgrounds in the field of information and library studies.

- Our experience in creating information architectures for large, complex web sites, primarily for corporate clients.

Many librarians have responded slowly to new information technologies like the Web. Some librarians feel that their value as professionals will be diminished as "virtual libraries" supplant those filled with physical books and periodicals. Many librarians fear that the public will bypass them and go directly to the source via the Internet. The truth is, however, that skills in information organization and access are more and more necessary in this era of information explosion. We have found that the demand for our skills in classifying and organizing information in web sites has grown beyond our wildest dreams, so we believe that you, your sites, and their users will benefit from our profession's perspective.

Between us, we have many years of experience in creating information architectures for web sites and intranets. At Argus Associates, our consulting firm, we concentrate on this area almost exclusively, and we have helped lots of large clients develop architectures that provide firm foundations for high quality web sites. We also have the benefit of working with and learning from experts from other companies who have backgrounds in other disciplines (our joint venture is called, aptly, Allied Studios). Besides our positive experiences, being in the "business" has given us many opportunities to make mistakes and ample time to learn from them. We hope you will benefit by learning from our mistakes as well as our successes.

You don't need a library degree to be a successful information architect. Despite the requirements listed in some job descriptions, it's hard to have had years of experience within this fledgling medium. More important than either of these two factors is common sense, plain and simple. The Web is too new for anyone to feel secure in claiming that there is a "right way" to do things. Web sites are multifaceted, and can support many different ways of presenting information. This book clarifies different approaches to web site architecture, and provides you with the tools and concepts you need to determine the best approach for your site.

Who This Book Is For

We're convinced that *everyone*, novice and wizard, should invest considerable time and energy into their web site's information architecture, especially if the goal is to build a large, complex web site or intranet. As we don't use lots of technical jargon, and because the topic of information architecture is so centered around users, we wrote this book to be accessible to anyone who has used the World Wide Web more than once or twice.

The reality is that most novice site developers are blinded by the excitement created by the Web's technical and graphical possibilities and don't immediately key in on the intangible value of information architecture. So this book probably will be most beneficial to readers who already have a site under their belt, particularly:

- Anyone who maintains a web site, intranet, or extranet where users get lost.

- Anyone who maintains a web site, intranet, or extranet where users have difficulty finding the information they need.

- Anyone who faces huge amounts of complex content and wonders how they'll ever organize the terrible mess into a usable and useful web site or intranet.

- Anyone who confuses web *page* design with web *site* design.

The authors work exclusively as information architecture consultants for large corporate clients; knowing our background will help you understand our biases. However, this book isn't written solely for people who work as outside consultants to corporations. For example, when we talk about clients, don't let that stop you from reading on; chances are that, without knowing it, you also have clients. It might be your boss or other coworkers. It might be the other members of your web development team. Maybe in a way *you're* the client. The guidelines for working with a client will hold true regardless of whether the client is from your organization, another organization, or yourself.

How To Use This Book

This is not the typical O'Reilly animal book that tells you how to build a Unix firewall machine from a box of toothpicks and an old coffee maker. There are no code listings, no listings of function parameters, and no workarounds on little-known bugs in SunOS 4.1.4. While the content may be different, the format of this book is much the same: first we tell you why you need to know something, then we tell you what you need to know, and then we show you how to put it to practical use.

Here is a description of the contents:

Chapter 1, *What Makes a Web Site Work*, forces you to walk in the shoes of site users, ensuring that you'll consider their needs as you design the architecture.

Chapter 2, *Introduction to Information Architecture*, provides you with some context for the field, and describes the information architect's role in developing web sites.

Chapter 3, *Organizing Information*, describes options for building organization structures, the backbones of any site, and organization schemes that meet the needs of your site's various audiences.

Chapter 4, *Designing Navigation Systems*, helps you to choose from among the various ways that you can make your site browsable.

Chapter 5, *Labeling Systems*, provides you with approaches to determining and creating effective and descriptive content labels that your site's users will understand.

Chapter 6, *Searching Systems*, helps you to understand how people really search, and describes indexing and search interface improvements that result in better searching performance.

Chapter 7, *Research*, makes sure you're prepared to move forward by helping you to learn about the site's mission and vision, budget, timeline, audiences, content, and functionality.

Chapter 8, *Conceptual Design*, provides you with the tools and approaches you need to capture the ideas that will drive the information architecture.

Chapter 9, *Production and Operations*, describes how you and your blueprints will affect and guide the production of the site.

Chapter 10, *Information Architecture in Action*, is a case study that demonstrates the evolution of an information architecture for a real client.

While this book stands on its own, we also encourage you to learn more about the disciplines from which information architecture borrows many of its principles. In the *Selected Bibliography*, we've listed several publications that might be interesting to you as further reading.

Text Conventions

In this book, we follow these conventions:

Italics are used for email addresses, URLs, and for emphasis.

`Courier` is used for code examples.

Other (Really Important) Conventions

In this book, we talk about web sites. Not web pages, not home pages. *Web sites.*

Why are we so hung up on this term?

Because a great wrong has been committed, and it's time to right it. You see, somewhere, sometime way back in early Web pre-history when the terminology of the Web first got started, someone decided that home pages were cool.

So, the people who were creating content for the Web began thinking of their output as pages. Discrete, singular. Stand-alone. Sure, these pages were linked to other pages, but the emphasis was placed on the page as the ultimate product.

The Web is magical. It allows us to link together so many things in ways never before possible. It is fantastic that an image of Shakespeare can link to a page that provides a short biography of the great Bard, which can, in turn, link to another page that opens us up to the fascinating history of Elizabethan England. And so on.

The whole of those pages and their links is much greater than the sum of the parts. That whole is what we call a web site.

Thinking in terms of web pages or home pages too easily limits your field of vision to the trees and not the forest. The goal of this book is to help you master web architecture so that you can design wonderful forests. So from here on, think in terms of sites first and foremost. If we slip into incorrect usage, please email us your flames.*

We also should clarify that we use the term *web site* to include sites available via the Internet, intranets, and extranets. We hope you'll find this book useful regardless of what type of web site you are developing.

---

* Louis Rosenfeld and Peter Morville can be flamed at *lou@argus-inc.com* and *morville@argus-inc.com*, respectively.

We'd Like to Hear from You

We have tested and verified all of the information in this book to the best of our ability, but you may find that features have changed (or even that we have made mistakes!). Please let us know about any errors you find, as well as your suggestions for future editions, by writing:

O'Reilly & Associates, Inc.
101 Morris Street
Sebastopol, CA 95472
1-800-998-9938 (in US or Canada)
1-707-829-0515 (international/local)
1-707-829-0104 (FAX)

You can also send us messages electronically. To be put on the mailing list or request a catalog, send email to:

nuts@oreilly.com (via the Internet)

To ask technical questions or comment on the book, send email to:

bookquestions@oreilly.com (via the Internet)

Acknowledgments

Acknowledgments are both the most enjoyable and most treacherous part of writing a book. It's a wonderful feeling to reach the point where thanks are in order and to recognize the many people who participated in the experience, directly or indirectly. Yet it's awfully frightening to consider the strong possibility that we've left someone out. So we'd like to offer our apologies to anyone we have forgotten, and thank the rest:

Linda Mui and the rest of the editorial staff for their availability, high standards, and professionalism. The production team, which included Jane Ellin, the production editor; Mike Sierra, who converted the book and provided Tools support; Seth Maislin, the indexer; Robert Romano, the illustrator; Nancy Priest, the interior designer; Edie Freedman, who designed the cover; Elissa Haney and Claire Cloutier LeBlanc for production support; and Madeleine Newell, Nicole Gipson Arigo, Clairemarie Fisher O'Leary, and Sheryl Avruch for quality control. We now know firsthand why O'Reilly & Associates enjoys its reputation.

Lorrie LeJeune, O'Reilly's Product Marketing Manager, who got us into this mess in the first place, but kept prodding good-naturedly throughout the process. Without her this book would never have been written.

O'Reilly & Associates, for its willingness to delve into the risky waters of publishing a book on the slippery topic of information architecture. We also really appreciated the free books and tee shirts.

Our reviewers, Steve Champeon, Jennifer Fleming, Andrew Gent, David Golumbia, Peter Mahnke, Paul Morville, Jeff Stuit, and Roy Tennant. It was our dumb luck that such a cast was available and willing to provide us with their expert feedback.

The sponsors of the many sites profiled in this book. We greatly appreciate their granting permission to allow us to use images of their sites to give information architecture a more tangible treatment.

Our colleagues at Argus Associates, Samantha Bailey, Stephen Toub, and Christopher Farnum. They read our drafts, gave us critical feedback and ideas, kept the Argus ship afloat, humored us, and put up with our crankiness while we worked on this book.

Our colleagues at Allied Studios, who have taught us volumes about interdisciplinary design and teamwork: John Bidwell, Jeff Callender, Hans Masing, Tom Rieke, Peter Wyngaard, and all the other creative people at Q LTD and InterConnect of Ann Arbor.

Our teachers and mentors from the University of Michigan's School of Information: Dan Atkins, David Blair, Michael Cohen, David Hessler, Maurita Holland, Joe Janes, Dave Rodgers, Victor Rosenberg, Amy Warner, and the late Miranda Pao.

Our friends in the Internet and library communities for their good works and generous help: Scott Brylow, Abbot Chambers, Larry Coppard, John December, Andrea Gallagher, Tony Grant, Charles Harmon, Randy Horton, Keith Instone, Jakob Nielsen, Anna Noakes, Pat Schuman, Phil Sutherland, Heidi Weise, Rich Wiggins, and Ed Vielmetti.

Finally, we'd like to say a special thanks to our families for their love and support, and to our respective partners, Mary Jean Babic and Susan Joanne Morville, who put up with us during the whole ordeal. Thanks to all!

Louis Rosenfeld
Peter Morville
January, 1998

In this chapter:
- *Consumer Sensitivity Boot Camp*
- *If You Don't Like to Exercise...*

1

What Makes a Web Site Work

What is it about buildings that stir us? Regardless of whether we consider ourselves architectural connoisseurs or just plain folks, we all encounter different physical structures every day. Each building affects us emotionally, whether we realize it or not.

Just this evening, I spent time in a dark, smoky bar with original tin ceilings and exposed brick walls. The bar has been around forever, as have some of the patrons, but I chose to spend time sipping beer there rather than in the neighboring gleaming microbrewery that opened last year. The new place has a wider menu of beers, better food, and non-smoking sections, but tonight I preferred the old joint with the great graffiti on the bathroom walls.

After the bar, I went to a café to read. Ann Arbor has about 25 cafés, 10 of which are within walking distance of each other, and they're all decent places. So why did I go to this one? It has a great nook with soft chairs and a low ceiling, providing an almost totally enclosed space where I can have the privacy I want.

And now I'm back at the office. Our space is located in an old building that originally was a mechanic's garage. What was once the oil pit is now a sunken-level workspace for graphic designers. Exposed timber beams lift the roof high over an eclectic space conducive to creativity. After the garage closed, the building was a greasy spoon; my office is where the kitchen used to be. Repurposed every decade or so, our building has worn many hats over time and overflows with history. Back in 1918, the builder could never have conceived that it eventually would be occupied by a Cajun restaurant or a travel agency, much less an information architecture firm.

Why so much talk about the impressions that physical structures make on us? Because they are familiar to us in ways that web sites are not. Like web sites, buildings have architectures that cause us to react. Buildings and their architectures therefore provide us with great opportunities to make analogies about web sites and their architectures.

Buildings and their architectures are diverse. Consider the extent of architectural ground I covered in my brief evening jaunt. Buildings look different—or are architected differently—because they must cater to so many different uses, users, and moods. Warehouses, strip malls, and Chinese restaurants look and work the way they do because they are designed for varying uses. Drinking beer with friends, reading quietly, and working all require different environments to succeed. Web sites are the same; we visit them to learn about alternative medicine, play games, or vent our frustration. So each web site requires a different architecture, designed with its particular users and uses in mind.

Some architectures disgust us. Ask someone who owns a house with a flat roof how they feel about its architecture. Or someone who spends too much time in a kitchen with no counter space right next to the refrigerator. Or someone who works in a steel-and-glass high-rise with fixed windows that prevent the building's occupants from opening them and letting in fresh air.

Why do bad architectures happen so often? Because their architects generally don't live or work in the buildings they design. That hardly seems fair. The same is true of so many web sites. Why does that main page contain over a hundred and forty links? How come the contact information is buried so deep in the site? Why do I keep getting lost? Don't these web sites' architects ever use their own sites?

That's exactly what the next section is about. You can't really become a proficient web site architect unless you first know what it's like to really use the Web on a regular basis. In other words, the best web site producer is an experienced consumer. You must become the toughest, most critical consumer of web sites you possibly can. Determining what you love, what you hate, and why, will shape your own personal web design philosophy. In turn, drawing on your new sensitivity to web consumers' needs will make a great difference as you start designing and building your own web site. Reaching such a level of user-centered awareness sets you aside from every other web site developer; in a profession with such a low barrier of entry, it may be all you have to ensure that your work stands out.

Consumer Sensitivity Boot Camp

Regardless of your level of experience producing web sites, you should revisit Consumer Sensitivity Boot Camp before beginning a new site or new phase of an existing site. Why? Well, if you are an experienced site developer, you're probably too jaded to remember what it's like to be a new user (this has certainly happened to us). If you're new at this, then it's likely that you're so excited by design and technical options that you're too distracted to worry about the user. If you work for a large organization, its personality, jargon, and self-perspective may be so instilled in you that you can't begin to imagine what an outsider encounters when confronted by your corporate culture. So now is a good time to run through our Consumer Sensitivity Boot Camp exercise.

Start by assembling the people who will work on developing the site. If this is just you, bring some other folks on board so you have a broader set of perspectives to draw on. So pull together some friends, coworkers, or anyone with at least a little experience using the Web.

Just about everyone in the group knows from their own experiences that using a web site has both good and bad aspects; the secret is to unlock those sentiments by forcing the participants to articulate them. Do this by asking your group (and yourself) to brainstorm answers for the following two simple questions:

- What do you hate about the Web?
- What do you like about the Web?

Usually we start with the hate question, because, interestingly (and sadly) enough, it's almost always easier for people to talk about negatives than positives. In group settings, it's a great way to break the ice. As the participants spew their venom (or offer their niceties), jot each point down on a white board or flip chart.

Once these issues are aired, run through the positives and negatives. Discuss any natural groupings that you notice. We almost always find that the issues raised fall into three general areas: 1) Technical (e.g., effective use of interactivity, bandwidth/download issues); 2) Look and Feel (e.g., complementary aesthetics and functionality, the importance of good copyediting); and 3) Something Else (e.g., finding information sites, site navigation issues). Interestingly, these Something Else issues often directly relate to information architecture. As this is likely the first time the participants have ever been introduced to the concept of information architecture, we like to emphasize strongly that it really does exist and does merit the same consideration as more obvious, tangible areas such as graphic and technical design.

While the group categorizes these issues, some interesting paradoxes often emerge. For example, a common like about web sites is their compelling use of images. Yet a common dislike is gratuitous use of images, many of which take a long time to download without providing useful information or adding any benefit. As such paradoxes emerge, light bulbs ought to appear over the heads of everyone in the group (at least those who thought that building a web site would be easy). It should now be obvious that building a web site and doing it well are two hugely different tasks. If not, be concerned; your colleagues may not be up to the arduous site design and production process that awaits them.

The final step is to see if the members of your group reach consensus on these issues. If you'll be working together on developing the site, it's important that the team comes to a consensus regarding what works and what doesn't. If there are disagreements on certain issues, it's important to acknowledge those and explore why they exist. We often find that these disagreements are directly tied to disciplinary backgrounds. Pointing them out now is a good way to sensitize the participants to something that ought to be, but unfortunately isn't, always obvious: different points of view are represented among both consumers and producers of web content. There isn't necessarily a Right Way or Wrong Way of going about things, but discussing these issues in advance gets them on the table, and gets you that much closer to making a sound and defensible decision once you are ready to begin developing your site.

Of course, you and your colleagues will ideally carry over into the development process your bittersweet memories of what it's like to actually use web sites, resulting in a more user-centered product.

If You Don't Like to Exercise...

Maybe you don't really want to go to Consumer Sensitivity Boot Camp. So we've decided to give you a break and share with you the types of likes and dislikes we often hear from our own clients and colleagues, sprinkled liberally with our own biases.

What Do You Hate About the Web?

We found that compiling this list was quick work, as we see these design sins every day, and have committed quite a few over the years ourselves.

Can't find it

You know great information is available in a certain web site. At least, that's what you've heard, but every time you look for it, you can't find it. Maybe you were even bounced out of the site altogether through some external link. Sites like these often provide no index, table of contents, or site map, and no search facility. Even worse, the labels they use for their information are obscure; they may mean something to someone else, but not to you. Another problem can be when the content is moved around repeatedly, so that something here today is gone tomorrow.

Even when users aren't looking for particular information within a site, they can often be befuddled by a poor navigation system. A common example of this phenomenon is navigational headers and footers that are inconsistent from page to page. Another example: backgrounds and color schemes that radically change from page to page within the same site. Users may wonder if they are even using the same site at all.

Poor graphic design and layout

It's becoming almost passé to complain about web sites with huge image files that take a long time to download, but people tend to hate a host of other graphic design-related problems. Pages crowded with text, links, graphics, and other components make it harder for users to find information on those pages. Many designers forget that white space is as important a component of a page as anything else. Crowding results in long pages that require scrolling to get to important items.

Paradoxically, people also complain about graphic design on the Web being both dull and excessive. We've all yawned our way through long pages of text after text after text, without a break for the eye, all against the backdrop of a dismal gray background. We've also encountered high-octane graphics with loudly crashing colors that make our eyes burn, or purposely minimalist designs that sacrifice usability for a bizarre sense of aesthetics (e.g., using the same colors for both links and unlinked text).

A large part of the problem, of course, is that graphic design is a profession whose mastery requires more than just picking up a copy of Adobe Photoshop or Illustrator and the URL for a clip art archive. Effective graphic designers step back and think about the objectives of the site, its sponsor, and the particular challenges of their project before plunging in. Also, good graphic designers don't tend to see every project as an opportunity to exclusively showcase their own work. Like it or not, the Web doesn't require us to have MFAs to design graphics for our sites.

Gratuitous use of bells and whistles

Technology is great: it allows us to do so many neat things! It's often hard to resist showing all the neat things we can do with web technologies. Wonderful things, from trite counters to moderately annoying, revolving "NEW!" animated GIFs to frustrating frames to the Java applets that, after taking eons to download, don't add any functionality.

This may seem to be a very Luddite perspective, but, like graphics and other aspects of web site design, technologies should directly aid users in getting what they want out of a site. There shouldn't be any unnecessary bells and whistles. If the desired effect of the technology is to attract and captivate the user, then it must be very carefully applied; unless the technical designer is quite talented, the user will have likely seen it before and seen it done better.

Inappropriate tone

An interesting aspect of designing user interfaces for *any* medium, Web or otherwise, is deciding what you can expect from the user. If a site is designed to speak one language (e.g., it makes liberal use of organizational jargon) and the user speaks another (e.g., he or she is a medical professional who is used to communicating with scientific terms), who should make the effort to learn the other's language? It's generally assumed that the burden is on the site and its designer to communicate in the language of the user, and not vice versa. In the heat of the moment, it's very easy to forget about the audience and instead concentrate on self-expression, technological options, or some other distraction from user-centered design. The result is a site that doesn't speak to the user, but forces the user to try to get inside the mind of the site's copyeditor.

Designer-centeredness

There's nothing wrong with self-expression, but most large, complex web sites aren't geared toward the self; the huge investment made in them requires that they be designed for use by many people. Yet we've all encountered sites ostensibly set up for companies that are little more than avenues for webmaster self-expression, including such oldies as lists of "my favorite links" and an image of said page designer. There is an ongoing debate at many companies as to whether or not to allow their employees to maintain their own personal information on the Web; keeping that stuff off the official web site seems to be a good practice.

Under construction

We always encounter sites that are under construction. In fact, sometimes they seem to have been abandoned. If a site's content and functionality don't merit launching, then why launch it? If it has already launched, it's generally understood that no site is ever really finished. Users would probably prefer to know nothing of far-down-the-road changes than see an under construction graphic or read a note explaining what's happening, why it's taking so long, or whose fault it is.

Lack of attention to detail

Then there are sites full of haphazard information, rife with typos, broken links, out-of-date content, factual errors, or poorly executed HTML. A lack of proofreading, link checking, HTML validation, and, in general, any attention to detail demonstrates a lack of professionalism and sensitivity to the user.

What Do You Like About the Web?

This section is considerably shorter than its predecessor. Does this mean that there is less to like about the Web than there is to hate? Not at all. It means that, as with anything else, we take success for granted. While poor design actively frustrates and angers us, quality is quiet, passive, and often transparent. Whether we're discussing everyday things such as door knobs and keyboards, or the look and feel of a web site, we generally take note only when things don't work. You will notice, however, that the sites we love all share the same characteristic: they integrate each of the key aspects of web site design: information architecture, technical design, and graphic design. Later we'll discuss many quiet techniques to aid in web site design and development, but for the time being, let's stay in web consumer mode.

Aesthetics

Superficial though it may seem, we use and enjoy some sites simply because they are aesthetically pleasing. However, it is rarely because they simply contain the most pleasing graphics. An attractive site is distinguished by a cohesive and consistent look that presents a unique identity for the site and, ideally, for its sponsors. These sites' graphics and page layouts are integrated with their other features, such as navigation systems, custom applications, editorial style, and so forth. Therefore, the user doesn't notice the individual images so much as he or she enjoys the overall atmosphere and experience created by the site. Behind such sites stand graphic designers for whom design is about the whole page, not just the images (just as information architects concentrate on the whole site, not just pages). The intangible qualities of this type of site are its consistent and functional graphic elements, as well as its integration of page layout and graphic elements.

Big ideas

Some sites are thought provoking: they present ideas that may change the way you look at things. The copy in these sites may be written in styles that are reminiscent of mystery novels, gossip, manifestoes, poetry, or Sunday morning political discourse. You might completely forget that you are using the Web. Great writing and intelligent page layout aren't what's obvious about these sites; their ideas are. The intangible qualities of this type of site are its quality writing, copyediting, and overall ability to communicate ideas effectively.

Utility

Above all, we visit and return to a web site because we find it useful in some way. Ideally, all sites incorporate special technologies seamlessly, but some have no choice: their end-all and be-all is to serve you some nifty application. Search engine sites, for example, are more engine and less web site. Or with Web-based games, the HTML files are really quite secondary. You don't go to any of these places because they are web sites. You go to them to do research, keep up with the news, or have fun. For that matter, you won't go to them if they don't function well. Can you imagine if AltaVista were down for an afternoon? The intangible quality of this type of site is that its applications work well and match the site's goals, or perhaps *are* the site's goals.

"Findability"

While one of the most painful parts of using the Web is trying to find something on a bad site, a real joy can come from a site that makes it easy to find its useful content. Sites that use well-planned information architectures are as magical as the phenomenon of the Internet itself: both are incredibly effective at the tricky task of routing users and packets respectively. Strong information architectures are especially important for large web sites: to unlock the power found in those huge volumes of content, these sites need navigation systems and organizational schemes that feature the information that people need to know and hide the stuff that would otherwise get in the way. The intangible qualities of this type of site are organization, navigational ease, and the fact that the site doesn't get between the users and the information they need.

Personalization

Users increasingly demand from web sites the ability to get information that is customized to their interests and needs. Many web sites now tailor their content through the use of architectures designed to support multiple audience types, or through technologies that allow users to profile their personal interests. These kinds of sites demonstrate that their designers are sensitive to the fact the users aren't all the same. Besides the influence of users, marketing efforts have driven this trend to a large degree: why present general information to the broadest audience (e.g., trying to sell tobacco products to everyone, including the anti-smoking activists) when you can target information to prequalified market segments (e.g., selling expensive cigars to yuppies)? The intangible quality of this type of site is that its designers realize that users are different, and make provisions to address their unique needs.

A Last Word About Consumers

Web consumers have an almost mythically short attention span. No medium compares. When visiting a new site, users often give up on it *before* its main page has fully downloaded. Sure, cable TV watchers can surf channels rapid-fire, but few systems carry more than 60 or 70 channels. The Web, on the other hand, has hundreds of thousands of "channels" only a click away.

Considering the challenge of designing sites that users love while also accommo-dating their microscopic attention spans, it may seem that the web site designer has a snowball's chance in hell of succeeding. However, if completing our Boot Camp exercise doesn't make the prospective web site designer at least a little uncomfortable, then there is an even bigger reason to worry. Besides producing a useful list of likes and dislikes, this exercise should strike some fear into the hearts of all web site designers. It should now be apparent that, regardless of how low the barrier of entry is for writing HTML pages, designing successful sites is an incredible challenge.

Completing the Boot Camp exercise makes you a more advanced web site consumer. It may force you to take a thoughtful step back before diving into the inviting but treacherous pool of web site design. As you jump in, your next step will be to decompose the huge problems discussed here into something more manageable. You'll do this by asking important questions, such as:

- What is it that we are designing, and why?
- Who will use it?
- How will we know if we've been successful?

Helping you answer those questions is the purpose of this book.

2

In this chapter:
- *The Role of the Information Architect*
- *Who Should Be the Information Architect?*
- *Collaboration and Communication*

Introduction to Information Architecture

Information Architect: 1) the individual who organizes the patterns inherent in data, making the complex clear; 2) a person who creates the structure or map of information which allows others to find their personal paths to knowledge; 3) the emerging 21st century professional occupation addressing the needs of the age focused upon clarity, human understanding and the science of the organization of information.*

—Richard Saul Wurman

The Role of the Information Architect

Now that you know right from wrong from the web consumer's perspective, you're in a much better position to develop a web site. But besides needing a sophisticated knowledge of what works for consumers of the Web, what's actually involved in creating a web site?

Obviously, you need HTML pages. Maybe you'll grab a good HTML book or a decent HTML editing package. Maybe a high school kid can do the trick for peanuts. What about the copy for those pages? It needs to come from somewhere—perhaps existing brochures and documentation; perhaps it needs to be written from scratch. You'll also need some graphic design expertise to make sure that the pages are laid out with effective use of text, white space, and attractive images. Of course you'll need a server that is connected to the Internet; this you can lease, or you can buy one of your own. If you do, just be sure to hire someone sufficiently technically astute to administer that server. Perhaps that

---

* Richard Saul Wurman, *Information Architects,* ed. Peter Bradford (Zurich: Graphis Press Corp, 1996).

person should also write the CGI, Perl, ActiveX, Java, and other scripts that make the site interactive. What's missing? Maybe a project manager to make sure all these folks work together to develop the site without running behind schedule and over budget.

So now you're all set to design your web site, right?

Well, not quite. What's missing from this picture is a definition of *what the site will actually be, and how it will work.*

This may sound obvious, but for most web sites, it's true: design and production storm ahead without any unifying principle to guide the site's development. A web site essentially can be anything you want it to be and could cost millions of dollars, take years to complete, and cost thousands of lives to develop. To avoid such overkill, it will need to be defined somehow: it will need a *definition.*

That's the main job of the information architect, who:

- Clarifies the *mission* and *vision* for the site, balancing the needs of its sponsoring organization and the needs of its audiences.

- Determines what *content* and *functionality* the site will contain.

- Specifies how users will find information in the site by defining its *organization, navigation, labeling,* and *searching systems.*

- Maps out how the site will accommodate *change* and *growth* over time.

Although these sound obvious, information architecture is really about what's *not obvious.* Users don't notice the information architecture of a site unless it isn't working. When they do notice good architectural features within a site, they instead attribute these successes to *something else,* like high-quality graphic design or a well-configured search engine. Why? When you read or hear about web site design, the language commonly used pertains to pages, graphic elements, technical features, and writing style. However, no terms adequately describe the relationships among the intangible elements that constitute a web site's architecture. The elements of information architecture—navigation systems, labeling systems, organization systems, indexing, searching methods, metaphors—are the glue that holds together a web site and allows it to evolve smoothly. To a novice, this terminology is not very clear. These elements are extremely difficult to measure, and therefore even harder to compare. You really have to spend time using a site and get a feel for it before you can confidently talk about a site's information architecture.

Yet, we know these things are important. How? Well, consider your responses to the Boot Camp exercise in Chapter 1. How many of the likes and dislikes are *not* related to technical issues, copyrighting, or graphic design? Remaining issues are probably tied to information architecture. Although perhaps indirectly, a poorly planned information architecture will adversely affect those other areas.

Well-planned information architectures greatly benefit both consumers and producers. Accessing a site for the first time, consumers can quickly understand it effortlessly. They can quickly find the information they need, thereby reducing the time (and costs) wasted on both finding information and *not* finding information. Producers of web sites and intranets benefit because they know where and how to place new content without disrupting the existing content and site structure. Perhaps most importantly, producers can use an information architecture to greatly minimize the politics that come to the fore during the development of a web site.

The Consumer's Perspective

Consumers, or users as we more commonly refer to them, want to find information quickly and easily. Contrary to what you might conclude from observing the architectures of many large, corporate web sites, users do not like to get lost in chaotic hypertextual webs. Poor information architectures make busy users confused, frustrated, and angry.

Because different users have varying needs, it's important to support multiple modes of finding information. Some users know exactly what they're looking for. They know what it's called (or labeled), and they know it exists. They just want to find it and leave, as quickly and painlessly as possible. This is called known-item searching.

Other users do not know what they're looking for. They come to the site with a vague idea of the information they need. They may not know the right labels to describe what they want or even whether it exists. As they casually explore your site, they may learn about products or services that they'd never even considered. Iteratively, through serendipity and associative learning, they may leave your site with knowledge (or products) that they hadn't known they needed.

These modes of finding information are not mutually exclusive. In a well-designed system, many users will switch between known-item searching and casual browsing as they explore the site. If you care about the consumer, make sure your architecture supports both modes. While attractive graphics and reliable technologies are essential to user satisfaction, they are not enough.

The Producer's Perspective

Since few organizations are completely altruistic, they usually want to know the return on their investment for information architecture design. In other words, what's in it for them? First, a disclaimer. Buying information architecture services is not like investing in a mutual fund. You can't calculate hard and fast numbers to show the exact benefit of your investment over time.

Nonetheless, you *can* demonstrate the value to the organization through less scientific means. Depending upon the goals and nature of your site, you may even be able to defend your investment with some not-so-hard numbers.

Consideration of value to the producer takes us back to the consumer. If you're producing an external web site, this involves actual and prospective customers, investors, employees, and business partners, not to mention the media and senior executives within your organization. Do you really want to frustrate any of these people? What is the value of quickly and easily helping them find the information they need?

If you're producing an intranet, the employees of your organization are the consumers. What is the cost of their time spent to find the information they need? What is the cost when employees don't find the information they need?

Finally, we need to consider the actual costs of designing and implementing the architecture. A well-designed, diplomatic architecture can prevent costly political battles that can stop a project in its tracks. The cost of time spent by high-level executives arguing over which department's information belongs on the main page can skyrocket if you're not careful. A well-designed scaleable architecture can prevent doing it all over a year later. Far too many architectures are crushed under the weight of their own content. Redesign of the information architecture impacts all other aspects of the web site, from graphical navigation bars to the content itself, and it can be a very costly adventure.

Let's illustrate with a real-life example. Recently, we met with about ten members of a large client's web site development team. Because we were in the early stages of the planning process, we had just reviewed the client's likes and dislikes, and were determining their web design philosophy. Now we were ready to begin *defining* what their site would be.

In discussing the site's likely users, around seven or eight audiences were suggested. Five or six major goals of the site were determined. Finally, we talked about the main areas of content and functionality that the site would include. This wish list included thirty or forty items. We now had a lot of useful lists and ideas, but was the web site ready to be designed yet?

At this point, many site designers would happily dive in head first. Their work would be a site headed by a main page that included thirty or forty items and links, tried to please seven or eight different audiences, and ultimately failed at achieving its five or six goals. This is what happens when the big picture of a site is ignored.

Consider what happens to a site with a single designer who sees only the trees, not the forest. Now add an order of magnitude: large organizations, rife with complex goals and messy politics, often have sites designed by ten individuals with their own vision of the site, their own deadlines and goals to meet, and their own politics to play. Is it any wonder that these sites often work so poorly, even when huge investments of time and money are made in them?

Succinctly, information architecture is about understanding and conveying the big picture of a web site.

Back to our client's committee of ten tree-people. They were still struggling over what the site would ultimately be. Which goals are the most important? Should the site be informational, entertaining, or educational? Should there be one main page for all audiences, or one for each audience? Should we design an architecture that organizes the site's information by topic, by function, or in some other way? Who within their organization should own and maintain the information in the site? What kind of navigation and wording would make the most sense?

Our last meeting ended in frustration, as the committee members argued but never resolved these points. They were especially unhappy, as they'd thought that designing a web site was supposed to be fun, without the haggling over audience definitions, dredging up of organizational politics, and dealing with other unpleasantries that had come up in the discussion. Some even expressed concern that we shouldn't even bother wading into this swamp and instead should start *doing* something, like gathering together the site's content, pushing forward on the graphic design, and so on.

Having exposed so much frustration, we were obviously on the right track. Why?

Because these thorny and confounding issues of information architecture must be resolved during the design process, *before the site is built.* If we were to avoid answering these questions and the site's development was to proceed, these issues wouldn't go away. Instead, *the burden would be on the site's users* to understand how to use and find information in a confusing, poorly-designed web site. Of course, we know that a frustrated user will click and leave with a bad memory of the site, likely to never return. Without a clear information architecture, the site's maintainers wouldn't know where to locate the new information that the site would eventually include; they'd likely begin to quarrel over whose content was more important and deserved visibility on the main page, and so on.

Who Should Be the Information Architect?

The information architect of a large, complex web site should be two things: someone who can think as an outsider and be sensitive to the needs of the site's users, and at the same time is enough of an insider to understand the site's sponsoring organization, its mission, goals, content, audiences, and inner workings. In terms of disciplinary background, the information architect should combine the generalist's ability to understand the perspectives of other disciplines with specialized skills in visualizing, organizing, and labeling information. As it's very difficult for someone to retain all of these characteristics, you'll have to make some compromises, but it's important to consider them as you search for that elusive information architect.

Thinking Like an Outsider

Because information architecture is largely about the big picture view of the organization, its goals, and its politics, a logical choice for the architect role is a senior person who knows the organization as a whole and who isn't involved exclusively within the activities of one department. A senior person can often think like an outsider even though being on the inside, and has enough clout to enlist other departments' resources when necessary. One drawback to choosing a senior level manager is that he or she may have so many other responsibilities that the work gets delegated out to staff, thereby negating the original goal of using a single, organizationally savvy person.

Another approach is bringing in a true outsider: a new hire or a consultant (we typically function in the latter role, but we are trying to avoid biasing our discussion too greatly). The great thing about outsiders is that they can get away with asking naive questions considered suicidal by insiders, such as "Why does your organization have two completely separate order fulfillment departments? The web site will confuse users if they can order products in two different, unresolved ways. Are there any politics going on here that we can get past to improve the site's design?"

Further, an outsider can ensure that the organization chart isn't the site's architecture, and challenge confusing orgspeak labels: "'Total Quality Product Dissemination Systems'? Oh, you mean 'Product Shipping Options.'" The drawbacks of bringing in a true outsider are that they can be expensive and can lack sufficient knowledge of the organization to do the job, thus delaying the project's progress.

Thinking Like an Insider

As many organizations can't afford to outsource information architecture services or move a head honcho into the role, the responsibility often goes to an insider who is not a senior level manager. Sometimes this is ideal; it's the people in the trenches who often know the most about an organization's processes, and how to get things done within that organization. For example, who knows an external web site's audiences better than a marketing specialist, sales rep, or product manager? Who knows an intranet's intended audiences better than a human resources specialist, corporate librarian, or switchboard operator? How many senior level managers can describe every step of their organization's fulfillment process, from product ordering to computing sales tax and shipping charges to warehouse picking to delivery? Someone needs this knowledge to mirror the process on the web site.

The problem with a lower-level person is that his or her knowledge may be too specific. Additionally, such a person often lacks the political base required to mobilize cooperation from others in the organization. A possible solution is to make information architecture this person's only job responsibility. This could allow him or her to step away from original duties and focus on the broader needs of the organization and the users of its site.

Disciplinary Background

Since information architecture is a relatively new field, you can't just post a job description and expect a flock of interested, competent, and experienced candidates to show up on your doorstep. Instead, you'll need to actively recruit, outsource, or perhaps *become* the information architect for your site. If you are looking for someone else, you might consider the disciplines listed below as potential sources. If you're on your own, it might be worthwhile to learn a little bit about each of these disciplines yourself. Or, if possible, find someone knowledgeable about them to work with you and complement your own expertise. In either case, remember that no single discipline is the obvious source for information architects; each presents its own strengths and weaknesses.

Graphic design

Most people who have written about and practice information architecture are graphic designers by training. This is not surprising; as mentioned, graphic design is much more than creating pretty pictures. It is geared more toward creating *relationships* between visual elements and determining their effective integration as a whole. On a page, printed or HTML, these elements include white space and typography as well as images. So graphic designers traditionally have been focused on the architectures of individual pages of information, which can be a weakness when building a web *site*.

Information and library science

We've found that our backgrounds in information science and librarianship have proven very useful in dealing with the relationships between pages and other elements that make up a whole site. By definition, librarians deal with organization of and access to information within information systems and are trained to work with searching, browsing, and indexing technologies. Forward-looking librarians (recently described as *cybrarians*) see that their expertise applies in new arenas unrelated to providing access to printed information stored in traditional libraries. So librarianship is an important discipline to turn to for information architecture expertise. Just remember that librarians are also prone to get lost in details, a weakness that can distract from determining the big picture of a web site.

Journalism

Journalists, like librarians, are trained at organizing information, but in a different setting. If your web site delivers highly dynamic information, like a news wire or a push technology-based service, someone with a journalism background might have a great sense of how to best organize and deliver this information. Because of their writing experience, journalists are also good candidates for architecting sites that will have high levels of edited content. Occasionally, journalists who move into information architecture find themselves intellectually constrained by their experience in organizing information for print and other traditional media.

Usability engineering

Usability engineers are experts at testing and evaluating how systems work. For information systems, they measure such criteria as how long it takes users to learn how to use a system, how long it takes them to find information in a system, and how many errors they make along the way. Of all the disciplines we list, usability engineering is probably the most scientific in its view of users and the quality of their experiences with information systems. Keep in mind that usability engineers concentrate on measuring a system's performance, not in designing or redesigning a system. (Of course, measurements of a site's performance can greatly determine how redesign should proceed.)

Marketing

Marketing specialists are expert at understanding audiences and communicating a message effectively to different audiences. This skill is especially valuable not only in designing externally oriented web sites, but also for intranets, which often have multiple audiences with very different needs. Marketing expertise can ensure that the message is presented in a user-oriented manner and not buried in organizational jargon. If your site is geared especially toward selling products and building brand-awareness, someone from your organization's marketing department might do the trick. The drawback to marketing-based approaches is the danger that they are more geared toward selling rather than helping users, and so may not be appropriate for certain types of web sites and audiences.

Computer science

Programmers and computer specialists bring an important skill to information architecture, especially to architecting information from the bottom up. For example, often a site requires a database to serve the content; this minimizes maintenance and data integrity problems. Computer scientists have the best skills for modeling content for inclusion in a database. However, unlike librarians or usability engineers, computer scientists aren't necessarily trained in user-centered approaches to designing information systems.

So, an information architect might come from one of many different disciplines. He or she will certainly need to know at least a little about every type of expertise involved in the entire web site design and development process, because his or her work will affect every part of the process. The architect also needs to be the keeper of the big picture as this process unfolds and the details of design and production become the main focus of all involved.

Perhaps the most important quality in an information architect is the ability to think outside the lines, to come up with new approaches to designing information systems. The Web provides many opportunities to do things in ways that haven't been done before. Many sites are pushing the envelope of design, architecture, and technology. While it's tempting to create a site that mirrors the same old things that an organization already does in other media (e.g., product brochures, annual reports), this approach could severely damage your site's chances for success. If a site doesn't rise to the occasion for its users, it won't fare well in head-to-head competition with other sites. This medium is more competitive than any other. One click, and a site becomes one of thousands that the user visits once but never returns to. It's the responsibility of the architect more than anyone else to prevent this outcome and ensure that the user encounters a site designed to take best advantage of the medium.

Balance Your Perspective

Whomever you do use as an information architect, remember: everyone (including us) is biased by their disciplinary perspective. If possible, try to ensure that other disciplines are represented on your web site development team to guarantee a balanced architecture.

Also, no matter your perspective, the information architect ideally should be solely responsible for the site's architecture, and *not* for its other aspects. It can be distracting to be responsible for other, more tangible aspects of the site, such as its graphic identity. In this case, the site's architecture can easily, if unintentionally, get relegated to secondary status because the architect is concentrating, naturally, on the tangible stuff.

However, with smaller organizations, limited resources mean that all or most aspects of the site's development—design, editorial, technical, architecture, and production—are likely to be the responsibility of one person. Our best advice for someone in this position is obvious but worth mentioning: 1) find a group of friends and colleagues who are willing to be a sounding board for your ideas, and 2) practice a sort of controlled schizophrenia in which you make a point to look at your site from different perspectives; first from the architect's, then from the designer's, and so on.

Collaboration and Communication

The information architect must communicate effectively with the web site development team. This is challenging, since an information architecture is highly abstract and intangible. Besides communicating the architecture verbally, documents (such as blueprint diagrams) must be created in ways that can be understood by the rest of the team regardless of their own disciplinary backgrounds.

In the early days of the Web, web sites were often designed, built, and managed by a single individual through sheer force of will. This webmaster was responsible for assembling and organizing the content, designing the graphics, and hacking together any necessary CGI scripts. The only prerequisites were a familiarity with HTML and a willingness to learn on the job. People with an amazing diversity of backgrounds suddenly became webmasters overnight, and soon found themselves torn in many directions at once. One minute they were information architects, then graphic designers, then editors, then programmers.

Then companies began to demand more of their sites and, consequently, of their webmasters. Simple home pages quickly evolved into complex web sites. People wanted more content, better organization, greater function, and prettier graphics. Extensions, plug-ins, and languages proliferated. Tables, VRML, frames, Shockwave, Java, and ActiveX were added to the toolbox. No mortal webmaster could keep up with the rising expectations and the increasing complexity of the environment.

Increasingly, webmasters and their employers began to realize that the successful design and production of complex web sites requires an interdisciplinary team approach. An individual cannot be an expert in all facets of the process. Rather, a team of individuals with complementary areas of expertise must work together. The composition of this team will vary, depending upon the needs of a particular project, available budget, and the availability of expertise. However, most projects will require expertise in marketing, information architecture, graphic design, writing and editing, programming, and project management.

Marketing

> The marketing team focuses on the intended purposes and audiences for the web site. They must understand what will bring the right people to the web site and what will bring them back again.

Information Architecture

> The information architects focus on the design of organization, indexing, labeling, and navigation systems to support browsing and searching throughout the web site.

Graphic Design

> The designers are responsible for the graphic design and page layout that defines the graphic identity or look of the web site. They strive to create and implement a design philosophy that balances form and function.

Editorial

> Editors focus on the use of language throughout the web site. Their tasks may involve proofreading and editing copy, massaging content to ensure a common voice for the site, and creating new copy.

Technical

> The technical designers and programmers are responsible for server administration and the development or integration of site production tools and web site applications. They advise the other teams regarding technology-related opportunities and limitations.

Project Management

> The project manager keeps the project on schedule and within budget. He or she facilitates communication between the other teams and the clients or internal stakeholders.

The success of a web site design and production project depends on successful communication and collaboration between these specialized team members. A linear, black-box, throw-it-over-the-wall methodology just won't work. Everyone needs to understand the goals, perspectives, and approaches of the other members of the team. For example, while the marketing specialist may lead the audience analysis process, he or she needs to anticipate the types of questions about the audience that the specialists will have. Otherwise, each will need to start from scratch in learning about that audience, wasting substantial time and resources.

For the information architect, communication is a special challenge because of the intangible nature of the work. Anyone who has played Pictionary knows that it is much harder to draw an abstract concept such as *science* than a physical object such as *moon*. As an information architect, you face the daunting challenge of helping others visualize such abstract concepts as a *metaphor-based architecture* and *indexing systems*.

The information architect has to identify both the goals of the site and the content that it will be built on. This means getting the people who drive the business, whether bosses or clients, to articulate their vision of the site and who its users are. Once you've collected the data and developed a plan, you need to present your ideas for an information architecture and move the group toward consensus. All in all, this significantly burdens the architect to communicate effectively.

This is the point of the rest of this book. The next four chapters introduce the foundations of information architecture to support your efforts to communicate an information architecture by providing useful terms, definitions, and concepts. Chapters 7 through 10 provide a framework for these communications, and for the role of architecture in site development as a whole.

3

Organizing Information

> *The beginning of all understanding is classification.*
> —Hayden White

Our understanding of the world is largely determined by our ability to organize information. Where do you live? What do you do? Who are you? Our answers reveal the systems of classification that form the very foundations of our understanding. We live in towns within states within countries. We work in departments in companies in industries. We are parents, children, and siblings, each an integral part of a family tree.

We organize to understand, to explain, and to control. Our classification systems inherently reflect social and political perspectives and objectives. We live in the *first* world. They live in the *third* world. She is a freedom fighter. He is a terrorist. The way we organize, label, and relate information influences the way people comprehend that information.

As information architects, we organize information so that people can find the right answers to their questions. We strive to support casual browsing and directed searching. Our aim is to apply organization and labeling systems that make sense to users.

The Web provides us with a wonderfully flexible environment in which to organize. We can apply multiple organization systems to the same content and escape the physical limitations of the print world. So why are many large web sites so difficult to navigate? Why can't the people who design these sites make it easy to find information? These common questions focus attention on the very real challenge of organizing information.

Organizational Challenges

In recent years, increasing attention has been focused on the challenge of organizing information. Yet, this challenge is not new. People have struggled with the difficulties of information organization for centuries. The field of librarianship has been largely devoted to the task of organizing and providing access to information. So why all the fuss now?

Believe it or not, we're all becoming librarians. This quiet yet powerful revolution is driven by the decentralizing force of the global Internet. Not long ago, the responsibility for labeling, organizing, and providing access to information fell squarely in the laps of librarians. These librarians spoke in strange languages about Dewey Decimal Classification and the Anglo-American Cataloging Rules. They classified, cataloged, and helped us find the information we needed.

The Internet is forcing the responsibility for organizing information on more of us each day. How many corporate web sites exist today? How many personal home pages? What about tomorrow? As the Internet provides us all with the freedom to publish information, it quietly burdens us with the responsibility to organize that information.

As we struggle to meet that challenge, we unknowingly adopt the language of librarians. How should we *label* that content? Is there an existing *classification system* we can borrow? Who's going to *catalog* all of that information?

We're moving towards a world where tremendous numbers of people publish and organize their own information. As we do so, the challenges inherent in organizing that information become more recognized and more important. Let's explore some of the reasons why organizing information in useful ways is so difficult.

Ambiguity

Classification systems are built upon the foundation of language, and language is often ambiguous. That is, words are capable of being understood in two or more possible ways. Think about the word *pitch*. When you say *pitch*, what do I hear? There are actually more than 15 definitions, including:

- A throw, fling, or toss.
- A black, sticky substance used for waterproofing.
- The rising and falling of the bow and stern of a ship in a rough sea.
- A salesman's persuasive line of talk.
- An element of sound determined by the frequency of vibration.

This ambiguity results in a shaky foundation for our classification systems. When we use words as labels for our categories, we run the risk that users will miss our meaning. This is a serious problem. See Chapter 5, *Labeling Systems*, for more on this issue.

It gets worse. Not only do we need to agree on the labels and their definitions, we also need to agree on which documents to place in which categories. Consider the common tomato. According to Webster's dictionary, a tomato is *a red or yellowish fruit with a juicy pulp, used as a vegetable: botanically it is a berry*. Now I'm confused. Is it a fruit or a vegetable or a berry?*

If we have such problems classifying the common tomato, consider the challenges involved in classifying web site content. Classification is particularly difficult when you're organizing abstract concepts such as subjects, topics, or functions. For example, what is meant by *alternative healing* and should it be cataloged under *philosophy* or *religion* or *health and medicine* or all of the above? The organization of words and phrases, taking into account their inherent ambiguity, presents a very real and substantial challenge.

Heterogeneity

Heterogeneity refers to an object or collection of objects composed of unrelated or unlike parts. You might refer to grandma's homemade broth with its assortment of vegetables, meats, and other mysterious leftovers as heterogeneous. At the other end of the scale, homogeneous refers to something composed of similar or identical elements. For example, Oreo cookies are homogeneous. Every cookie looks and tastes the same.

An old-fashioned library card catalog is relatively homogeneous. It organizes and provides access to books. It does not provide access to chapters in books or collections of books. It may not provide access to magazines or videos. This homogeneity allows for a structured classification system. Each book has a record in the catalog. Each record contains the same fields: author, title, and subject. It is a high-level, single-medium system, and works fairly well.

Most web sites, on the other hand, are highly heterogeneous in two respects. First, web sites often provide access to documents and their components at varying levels of *granularity*. A web site might present articles and journals and journal databases side by side. Links might lead to pages, sections of pages, or to

---

* "The tomato is technically a berry and thus a fruit, despite an 1893 U.S. Supreme Court decision that declared it a vegetable. (John Nix, an importer of West Indies tomatoes, had brought suit to lift a 10 percent tariff, mandated by Congress, on imported vegetables. Nix argued that the tomato is a fruit. The Court held that since a tomato was consumed as a vegetable rather than as a dessert like fruit, it was a vegetable.)" "Best Bite of Summer" by Denise Grady, *Self*, July 1997, Vol. 19 (7), pp. 124–125.

other web sites. Second, web sites typically provide access to documents in *multiple formats*. You might find financial news, product descriptions, employee home pages, image archives, and software files. Dynamic news content shares space with static human resources information. Textual information shares space with video, audio, and interactive applications. The web site is a great multimedia melting pot, where you are challenged to reconcile the cataloging of the broad and the detailed across many mediums.

The heterogeneous nature of web sites makes it difficult to impose highly structured organization systems on the content. It doesn't make sense to classify documents at varying levels of granularity side by side. An article and a magazine should be treated differently. Similarly, it may not make sense to handle varying formats the same way. Each format will have uniquely important characteristics. For example, we need to know certain things about images such as file format (GIF, TIFF, etc.) and resolution (640x480, 1024x768, etc.). It is difficult and often misguided to attempt a one-size-fits-all approach to the organization of heterogeneous web site content.

Differences in Perspectives

Have you ever tried to find a file on a coworker's desktop computer? Perhaps you had permission. Perhaps you were engaged in low-grade corporate espionage. In any case, you needed that file. In some cases, you may have found the file immediately. In others, you may have searched for hours. The ways people organize and name files and directories on their computers can be maddeningly illogical. When questioned, they will often claim that their organization system makes perfect sense. "But it's obvious! I put current proposals in the folder labeled /*office/clients/red* and old proposals in /*office/clients/blue*. I don't understand why you couldn't find them!"

The fact is that labeling and organization systems are intensely affected by their creators' perspectives. We see this at the corporate level with web sites organized according to internal divisions or org charts. In these web sites, we see groupings such as *marketing, sales, customer support, human resources,* and *information systems.* How does a customer visiting this web site know where to go for technical information about a product they just purchased? To design usable organization systems, we need to escape from our own mental models of content labeling and organization.

You must put yourself into the shoes of the intended user. How do they see the information? What types of labels would they use? This challenge is further complicated by the fact that web sites are designed for multiple users, and all users will have different perspectives or ways of understanding the information. Their levels of familiarity with your company and your web site will vary. For these reasons, it is impossible to create a perfect organization system. One site does not fit all! However, by recognizing the importance of perspective and striving to understand the intended audiences, you can do a better job of organizing information for public consumption than your coworker on his or her desktop computer.

Internal Politics

Politics exist in every organization. Individuals and departments constantly position for power or respect. Because of the inherent power of information organization in forming understanding and opinion, the process of designing information architectures for web sites and intranets can involve a strong undercurrent of politics. The choice of organization and labeling systems can have a big impact on how users of the site perceive the company, its departments, and its products. For example, should we include a link to the library site on the main page of the corporate intranet? Should we call it *The Library* or *Information Services* or *Knowledge Management*? Should information resources provided by other departments be included in this area? If the library gets a link on the main page, then why not corporate communications? What about daily news?

As an information architect, you must be sensitive to your organization's political environment. In certain cases, you must remind your colleagues to focus on creating an architecture that works for the user. In others, you may need to make compromises to avoid serious political conflict. Politics raise the complexity and difficulty of creating usable information architectures. However, if you are sensitive to the political issues at hand, you can manage their impact upon the architecture.

Organizing Web Sites and Intranets

The organization of information in web sites and intranets is a major factor in determining success, and yet many web development teams lack the understanding necessary to do the job well. Our goal in this chapter is to provide a foundation for tackling even the most challenging information organization projects.

Organization systems are composed of *organization schemes* and *organization structures*. An organization scheme defines the shared characteristics of content items and influences the logical grouping of those items. An organization structure defines the types of relationships between content items and groups.

Before diving in, it's important to understand information organization in the context of web site development. Organization is closely related to navigation, labeling, and indexing. The hierarchical organization structures of web sites often play the part of primary navigation system. The labels of categories play a significant role in defining the contents of those categories. Manual indexing is ultimately a tool for organizing content items into groups at a very detailed level. Despite these closely knit relationships, it is both possible and useful to isolate the design of organization systems, which will form the foundation for navigation and labeling systems. By focusing solely on the logical grouping of information, you avoid the distractions of implementation details and design a better web site.

Organization Schemes

We navigate through organization schemes every day. Phone books, supermarkets, and television programming guides all use organization schemes to facilitate access. Some schemes are easy to use. We rarely have difficulty finding a friend's phone number in the alphabetical organization scheme of the white pages. Some schemes are intensely frustrating. Trying to find marshmallows or popcorn in a large and unfamiliar supermarket can drive us crazy. Are marshmallows in the snack aisle, the baking ingredients section, both, or neither?

In fact, the organization schemes of the phone book and the supermarket are fundamentally different. The alphabetical organization scheme of the phone book's white pages is exact. The hybrid topical/task-oriented organization scheme of the supermarket is ambiguous.

Exact organization schemes

Let's start with the easy ones. Exact organization schemes divide information into well defined and mutually exclusive sections. The alphabetical organization of the phone book's white pages is a perfect example. If you know the last name of the person you are looking for, navigating the scheme is easy. *Porter* is in the P's which is after the O's but before the Q's. This is called "known-item" searching. You know what you're looking for and it's obvious where to find it. No ambiguity is involved. The problem with exact organization schemes is that they require the user to know the specific name of the resource they are looking for. The white pages don't work very well if you're looking for a plumber.

Exact organization schemes are relatively easy to design and maintain because there is little intellectual work involved in assigning items to categories. They are also easy to use. The following sections explore three frequently used exact organization schemes.

Alphabetical. An alphabetical organization scheme is the primary organization scheme for encyclopedias and dictionaries. Almost all nonfiction books, including this one, provide an alphabetical index. Phone books, department store directories, bookstores, and libraries all make use of our 26-letter alphabet for organizing their contents. Alphabetical organization often serves as an umbrella for other organization schemes. We see information organized alphabetically by last name, by product or service, by department, and by format. See Figure 3-1 for an example.

Figure 3-1. An alphabetical index supports both rapid scanning for a known item and more casual browsing of a directory.

Chronological. Certain types of information lend themselves to chronological organization. For example, an archive of press releases might be organized by the date of release (see Figure 3-2). History books, magazine archives, diaries, and television guides are organized chronologically. As long as there is agreement on when a particular event occurred, chronological schemes are easy to design and use.

Geographical. Place is often an important characteristic of information. We travel from one place to another. We care about the news and weather that affects us in our location. Political, social, and economic issues are frequently location-dependent. With the exception of border disputes, geographical organization schemes are fairly straightforward to design and use. Figure 3-3 shows an example of a geographic organization scheme.

Figure 3-2. Press release archives are obvious candidates for chronological organization schemes. The date of announcement provides important context for the release. However, keep in mind that users may also want to browse the releases by title or search by keyword. A complementary combination of organization schemes is often necessary.

Ambiguous organization schemes

Now for the tough ones. Ambiguous organization schemes divide information into categories that defy exact definition. They are mired in the ambiguity of language and organization, not to mention human subjectivity. They are difficult to design and maintain. They can be difficult to use. Remember the tomato? Do we put it under fruit, berry, or vegetable?

However, they are often more important and useful than exact organization schemes. Consider the typical library catalog. There are three primary organization schemes. You can search for books by author, by title, or by subject. The author and title organization schemes are exact and thereby easier to create, maintain, and use. However, extensive research shows that library patrons use ambiguous subject-based schemes such as the Dewey Decimal and Library of Congress Classification Systems much more frequently.

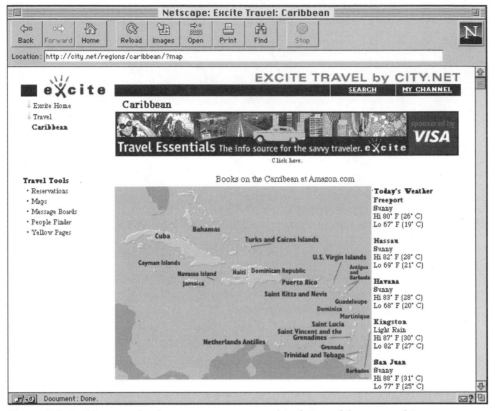

Figure 3-3. In this example, the map presents a graphical view of the geographic organization scheme. Users can select a location from the map using their mouse.

There's a simple reason why people find ambiguous organization schemes so useful: *We don't always know what we're looking for.* In some cases, you simply don't know the correct label. In others, you may only have a vague information need that you can't quite articulate. For these reasons, information seeking is often iterative and interactive. What you find at the beginning of your search may influence what you look for and find later in your search. This information seeking process can involve a wonderful element of associative learning. Seek and ye shall find, but if the system is well-designed, you also might learn along the way. This is web surfing at its best.

Ambiguous organization supports this serendipitous mode of information seeking by grouping items in intellectually meaningful ways. In an alphabetical scheme, closely grouped items may have nothing in common beyond the fact that their names begin with the same letter. In an ambiguous organization scheme, someone other than the user has made an intellectual decision to group items together. This grouping of related items supports an associative learning process that may enable the user to make new connections and reach better conclusions. While ambiguous organization schemes require more work and introduce a messy element of subjectivity, they often prove more valuable to the user than exact schemes.

The success of ambiguous organization schemes depends on the initial design of a classification system and the ongoing indexing of content items. The classification system serves as a structured container for content items. It is composed of a hierarchy of categories and subcategories with scope notes that define the types of content to be included under each category. Once this classification system has been created, content items must be assigned to categories accurately and consistently. This is a painstaking process that only a librarian could love. Let's review a few of the most common and valuable ambiguous organization schemes.

Topical. Organizing information by subject or topic is one of the most challenging yet useful approaches. Phone book yellow pages are organized topically. That's why they're the right place to look when you need a plumber. Academic courses and departments, newspapers, and the chapters of most nonfiction books are all organized along topical lines.

While few web sites should be organized solely by topic, most should provide some sort of topical access to content. In designing a topical organization scheme, it is important to define the breadth of coverage. Some schemes, such as those found in an encyclopedia, cover the entire breadth of human knowledge (see Figure 3-4 for an example). Others, such as those more commonly found in corporate web sites, are limited in breadth, covering only those topics directly related to that company's products and services. In designing a topical organization scheme, keep in mind that you are defining the universe of content (both present and future) that users will expect to find within that area of the web site.

Task-oriented. Task-oriented schemes organize content and applications into a collection of processes, functions, or tasks. These schemes are appropriate when it's possible to anticipate a limited number of high-priority tasks that users will want to perform. Desktop software applications such as word processors and spreadsheets provide familiar examples. Collections of individual actions are organized under task-oriented menus such as *Edit*, *Insert*, and *Format*.

On today's Web, task-oriented organization schemes are less common, since most web sites are content rather than application intensive. This should change as sites become increasingly functional. Intranets and extranets lend themselves well to a task orientation, since they tend to integrate powerful applications as well as content. Figure 3-5 shows an example of a task-oriented site.

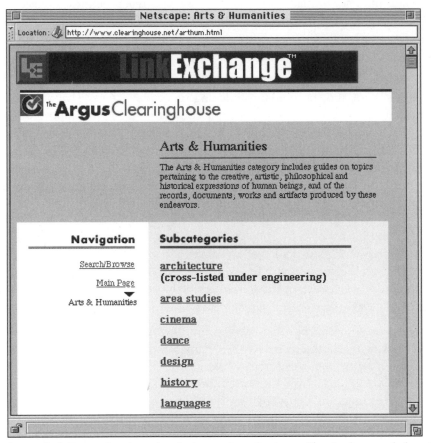

Figure 3-4. Research-oriented web sites such as the Argus Clearinghouse rely heavily on their topical organization scheme. In this example, the scope note for the Arts and Humanities category is presented as well as the list of subcategories. This helps the user to understand the reasoning behind the inclusion or exclusion of specific subcategories.

Audience-specific. In cases where there are two or more clearly definable audiences for a web site or intranet, an audience-specific organization scheme may make sense. This type of scheme works best when the site is frequented by repeat visitors who can bookmark their particular section of the site. Also, it works well if there is value in customizing the content for each audience. Audience-oriented schemes break a site into smaller, audience-specific mini-sites, thereby allowing for clutter-free pages that present only the options of interest to that particular audience. See Figure 3-6 for an example.

Audience-specific schemes can be open or closed. An open scheme will allow members of one audience to access the content intended for other audiences. A closed scheme will prevent members from moving between audience-specific

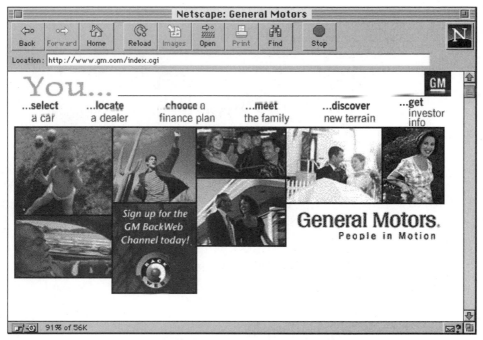

Figure 3-5. In this example, General Motors anticipates some of the most important needs of users by presenting a task-based menu of action items. This approach enables GM to quickly funnel a diverse user base into specific action-oriented areas of the web site.

sections. A closed scheme may be appropriate if subscription fees or security issues are involved.

Metaphor-driven. Metaphors are commonly used to help users understand the new by relating it to the familiar. You need not look further than your *desktop* computer with its *folders*, *files*, and *trash can* or *recycle bin* for an example. Applied to an interface in this way, metaphors can help users understand content and function intuitively. In addition, the process of exploring possible metaphor-driven organization schemes can generate new and exciting ideas about the design, organization, and function of the web site (see "Metaphor Exploration" in Chapter 8, *Conceptual Design*).

While metaphor exploration can be very useful while brainstorming, you should use caution when considering a metaphor-driven global organization scheme. First, metaphors, if they are to succeed, must be familiar to users. Organizing the web site of a computer hardware vendor according to the internal architecture of a computer will not help users who don't understand the layout of a motherboard.

Second, metaphors can introduce unwanted baggage or be limiting. For example, users might expect a virtual library to be staffed by a librarian that will answer

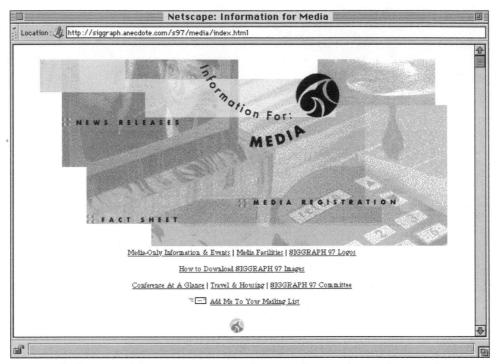

Figure 3-6. This area of the SIGGRAPH 97 conference web site is designed to meet the unique needs of media professionals covering the conference. Other SIGGRAPH audiences with special needs include contributors and exhibitors.

reference questions. Most virtual libraries do not provide this service. Additionally, you may wish to provide services in your virtual library that have no clear corollary in the real world. Creating your own customized version of the library is one such example. This will force you to break out of the metaphor, introducing inconsistency into your organization scheme.

Figure 3-7 shows a more offbeat metaphor example.

Hybrid schemes

The power of a pure organization scheme derives from its ability to suggest a simple mental model for users to quickly understand. Users easily recognize an audience-specific or topical organization. However, when you start blending elements of multiple schemes, confusion is almost guaranteed. Consider the example of a hybrid scheme in Figure 3-8. This hybrid scheme includes elements of audience-specific, topical, metaphor-based, and task-oriented organization schemes. Because they are all mixed together, we can't form a mental model. Instead, we need to skim through each menu item to find the option we're looking for.

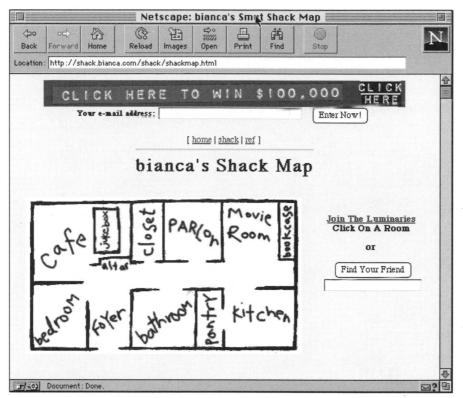

Figure 3-7. In this offbeat example, Bianca has organized the contents of her web site according to the metaphor of a physical shack with rooms. While this metaphor-driven approach is fun and conveys a sense of place, it is not particularly intuitive. Can you guess what you'll find in the pantry? Also, note that features such as Find Your Friend don't fit neatly into the metaphor.

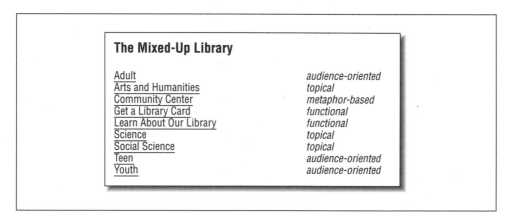

Figure 3-8. A hybrid organization scheme

Examples of hybrid schemes are common on the Web. This happens because it is often difficult to agree upon any one scheme to present on the main page, so people throw the elements of multiple schemes together in a confusing mix. There is a better alternative. In cases where multiple schemes must be presented on one page, you should communicate to designers the importance of retaining the integrity of each scheme. As long as the schemes are presented separately on the page, they will retain the powerful ability to suggest a mental model for users (see Figure 3-9 for an example).

Figure 3-9. Notice that the audience-oriented scheme (contributors, exhibitors, media) has been presented as a pure organization scheme, separate from the others on this page. This approach allows you to present multiple organization schemes on the same page without causing confusion.

Organization Structures

Organization structure plays an intangible yet very important role in the design of web sites. While we interact with organization structures every day, we rarely think about them. Movies are linear in their physical structure. We experience them frame by frame from beginning to end. However, the plots themselves may be non-linear, employing flashbacks and parallel subplots. Maps have a spatial structure. Items are placed according to physical proximity, although the most useful maps cheat, sacrificing accuracy for clarity.

The structure of information defines the primary ways in which users can navigate. Major organization structures that apply to web site and intranet architectures include the hierarchy, the database-oriented model, and hypertext. Each organization structure possesses unique strengths and weaknesses. In some cases, it makes sense to use one or the other. In many cases, it makes sense to use all three in a complementary manner.

The hierarchy: A top-down approach

The foundation of almost all good information architectures is a well-designed hierarchy. In this hypertextual world of nets and webs, such a statement may seem blasphemous, but it's true. The mutually exclusive subdivisions and parent-child relationships of hierarchies are simple and familiar. We have organized information into hierarchies since the beginning of time. Family trees are hierarchical. Our division of life on earth into kingdoms and classes and species is hierarchical. Organization charts are usually hierarchical. We divide books into chapters into sections into paragraphs into sentences into words into letters. Hierarchy is ubiquitous in our lives and informs our understanding of the world in a profound and meaningful way. Because of this pervasiveness of hierarchy, users can easily and quickly understand web sites that use hierarchical organization models. They are able to develop a mental model of the site's structure and their location within that structure. This provides context that helps users feel comfortable. See Figure 3-10 for an example of a simple hierarchical model.

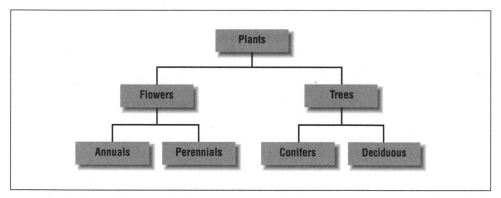

Figure 3-10. A simple hierarchical organization model.

Because hierarchies provide a simple and familiar way to organize information, they are usually a good place to start the information architecture process. The top-down approach allows you to quickly get a handle on the scope of the web site without going through an extensive content inventory process. You can begin identifying the major content areas and exploring possible organization schemes that will provide access to that content.

Designing hierarchies

When designing information hierarchies on the Web, you should remember a few rules of thumb. First, you should be aware of, but not bound by, the idea that hierarchical categories should be mutually exclusive. Within a single organization scheme, you will need to balance the tension between exclusivity and inclusivity. Ambiguous organization schemes in particular make it challenging to divide content into mutually exclusive categories. Do tomatoes belong in the fruit or vegetable or berry category? In many cases, you might place the more ambiguous items into two or more categories, so that users are sure to find them. However, if too many items are cross-listed, the hierarchy loses its value. This tension between exclusivity and inclusivity does not exist across different organization schemes. You would expect a listing of products organized by format to include the same items as a companion listing of products organized by topic. Topic and format are simply two different ways of looking at the *same* information.

Second, it is important to consider the balance between breadth and depth in your information hierarchy. Breadth refers to the number of options at each level of the hierarchy. Depth refers to the number of levels in the hierarchy. If a hierarchy is too narrow and deep, users have to click through an inordinate number of levels to find what they are looking for (see Figure 3-11). If a hierarchy is too broad and shallow, users are faced with too many options on the main menu and are unpleasantly surprised by the lack of content once they select an option.

In considering breadth, you should be sensitive to the cognitive limits of the human mind. Particularly with ambiguous organization schemes, try to follow the seven plus-or-minus two rule.* Web sites with more than ten options on the main menu can overwhelm users.

In considering depth, you should be even more conservative. If users are forced to click through more than four or five levels, they may simply give up and leave your web site. At the very least, they'll become frustrated.

For new web sites and intranets that are expected to grow, you should lean towards a broad and shallow rather than narrow and deep hierarchy. This approach allows for the addition of content without major restructuring. It is less problematic to add items to secondary levels of the hierarchy than to the main page, for a couple of reasons. First, the main page serves as the most prominent and important navigation interface for users. Changes to this page can really hurt the mental model they have formed of the web site over time. Second, because of its prominence and importance, companies tend to spend lots of care (and

---

* G. Miller, "The Magical Number Seven, Plus or Minus Two: Some Limits on our Capacity for Processing Information," *Psychological Review* 63, no. 2 (1956): 81-97.

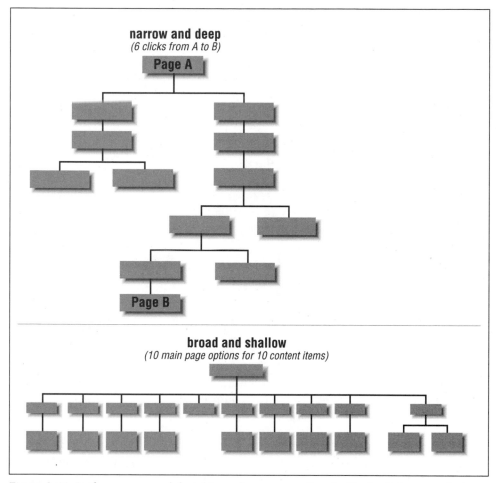

Figure 3-11. In the narrow and deep hierarchy, users are faced with six clicks to reach the deepest content. In the broad and shallow hierarchy, users must choose from ten options to reach a limited amount of content.

money) on the graphic design and layout of the main page. Changes to the main page can be more time consuming and expensive than changes to secondary pages.

Finally, when designing organization structures, you should not become trapped by the hierarchical model. Certain content areas will invite a database or hypertext-based approach. The hierarchy is a good place to begin, but is only one component in a cohesive organization system.

Hypertext

Hypertext is a relatively new and highly nonlinear way of structuring information. A hypertext system involves two primary types of components: the items or chunks of information which are to be linked, and the links between those chunks. These components can form hypermedia systems that connect text, data, image, video, and audio chunks. Hypertext chunks can be connected hierarchically, non-hierarchically, or both (see Figure 3-12).

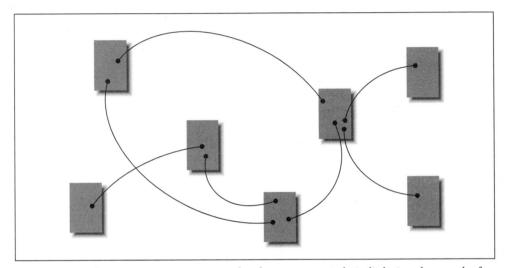

Figure 3-12. In hypertext systems, content chunks are connected via links in a loose web of relationships.

Although this organization structure provides you with great flexibility, it presents substantial potential for complexity and user confusion. As users navigate through highly hypertextual web sites, it is easy for them to get lost. It's as if they are thrown into a forest and are bouncing from tree to tree, trying to understand the lay of the land. They simply can't create a mental model of the site organization. Without context, users can quickly become overwhelmed and frustrated. In addition, hypertextual links are often personal in nature. The relationships that one person sees between content items may not be apparent to others.

For these reasons, hypertext is rarely a good candidate for the primary organization structure. Rather, hypertext can be used to complement structures based upon the hierarchical or database models.

Hypertext allows for useful and creative relationships between items and areas in the hierarchy. It usually makes sense to first design the information hierarchy and then to identify ways in which hypertext can complement the hierarchy.

The relational database model: A bottom-up approach

Most of us are familiar with databases. In fact, our names, addresses, and other personal information are included in more databases than we care to imagine. A database is a collection of records. Each record has a number of associated fields. For example, a customer database may have one record per customer. Each record may include fields such as customer name, street address, city, state, ZIP code, and phone number. The database enables users to search for a particular customer or to search for all users with a specific ZIP code. This powerful field-specific searching is a major advantage of the database model. Additionally, content management is substantially easier with a database than without. Databases can be designed to support time-saving features such as global search and replace and data validation. They can also facilitate distributed content management, employing security measures and version control systems that allow many people to modify content without stepping on each others' toes.

Finally, databases enable you to repurpose the same content in multiple forms and formats for different audiences. For example, an audience-oriented approach might benefit from a context-sensitive navigation scheme in which each audience has unique navigation options (such as returning to the main page of that audience area). Without a database, you might need to create a separate version of each HTML page that has content shared across multiple audiences. This is a production and maintenance nightmare! In another scenario, you might want to publish the same content to your web site, to a printed brochure, and to a CD-ROM. The database approach supports this flexibility.

However, the database model has limitations. The records must follow rigid rules. Within a particular record type, each record must have the same fields, and within each field, the formatting rules must be applied consistently across records. This highly structured approach does not work well with the heterogeneous content of many web sites. Also, technically it's not easy to place the entire contents (including text, graphics, and hypertext links) of every HTML page into a database. Such an approach can be very expensive and time consuming.

For these reasons, the database model is best applied to subsites or collections of structured, homogeneous information within a broader web site. For example, staff directories, news release archives, and product catalogs are excellent candidates for the database model.

Designing databases

Typically, the top-down process of hierarchy design will uncover content areas that lend themselves to a database-driven solution. At this point, you will do well to involve a programmer, who can help not only with the database implementation but with the nitty-gritty data modeling issues as well (see Figure 3-13).

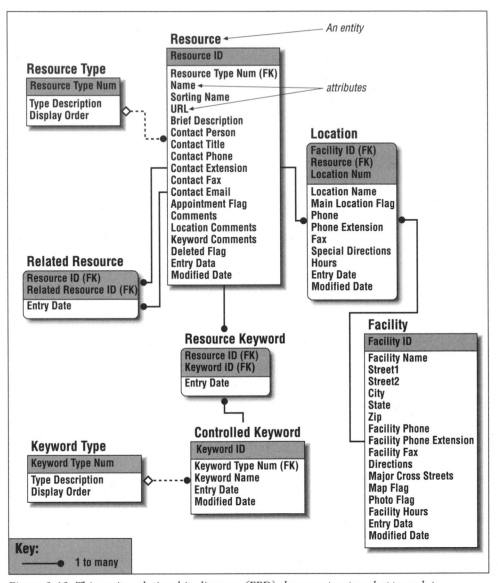

Figure 3-13. This entity relationship diagram (ERD) shows a structured approach to database design. We see that entities (e.g., Resource) have attributes (e.g., Name, URL). Ultimately, entities and attributes become records and fields in the database. An ERD also shows relationships between entities. For example, we see that each resource is available at one or more locations. The ERD is used to visualize and refine the data model, before design and population of the database. (This entity relationship diagram courtesy of InterConnect of Ann Arbor, a technical consulting and development firm.)

Within each of the content areas identified as candidates for a database-driven solution, you will need to begin a bottom-up approach aimed at identifying the content and structure of individual record types.

For example, a staff directory may have one record for each staff member. You will need to identify what information will be made available for each individual. Some fields such as name and office phone number may be required. Others such as email address and home phone number may be optional. You may decide to include an expertise field that includes keywords to describe the skills of that individual. For fields such as this, you will need to determine whether or not to define a controlled vocabulary.

A controlled vocabulary specifies the acceptable terms for use in a particular field. It may also employ scope notes that define each term.

For example, the table below lists the controlled vocabulary for keywords in the ecology area of the Argus Clearinghouse web site (see *http://www.clearing-house.net*). The scope notes explain that ecology is "the branch of biology dealing with the relation of living things to their environments." (See Figure 5-2 for an example of scope notes in action.) This information is useful for the staff who index resources and the users who navigate the web site.

Controlled Vocabulary
Argus Clearinghouse: Environment: Ecology

biodiversity	coastal zone management
conservation	ecology (general)
environment	environmental health
environmental resources	environmental science
environmental studies	land use
reef conservation	roadkill
water resources	wetlands conservation
wildlife	wildlife management
wildlife rehabilitation	

Use of a controlled vocabulary imposes an important degree of consistency that supports searching and browsing. Once users understand the controlled vocabulary, they know that a search on *biodiversity* should retrieve all relevant documents. They do not also need to try *biological diversity*. In addition, this consistency allows you to automatically generate browsable indexes. This is a great feature for users, is not very difficult to implement, and is extremely efficient from a site maintenance perspective (see Figure 3-14).

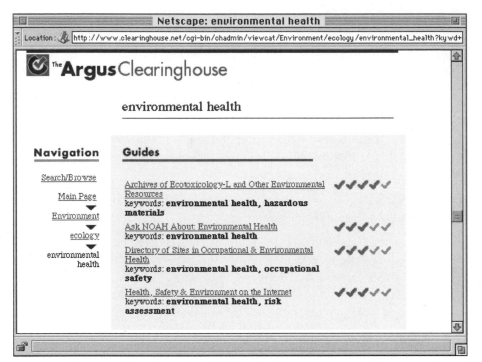

Figure 3-14. You can leverage a controlled vocabulary to automatically generate browsable indexes. In this example, after selecting Environmental Health from a menu of acceptable terms in the Ecology category, the user is presented with a list of relevant resources. These resources have been manually indexed according to the controlled vocabulary.

However, creating and maintaining a controlled vocabulary is not a simple task. In many cases, complementing a simple controlled vocabulary that divides the items into broad categories with an uncontrolled keyword field provides a good balance of structure and flexibility. (For more on creating controlled vocabularies, see "Controlled vocabularies and thesauri" in Chapter 5.)

Once you've constructed the record types and associated controlled vocabularies, you can begin thinking about how users should be able to navigate this information. One of the major advantages of a database-driven approach is the power and flexibility it affords for the design of searching and browsing systems (see Figure 3-15). Every field presents an additional way to browse or search the directory of records.

The database-driven approach also brings greater efficiency and accuracy to data entry and content management. You can create administrative interfaces that eliminate worry about HTML tags and ensure standard formatting across records through the use of templates. You can integrate tools that perform syntax and link

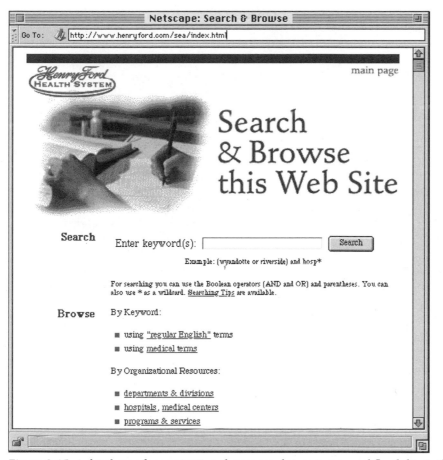

Figure 3-15. A database of organizational resources brings power and flexibility to the Henry Ford Health System web site. Users can browse by organizational resource or keyword, or perform a search against the collection of records. The browsing indexes and the records themselves are generated from the database. Site-wide changes can be made at the press of a button. This flexibility is made possible by a database-driven approach to content organization and management.

checking. Of course, the search and browse indexes can be rebuilt automatically after each addition, deletion, or modification.

Content databases can be implemented in a variety of ways. The database management software can be configured to produce static HTML pages in batch mode or to generate dynamic HTML pages on-the-fly as users navigate the site. These implementation decisions will be influenced by technical performance issues (e.g., bandwidth and CPU constraints) and have little impact upon the architecture.

Creating Cohesive Organization Systems

As you've seen in this chapter, organization systems are fairly complex. You need to consider a variety of exact and ambiguous organization schemes. Should you organize by topic, by task, or by audience? How about a chronological or geographical scheme? What about using multiple organization schemes?

You also need to think about the organization structures that influence how users can navigate through these schemes. Should you use a hierarchy or would a more structured database-model work best? Perhaps a loose hypertextual web would allow the most flexibility? Taken together, in the context of a large web site development project, these questions can be overwhelming. That's why it's important to break down the site into its components, so you can tackle one question at a time. Also, keep in mind that all information retrieval systems work best when applied to narrow domains of homogeneous content. By decomposing the content collection into these narrow domains, you can identify opportunities for highly effective organization systems.

However, it's also important not to lose sight of the big picture. As with cooking, you need to mix the right ingredients in the right way to get the desired results. Just because you like mushrooms and pancakes doesn't mean they will go well together. The recipe for cohesive organization systems varies from site to site. However, there are a few guidelines to keep in mind.

In considering which organization schemes to use, remember the distinction between exact and ambiguous schemes. Exact schemes are best for known-item searching, when users know precisely what they are looking for. Ambiguous schemes are best for browsing and associative learning, when users have a vaguely defined information need. Whenever possible, use both types of schemes. Also, be aware of the challenges of organizing information on the Web. Language is ambiguous, content is heterogeneous, people have different perspectives, and politics can rear its ugly head. Providing multiple ways to access the same information can help to deal with all of these challenges.

When thinking about which organization structures to use, keep in mind that large web sites and intranets typically require all three types of structure. The top-level, umbrella architecture for the site will almost certainly be hierarchical. As you are designing this hierarchy, keep a lookout for collections of structured, homogeneous information. These potential subsites are excellent candidates for the database model. Finally, remember that less structured, creative relationships between content items can be handled through hypertext. In this way, all three organization structures together can create a cohesive organization system.

4

Designing Navigation Systems

Just wait, Gretel, until the moon rises, and then we shall see the crumbs of bread which I have strewn about, they will show us our way home again.

—Hansel and Gretel

As our fairy tales suggest, getting lost is often a bad thing. It is associated with confusion, frustration, anger, and fear. In response to this danger, we have developed navigation tools to prevent people from getting lost. From bread crumbs to compass and astrolabe to maps, street signs, and global positioning systems, people have demonstrated great ingenuity in the design and use of navigation tools.

We use them to chart our course, to determine our position, and to find our way back. They provide a sense of context and comfort as we explore new places. Anyone who has driven through an unfamiliar city as darkness falls understands the importance that navigation tools play in our lives.

On the Web, navigation is rarely a life or death issue. However, getting lost in a large web site can be confusing and frustrating. While a well-designed hierarchical organization scheme will reduce the likelihood that users will become lost, a complementary navigation system is often needed to provide context and to allow for greater flexibility of movement within the site.

Navigation systems can be designed to support associative learning by featuring resources that are related to the content currently being displayed. For example, a page that describes a product may include *see also* links to related products and services (this type of navigation can also support a company's marketing goals). As users move through a well-designed navigation system, they learn about products, services, or topics associated to the specific content they set out to find.

Any page on a web site may have numerous opportunities for interesting *see also* connections to other areas of the site. The constant challenge in navigation system design is to balance this flexibility of movement with the danger of overwhelming the user with too many options.

Navigation systems are composed of a variety of elements. Some, such as graphical navigation bars and pop-up menus, are implemented on the content-bearing pages themselves. Others, such as tables of contents and site maps, provide remote access to content within the organization structure. While these elements may be implemented on each page, together they make up a navigation system that has important site-wide implications. A well-designed navigation system is a critical factor in determining the success of your web site.

Browser Navigation Features

When designing a navigation system, it is important to consider the environment the system will exist in. On the Web, people use web browsers such as Netscape Navigator and Microsoft Internet Explorer to move around and view web sites. These browsers sport many built-in navigation features.

Open URL allows direct access to any page on a web site. *Back* and *Forward* provide a bidirectional backtracking capability. The *History* menu allows random access to pages visited during the current session, and *Bookmark* enables users to save the location of specific pages for future reference. Web browsers also go beyond the Back button to support a "bread crumbs" feature by color-coding hypertext links. By default, unvisited hypertext links are one color and visited hypertext links are another. This feature helps users understand where they have and haven't been and can help them to retrace their steps through a web site.

Finally, web browsers allow for a prospective view that can influence how users navigate. As the user passes the cursor over a hypertext link, the destination URL appears at the bottom of the browser window, ideally hinting about the nature of that content (see Figure 4-1). If files and directories have been carefully labeled, prospective view gives the user context within the content hierarchy. If the hypertext link leads to another web site on another server, prospective view provides the user with basic information about this off-site destination.

Much research, analysis, and testing has been invested in the design of these browser-based navigation features. However, it is remarkable how frequently site designers unwittingly override or corrupt these navigation features. For example, designers often modify the unvisited and visited link colors with no consideration for the bread crumbs feature. They focus on aesthetics, attempting to match link colors with logo colors. It's common to see a complete reversal of the blue and

Figure 4-1. In this example, the cursor is positioned over the Investor Info button. The prospective view window at the bottom shows the URL of the Investor Info page.

purple standard. This is a classic sacrifice of usability* for aesthetics and belies a lack of consideration for the user and the environment. It's like putting up a green stop sign at a road intersection because it matches the color of a nearby building.

Given proper understanding of the aesthetic and usability issues, you can in fact modify the link colors and create an intelligent balance.† Unfortunately, this convention has been violated so frequently, the standard may no longer be standard.

A second common example of inadvertently disabling valuable browser navigation features involves prospective view. Image maps have become a ubiquitous navigation feature on web sites. The graphic navigation bar allows the aesthetically pleasing presentation of navigation options. Unfortunately, server-side image

---

* Analysis of a usability test that explored the impact of graphic design on users' ability to find information lead to the following conclusion: "Of all the graphic design elements we looked at, the only one that is strongly tied to user success was the use of browser-default link color....Our theory is that use of the default colors is helpful because users don't have to relearn every time they go to a new site." Jared Spool et al., *Web Site Usability* (Andover, MA: User Interface Engineering, 1997).

† For an example, see Michigan Comnet at *http://comnet.org/*. The link colors have been modified slightly to match the logo colors, but the red:purple/visited:unvisited link standard is maintained.

maps completely disable the prospective view feature of web browsers. Instead of the destination URL preview, the XY coordinates of the image map are presented. This information is distracting, not useful. Again, a solution that balances aesthetics and usability is available. Through an elegant use of tables (or by using client-side image maps), you can present a graphical navigation bar that leverages the browser-based prospective view feature.

Once you are sensitive to the built-in navigation features of web browsers, it is easy to avoid disabling or duplicating those features. In fact, it is both possible and desirable to find ways to leverage them. In designing navigation systems, you should consider all elements of that system. Web browsers are an extremely common and integral part of the user's navigation experience. From a philosophical perspective, we might say that web pages do not exist in the absence of a web browser. So, don't override or corrupt the browser!

Building Context

With all navigation systems, before we can plot our course, we must locate our position. Whether we're visiting Yellowstone National Park or the Mall of America, the *You Are Here* mark on fixed-location maps is a familiar and valuable tool. Without that landmark, we must struggle to triangulate our current position using less dependable features such as street signs or nearby stores. The *You Are Here* indicator can make all the difference between knowing where you stand and feeling completely lost.

In designing complex web sites, it is particularly important to provide context within the greater whole. Many contextual clues in the physical world do not exist on the Web. There are no natural landmarks and no north and south. Unlike physical travel, hypertextual navigation allows users to be transported right into the middle of a large unfamiliar web site. Links from remote web pages and search engine result pages allow users to completely bypass the front door or main page of the web site. To further complicate matters, people often print web pages to read later or to pass along to a colleague, resulting in even more loss of context.

You should always follow a few rules of thumb to ensure that your sites provide contextual clues. First, all pages should include the organization's name. This might be done as part of the title or header of the page. As a user moves through the levels of a site, it should be clear that they are still within that site. Carrying the graphic identity throughout the site supports such context and consistency. In addition, if a user bypasses the front door and directly accesses a subsidiary page of the site, it should be clear which site he or she is on.

Second, the navigation system should present the structure of the information hierarchy in a clear and consistent manner and indicate the location within that hierarchy. See Figure 4-2 for an example.

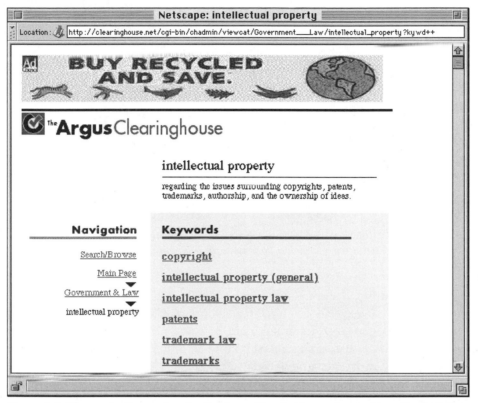

Figure 4-2. The navigation system for the Argus Clearinghouse clearly shows the path the user has taken through the hierarchy and indicates the user's current location. This helps the user to build a mental model of the organization scheme that facilitates navigation and helps them feel comfortable.

Improving Flexibility

As discussed in the previous chapter, hierarchy is a familiar and powerful way of organizing information. In many cases, it makes sense for a hierarchy to form the foundation for organizing content in a web site. However, hierarchies can be fairly limiting from a navigation perspective. If you have ever used the ancient information browsing technology and precursor to the World Wide Web known as Gopher, you will understand the limitations of hierarchical navigation. In Gopher-space, you were forced to move up and down the tree structures of content hierarchies (see Figure 4-3). It was not practical to encourage or even allow jumps across branches (lateral navigation) or between multiple levels (vertical navigation) of a hierarchy.

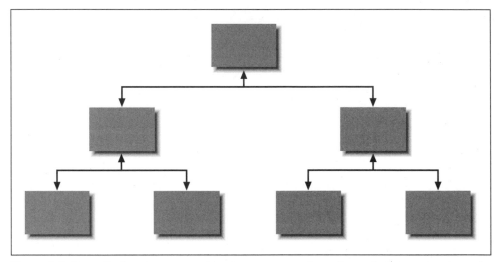

Figure 4-3. On a Gopher site, you could only move up or down through the tree structure of the hierarchy.

The Web's hypertextual capabilities removed these limitations, allowing tremendous freedom of navigation. Hypertext supports both lateral and vertical navigation (see Figure 4-4). From any branch of the hierarchy, it is possible and often desirable to allow users to laterally move into other branches. For example, as you explore the Programs and Events section of a conference web site, you may decide to register for that conference. A hypertext link should allow you to jump to Registration without first retracing your steps back up the Programs and Events hierarchy.

It is also possible and often desirable to allow users to move vertically from one level in a branch to a higher level in that same branch (e.g., from a specific Program back to the main Programs and Events page) or all the way back to the main page of the web site.

The trick with designing navigation systems is to balance the advantages of flexibility with the dangers of clutter. In a large, complex web site, the complete lack of lateral and vertical navigation aids can be very limiting. On the other hand, too many navigation aids can bury the hierarchy and overwhelm the user. Navigation systems should be designed with care to complement and reinforce the hierarchy by providing added context and flexibility.

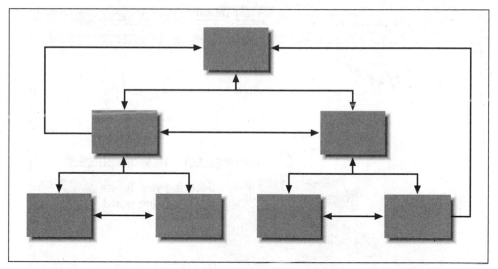

Figure 4-4. In a hypertext system, navigation links can completely bypass the hierarchy. You can enable users to get anywhere from anywhere. However, as you can see from this diagram, things can get confusing pretty quickly. It begins to look like an architecture from M.C. Escher.

Types of Navigation Systems

A complex web site often includes several types of navigation systems. To design a successful site, it is essential to understand the types of systems and how they work together to provide flexibility and context.

Hierarchical Navigation Systems

Although we may not typically think of it this way, the information hierarchy is the primary navigation system. From the main page to the destination pages that house the actual content, the main options on each page are taken directly from the hierarchy (see Figure 4-5). As noted earlier, the hierarchy is extremely important, but also rather limiting. It is these limitations that often require additional navigation systems.

Global Navigation Systems

A global or site-wide navigation system often complements the information hierarchy by enabling greater vertical and lateral movement throughout the entire site. At the heart of most global navigation systems are some standard rules that dictate the implementation of the system at each level of the site.

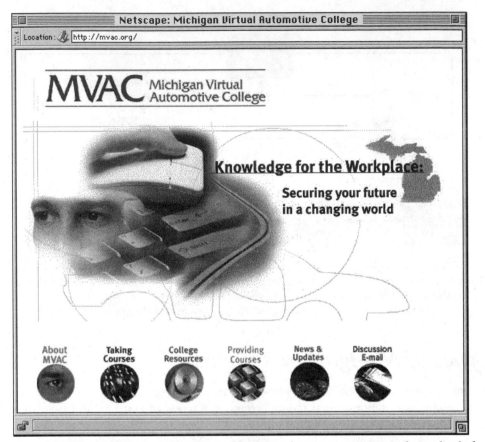

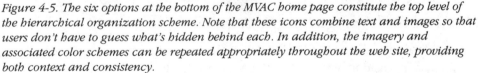

Figure 4-5. The six options at the bottom of the MVAC home page constitute the top level of the hierarchical organization scheme. Note that these icons combine text and images so that users don't have to guess what's hidden behind each. In addition, the imagery and associated color schemes can be repeated appropriately throughout the web site, providing both context and consistency.

The simplest global navigation system might consist of a graphical navigation bar at the bottom of each page on the site. On the main page, the bar might be unnecessary, since it would duplicate the primary options already listed on that page. On second level pages, the bar might include a link back to the home page and a link to the feedback facility, as in Figure 4-6.

A slightly more complex global navigation system may provide for area-specific links on third level pages and below. For example, if a user explores the products area of the web site, the navigation bar could include *Main Page*, *Products*, and *Search*. The obvious exception to this rule-based system is that pages should not include navigation links to themselves. For example, the main page of the products area should not include a *Products* link. However, this is a great opportunity

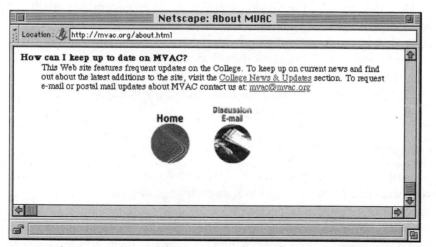

Figure 4-6. The MVAC Web site employs a very simple, icon-based global navigation system.

for the site's graphic designer to devise the navigation bar to show that you are currently on the main page of the products area. Designers often leverage a folder tab or button metaphor to accomplish this effect. (On the Argus web site, we use the @ sign from our corporate logo, as seen in Figure 4-7.)

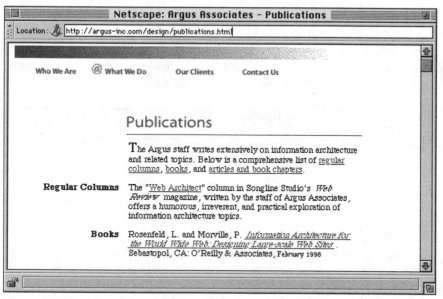

Figure 4-7. For the Argus web site, graphic designers from Q LTD came up with a creative and elegant solution to show context within the navigation system by leveraging the @ sign from our corporate logo. In this example, the @ sign indicates that the Publications page is within the What We Do area.

As you can see, this type of rule-based global navigation system can easily be applied throughout the entire web site. The navigation system and the graphic design system should be integrated to provide both flexibility and context. Note that the relative locations of the options should remain the same from one version of the bar to another and that, since people read from left to right, *Main Page* should be to the left of the other options. Both these factors enhance the context within the hierarchy.

Local Navigation Systems

For a more complex web site, it may be necessary to complement the global navigation system with one or more local navigation systems. To understand the need for local navigation systems, it is necessary to understand the concept of a *sub-site*.* The term sub-site was coined by Jakob Nielsen to identify the recurrent situation in which a collection of web pages within a larger site invite a common style and shared navigation mechanism unique to those pages.

For example, a software company may provide an online product catalog as one area in their web site. This product catalog constitutes a sub-site within the larger web site of the software company. Within this sub-site area, it makes sense to provide navigation options unique to the product catalog, such as browsing products by name or format or market.

However, it is also important to extend the global navigation system throughout the sub-site. Users should still be able to jump back to the main page or provide feedback. Local navigation systems should be designed to complement rather than replace the global navigation system (see Figure 4-8).

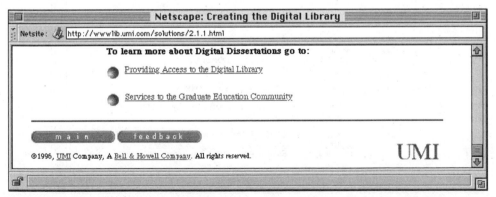

Figure 4-8. In this example, the bulleted options are part of a simple local navigation system that guides users through information about the Digital Dissertations project. The graphical buttons at the lower left of the page are part of the global navigation system.

---

* Jakob Nielsen, *The Rise of the Sub-Site*. Sept, 1996 (*http://www.useit.com/alertbox/9609.html*).

This integration can be challenging, particularly when the global and local navigation systems provide too many options. Alone they may each be manageable, but together on one page, the variety of options may overwhelm the user. In some cases, you may need to revisit the number of global and local navigation options. In others, the problem may be minimized through elegant page design.

Ad Hoc Navigation

Relationships between content items do not always fit neatly into the categories of hierarchical, global, and local navigation. An additional category of *ad hoc* links is more editorial than architectural. Typically an editor or content specialist will determine appropriate places for these types of links once the content has been placed into the architectural framework of the web site. In practice, this usually involves representing words or phrases within sentences or paragraphs (i.e., prose) as embedded hypertext links. This approach can be problematic if these ad hoc links are important, since usability testing shows "a strong negative correlation between embedded links (those surrounded by text) and user success in finding information."[*] Apparently, users tend to scan pages so quickly that they often miss these less conspicuous links. You can replace or complement the embedded link approach with external links that are easier for the user to see.

Embedded Links

As you can see, underlined embedded links are surrounded by text.

Users often miss these links.

One Solution to the Embedded Link Problem is to give links their own separate lines within the paragraph.

Another solution is to create a separate menu of ad hoc links at the top or bottom of the page that point to useful related resources:

- Embedded Links
- Users
- One Solution to the Embedded Link Problem

The approach you use should be determined by the nature and importance of the ad hoc links. For non-critical links provided as a point of interest, embedded links can be an elegant, unobtrusive solution.

---

[*] Spool et al., 41-42.

When using ad hoc links, it's important to consider whether the linked phrase provides enough context for the user. In Figure 4-9, it's fairly obvious where the Digital Dissertations Pilot Site link will take you. However, if 1861 or 1997 were underlined, you would be hard pressed to guess where those links would lead. In designing navigation systems for the Web, context is king.

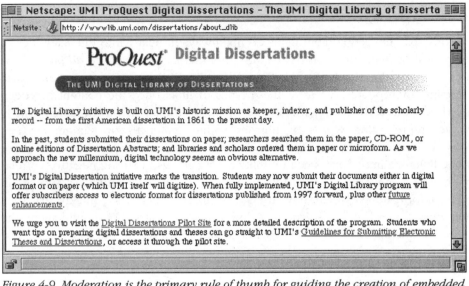

Figure 4-9. Moderation is the primary rule of thumb for guiding the creation of embedded ad hoc links. Used sparingly (as in this example), they can complement the existing navigation systems by adding one more degree of flexibility. Used in excess, ad hoc links can add clutter and confusion.

Integrated Navigation Elements

In global and local navigation systems, the most common and important navigation elements are those that are integrated into the content-bearing pages of the web site. As users move through the site or sub-site, these are the elements they see and use again and again. Most integrated navigation elements fit into one of two categories: navigation bars and pull-down menus.

Navigation Bars

You can implement navigation bars in many ways and use them for the hierarchical, global, and local navigation systems. In simplest form, a navigation bar is a collection of hypertext links grouped together on a page. Alternatively, the navigation bar may be graphical in nature, implemented as an image map or as graphic images within a table structure.

The decision to use text versus graphic navigation bars falls primarily within the realms of graphic design and technical performance rather than information architecture. Graphic navigation bars tend to look nicer but can significantly slow down the page loading speed (although, if you're able to reuse the same global navigation bar throughout the site, loading speed will only be hurt once, since the image will be cached locally). If you do use graphic navigation bars, you need to be sensitive to the needs of users with low bandwidth connections. You should also consider those users with text-only browsers (there are still quite a few out there) and those users with high-end browsers who turn off the graphical capabilities to get around more quickly. Appropriate use of the <ALT> attribute to define replacement text for the image will ensure that your site supports navigation for these users.

However, key issues related to the architecture should also influence this decision. For example, it is usually much easier to add options to a text menu than a graphic-based menu. If you anticipate substantial growth or change in a particular area, it may make sense to employ a textual navigation bar, like the one in Figure 4-10. Cost is also an issue, since graphic navigation bars require more work to create and change than text-based bars. In many cases, you might employ a graphic bar for global navigation and a textual menu for local navigation. A good graphic designer will strike an elegant balance between form and function in creating these navigation bars.

It is often best to place the navigation bar towards the top and/or bottom of the page, rather than at the side.* Placement at the top provides immediate access to the navigation system as well as an instant sense of context within the site. This supports the scenario in which a user quickly scans the first paragraph and decides to move on to other areas of the site. Placement at the bottom assumes navigation once the page has been fully read. Placement at both the top and bottom should be determined by the length of the content.

Graphical navigation bars may employ several techniques for conveying content and context, including textual labels and icons. Textual labels are the easiest to create and by far most clearly indicate the contents of each option. Icons, on the other hand, are relatively difficult to create and often fail to indicate the contents of each option. It's difficult to represent abstract concepts through images. A picture may say a thousand words, but often they're the wrong words. Icons can successfully be used to complement the textual labels. Since repeat users may become so familiar with the icons that they no longer take the time to read the textual labels, icons are useful in facilitating rapid menu selection for them. See Figure 4-11 for an example.

---

* One usability study showed that "Sites with navigation buttons or links at the top and bottom of pages did slightly better than sites with navigation buttons down the side of the page." Spool et al., 24.

Figure 4-10. C\Net provides a high-profile example of the use of text-based navigation options.

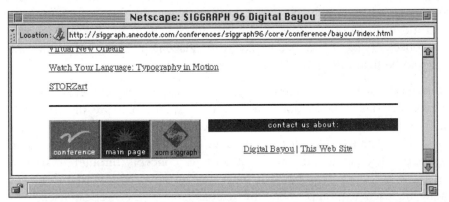

Figure 4-11. This navigation bar, which appears at the bottom of the page, demonstrates an interesting blend of graphic icons (with labels) and textual options. The global navigation icons provide a splash of color, while their labels ensure usability. The textual local navigation options allow for the creation of many footer navigation bars without restrictive costs.

However, hidden minefields may plague an iconic system. First, the Internet's global nature introduces the potential for confusion or even anger, since an image may have very different meanings from one culture to another. Second, the iconic system may work well for a limited number of menu options, but if the decision is made to add one or more options, creating an appropriate icon can be very challenging. While icons certainly work well sometimes, the skillful use of a color system can facilitate rapid menu selection without the inherent problems of iconic systems. (For more about the use of icons, see Chapter 5, *Labeling Systems*.)

Frames

Frames present an additional factor to consider in the application of textual or graphical navigation bars. Frames allow you to define one or more independently scrollable "panes" within a single browser window. Hypertextual links within one pane can control the content displayed in other panes within that same window. This enables the designer to create a static or independently scrolling navigation bar that appears on every page in that area of the web site. This frame-based navigation bar will be visible to the user in the same location in the browser window even while scrolling through long documents. By separating the navigation system from content in this way, frames can provide added context and consistency as users navigate a web site.

However, frames present several serious problems, both from the consumer's and producer's perspective. Architects should proceed very carefully in considering frame-based navigation solutions. Let's review a few of the major considerations.

Screen real estate

Static navigation bars implemented through frames often take up significant portions of valuable screen real estate (see Figure 4-12). No matter how far the user scrolls, the navigation bar always stays with them. The addition of winking, blinking banner advertisements into the static navigation bar often compounds this problem. On a large, high resolution monitor this may be only a minor irritation. On a standard 640 x 480 monitor, these frames can be really annoying. If you're going to use a frame-based navigation bar, keep it relatively small and non-obtrusive. You should also consider a vertical rather than horizontal frame, since left-to-right reading lends itself to narrow text columns like those found in newspapers and magazines.

The page model

The Web is built upon a model of pages, with each page having a unique address or URL. Users are familiar with the concept of pages. Frames confuse this issue, by slicing up pages into independent panes of content. By violating the page

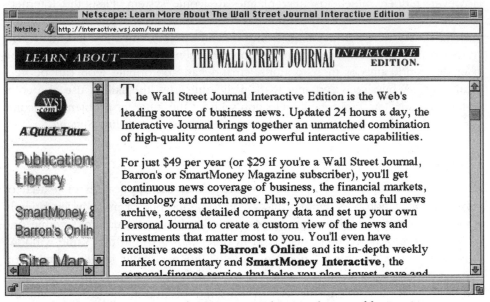

Figure 4-12. The Wall Street Journal*'s Interactive Edition makes use of frames. It's a relatively elegant implementation, but it limits screen real estate and disables basic navigation features.*

model, the use of frames frequently disables important browser navigation features such as bookmarking, visited and unvisited link discrimination, and history lists. Frames can also confuse and frustrate users executing simple tasks such as using the back button, reloading a page, and printing a page. While web browsers have improved in their ability to handle frames, they can't remove the confusion caused by violating the page model.

Display speed

Right off the bat, a web page with multiple panes will take a hit on display speed. Since each pane is a separate file with its own URL, loading and displaying each pane requires a separate client-server interaction. In other words, the user spends a lot of time watching "Host Contacted" messages fly by at the bottom of the screen. This problem is compounded by heavy graphics use.

Complex design

In theory, there are some compelling reasons to try frames. You can make global navigation bars or section headers (or advertisements) visible to the user at all times. However, in practice, designing user-friendly web sites using frames is quite challenging. Frames add a layer of complexity that many architects and designers deal with unsuccessfully. You must think about the multiple ways users will access your frame-based documents. What if they come from another frame-based document? Then you face the danger of frames within frames. In addition, while most web browsers now support frames, different browsers on different computer platforms display the frames and their contents slightly differently. This requires more testing and more careful design. Before using frames, make sure you consider the additional overhead in architecture and design.

Pull-Down Menus

Pull-down menus compactly provide for many navigation options. The user can expand what appears as a single-line menu to present dozens of options (as shown in Figure 4-13). The most common pull-down menus on the Web are implemented using the standard interactive forms syntax. Users must choose an option from the menu and then hit a Go or Submit button to move to that destination.

You can implement a more sophisticated version of the pull-down menu (also know as the *pop-up menu*) on the Web by using a programming language such as Java or JavaScript. As the user moves the cursor over a word or area on the page, a menu pops up. The user can directly select an option from that menu.

Use pull-down and pop-up menus with caution. These menus allow designers to pack lots of options on one page. This is usually what you are working hard to avoid. Additionally, menus hide their options and force the user to act before being able to see those options. However, when you have a very straightforward, exact organization scheme, these menus can work well.

Remote Navigation Elements

Remote navigation elements or supplemental navigation systems such as tables of contents, indexes, and site maps are external to the basic hierarchy of a web site and provide an alternative bird's-eye view of the site's content. Increasingly, we are seeing these remote navigation elements displayed outside of the main browser window, in either a separate target window or in a Java-based remote control panel. While remote navigation elements can enhance access to web site content by providing complementary ways of navigating, they should not be used as replacements or bandages for poor organization and navigation systems. In many ways, remote navigation elements are similar to software documentation or help systems. Documentation can be very useful but will never save a bad product. Instead, remote navigation elements should be used to complement a solid internal organization and navigation system. You should provide them but never rely on them.

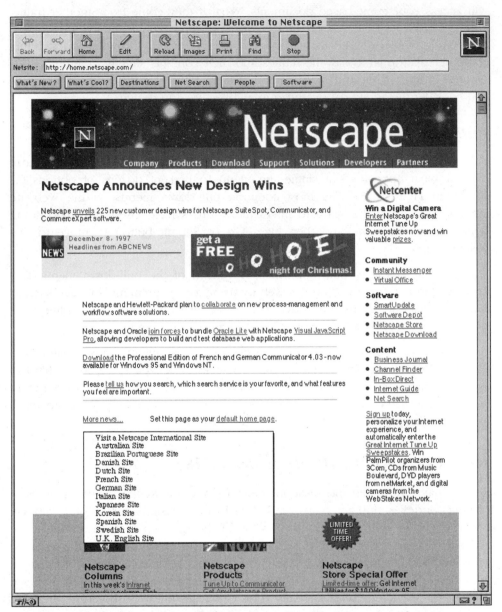

Figure 4-13. This pull-down menu enables users to select a location without first going to a separate web page. This approach avoids further cluttering the main page with a long list of locations.

The Table of Contents

The table of contents and the index are the state of the art in print navigation. Given that the design of these familiar systems is the result of testing and refinement over the centuries, we should not overlook their value for web sites.

In a book or magazine, the table of contents presents the top few levels of the information hierarchy. It shows the organization structure for the printed work and supports random as well as linear access to the content through the use of chapter and page numbers. Similarly, the table of contents for a web site presents the top few levels of the hierarchy. It provides a broad view of the content in the site and facilitates random access to segmented portions of that content. A web-based table of contents can employ hypertext links to provide the user with direct access to pages of the site.

You should consider using a table of contents for web sites that lend themselves to hierarchical organization. If the architecture is not strongly hierarchical, it makes no sense to present the parent-child relationships implicit in a structured table of contents. You should also consider the web site's size when deciding whether to employ a table of contents. For a small site with only two or three hierarchical levels, a table of contents may be unnecessary.

The design of a table of contents significantly affects its usability. When working with a graphic designer, make sure he or she understands the following rules of thumb:

1. Reinforce the information hierarchy so the user becomes increasingly familiar with how the content is organized.

2. Facilitate fast, direct access to the contents of the site for those users who know what they want.

3. Avoid overwhelming the user with too much information. The goal is to help, not scare, the user.

The *Search/Browse* area of the Argus Clearinghouse, shown in Figure 4-14, provides an example of a table of contents.

Graphics can be used in the design and layout of a table of contents, providing the designer with a finer degree of control over the presentation. Colors, font styles, and a variety of graphic elements can be applied to create a well-organized and aesthetically pleasing table of contents. However, keep in mind that a graphic table of contents will cost more to design and maintain and may slow down the page loading speed for the user. When designing a navigation tool such as a table of contents, form is less important than function.

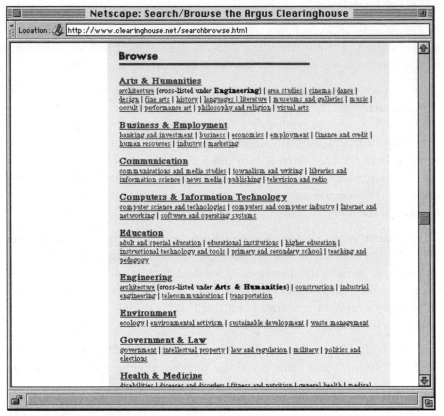

Figure 4-14. This table of contents allows users to select a category (e.g., Arts & Humanities) or jump directly to a subcategory (e.g., architecture). Because of the clean page layout, users can quickly scan the major and minor categories for the topic they're interested in.

The Index

For web sites that aren't conducive to strong hierarchical organization, a manually created index can be a good alternative to the more structured table of contents. Similar to an index found in print materials, a web-based index presents keywords or phrases alphabetically, without representing the hierarchy. Unlike a table of contents, indexes generally are flat and present only one or two levels of depth. Therefore, indexes work very well for users who already know the name of the item they are looking for. A quick scan of the alphabetical listing will get them where they want to go.

A major challenge in indexing a web site involves the level of granularity of indexing. Do you index web pages? Do you index individual paragraphs or concepts that are presented on web pages? Or do you index collections of web pages? In many cases, the answer may be *all of the above*. Perhaps a more valuable question is: *What terms are users going to look for?* Its answers should guide the index design. To answer this question, you need to know your audience and understand their needs. Before launch of the site, you can learn more about the terms that users will look for through focus group sessions and individual user interviews. After launch, you can employ a query tracking tool that captures and presents all search terms entered by users. Analysis of these actual user search terms should determine refinement of the index. (To learn more about query tracking tools, see Chapter 9, *Production and Operations.*)

In selecting items for the index, keep in mind that an index should point only to destination pages, not navigation pages. Navigation pages help users find (destination) pages through the use of menus that begin on the main page and descend through the hierarchy. They are often heavy on links and light on text. In contrast, destination pages contain the content that users are trying to find. The purpose of the index is to enable users to bypass the navigation pages and jump directly to these content-bearing destination pages.

A useful trick in designing an index involves term rotation, also known as permutation. A permuted index rotates the words in a phrase so that users can find the phrase in two places in the alphabetical sequence. For example, in the SIGGRAPH 96 index shown in Figure 4-15, users will find listings for both *New Orleans Maps* and *Maps (New Orleans)*. This supports the varied ways people look for information. Term rotation should be applied selectively. You need to balance the probability of users seeking a particular term with the annoyance of cluttering the index with too many permutations. For example, it would probably not make sense to present Sunday (Schedule) as well as Schedule (Sunday). If you have the time and budget to conduct focus groups or user testing, that's great. If not, you'll have to fall back on your common sense.

The Site Map

While the term *site map* is used indiscriminately in general practice, we define it narrowly as a graphical representation of the architecture of a web site. This definition excludes tables of contents and indexes that use graphic elements to enhance the aesthetic appeal of tools that are primarily textual. A real site map presents the information architecture in a way that goes beyond textual representation.

Unlike tables of contents and indexes, maps have not traditionally been used to facilitate navigation through bodies of text. Maps are typically used for navigating physical rather than intellectual space. This is significant for a few reasons. First, users are not familiar with the use of site maps. Second, designers are not familiar with the design of site maps. Third, most bodies of text (including most web sites) do not lend themselves to graphical representations. As we discussed in Chapter 3, *Organizing Information*, many web sites incorporate multiple organiza-

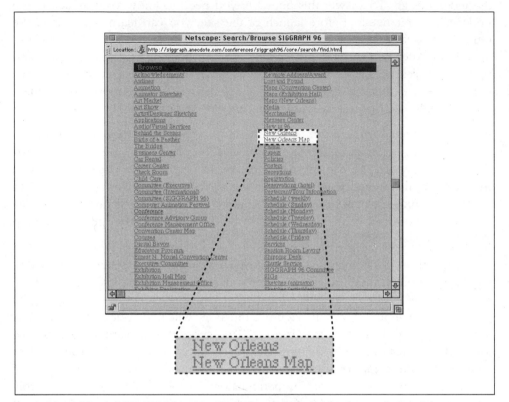

Figure 4-15. The SIGGRAPH 96 index allows for multiple levels of granularity. Selecting "New Orleans" will take you to a page that introduces this adventurous city and includes a number of links. One of those links takes you to a New Orleans map. Since this map is judged to be an important content item, it is also presented in the index.

tion schemes and structures. Presenting this web of hypertextual relationships visually is difficult. These reasons help explain why we see few good examples on the Web of site maps that can improve navigation systems.

Figure 4-16 shows a site map from *http://www.sgml.net*. To learn more about automatically generated site maps, see *http://www.webreview.com/97/05/16/arch/ index. html*.

If you decide to try a site map, consider physical versus symbolic representation. Maps of the physical world do not present the exact geography of an area. Accuracy and scale are often sacrificed for representative contextual clues that help us find our way through the maze of highways and byways to our destination. Often, the higher the level of abstraction, the more intuitive the map. This rule of thumb holds true for all of the remote navigation elements of web sites. When consulting a table of contents or index or site map, a user doesn't need to see every single link on every single page. They need to see the important links, presented in a clear and meaningful way.

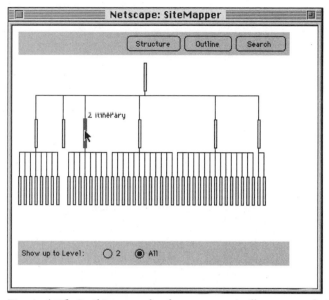

Figure 4-16. In this example of an automatically generated site map, gold bars represent pages within a web site. Users must roll their cursor over a gold bar to see the title of the page. Do you think this approach is more useful than a text-based table of contents?

The Guided Tour

A guided tour serves as a nice tool for introducing new users to the major content areas of a web site. It can be particularly important for restricted access web sites (such as online magazines that charge subscription fees) because you need to show potential customers what they will get for their money.

A guided tour should feature linear navigation (new users want to be guided, not thrown in), but a hypertextual navigation bar may be used to provide additional flexibility. The tour should combine screenshots of major pages with narrative text that explains what can be found in each area of the web site. See Figure 4-17 for an example.

Remember that a guided tour is intended as an introduction for new users and as a marketing opportunity for the web site. Many people may never use it, and few people will use it more than once. For that reason, you might consider linking to the tour from the gateway page* rather than the main page. Also, you should

---

* Web sites sometimes have a gateway page that first-time users encounter before reaching the main page. This gateway might serve as a splash page with fancy graphics and animation, as an audience-selection page that sends users to the appropriate area of a site, or as a preview page that shows users what they will get if they subscribe to that particular web site.

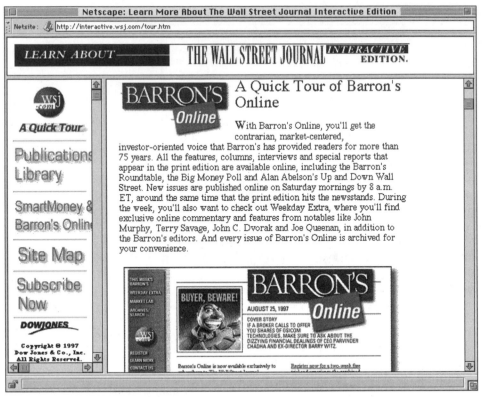

Figure 4-17. In this example, the navigation options on each screen allow users to move through the guided tour in a non-linear manner.

balance the inevitable big ideas about how to create an exciting, dynamic, interactive guided tour with the fact that it will not play a central role in the day to day use of the web site.

Designing Elegant Navigation Systems

Designing navigation systems that work well is challenging. You've got so many possible solutions to consider, and lots of sexy technologies such as pop-up menus and dynamic site maps can distract you from what's really important: building context, improving flexibility, and helping the user to find the information they need.

No single combination of navigation elements works for all web sites. One size does not fit all. Rather, you need to consider the specific goals, audience, and content for the project at hand, if you are to design the optimal solution.

However, there is a process that should guide you through the challenges of navigation system design. It begins with the hierarchy. As the primary navigation system, the hierarchy influences all other decisions. The choice of major categories at the highest levels of the web site will determine design of the global navigation system. Based on the hierarchy, you will be able to select key pages (or types of pages) that should be accessible from every other page on the web site. In turn, the global navigation system will determine design of the local and then ad hoc navigation systems. At each level of granularity, your design of the higher-order navigation system will influence decisions at the next level.

Once you've designed the integrated navigation system, you can consider the addition of one or more remote navigation elements. In most cases, you will need to choose between a table of contents, an index, and a site map. Is the hierarchy strong and clear? Then perhaps a table of contents makes sense. Does the hierarchy get in the way? Then you might consider an index. Does the information lend itself to visualization? If so, a site map may be appropriate. Is there a need to help new or prospective users to understand what they can do with the site? Then you might add a guided tour.

If the site is large and complex, you can employ two or more of these elements. A table of contents and an index can serve different users with varying needs. However, you must consider the potential user confusion caused by multiple options and the additional overhead required to design and maintain these navigation elements. As always, it's a delicate balancing act.

If life on the high wire unnerves you, be sure to build some usability testing into the navigation system design process. Only by learning from users can you design and refine an elegant navigation system that really works.

5

Labeling Systems

Labeling is a form of representation. Just as we use spoken words to represent thoughts, we use labels to represent larger chunks of information in our web sites. For example, Contact Us is a label that represents a chunk of information, including a contact name, an address, telephone, fax, email information, and maybe more. You cannot present all this information quickly and effectively on an already crowded page without overwhelming impatient users. Instead, we rely upon a label like Contact Us to trigger the right association in the user's mind *without* presenting all that stuff prominently. The user can then decide whether to click through or read on and get more contact information. So the goal of a label is to communicate information efficiently; that is, without taking up too much of a page's vertical space or a user's cognitive space.

Unlike the weather, no one ever talks about labeling (aside from a few deranged librarians and linguists), but everyone can do something about it. Web site designers and managers create labels for the site without even realizing it. Why? Because labeling is a natural outgrowth of creating organization and navigation systems that sites can't function without, and because labeling things comes very naturally to humans. It's too easy not to think about labeling. The point of this chapter is to get you to think about labeling before you dive in.

Pre-recorded or canned communications, including print, the Web, scripted radio, and TV, are very different from interactive real-time communications. When we talk with another person, we rely on constant user feedback to help us hone the way we get our message across. We subconsciously notice our conversation partner zoning out, getting ready to make their own point, or beginning to clench their fingers into an angry fist, so we immediately shift our style of communication, perhaps by raising our speaking volume, increasing our use of body language, changing a rhetorical tack, fleeing, etc.

Unfortunately, the Web isn't sufficiently interactive for us to know how well we're getting our message across. So, assuming we don't have extensive user testing budgets for our sites, we need to guess how the average user might best respond to our message and write it that way. "Tell 'em what you're going to tell 'em, tell 'em, and then tell 'em what you told 'em." This canned approach is completely contrary to real-time conversation, which is the way we're used to communicating. Therefore, as a form of pre-recorded communications, labeling is a great challenge for web developers.

Where does labeling fit with the other systems we've discussed? Well, labels are often the most obvious ways of clearly showing the user your organization and navigation systems. For example, a single web page might contain different groups of labels, with each group representing a different organization or navigation system: an overall organization system that matches the site's hierarchy (e.g., Resources for Dog Owners, Resources for Dog Groomers, Resources for Dogcatchers), a site-wide navigation system (e.g., Main, Search, Feedback), and a sub-site navigation system (e.g., Submit a Resource, Annotate a Resource). So before you begin creating labeling systems, you need to have already determined the site's organization and navigation systems.

Why You Should Care About Labeling

Squandering Attention Spans

Rock music lyrics were still pretty simple back in the early '60s. Even with folks like Little Richard screeching "A-wop-bop-a-loo-lop a-lop-bam-boo!" you could generally understand what the words meant. But the music matured so much so quickly during that decade that it soon supported the rise of a new pasttime: rock lyric interpretation. Serious brainpower was deployed to interpret what the heck it was that such lyrical giants as Bob Dylan, the Beatles, and Tiny Tim *really* meant.

But those innocent days of recreational head-scratching have given way to an era of abbreviated attention spans. Don't count on the Web maturing in the same way that rock music did; that is to say, web users are not likely to spend much time decoding what it was a web site designer *really* meant by labeling an item Info or Stuff.

Making Bad Impressions

Besides immeasurably affecting navigation, labeling influences your site's users in many other ways. The way you say or represent information in your site says a lot about you and your organization. If you've ever read an airline magazine, you're familiar with those ads for some educational cassette series that develops your vocabulary. "The words you use can make or break your business deals..." or something like that. This may sound silly and a bit overblown, but after visiting some purportedly professional organizations' sites that include such terms as Cool, Hot, and Stuff in their labels, you'll start to agree with those purveyors of vocabulary-improving cassettes. Your organization has probably mortgaged its future to create a professional graphic identity and presence in its industry. Poor, unprofessional labeling can betray that investment and destroy a user's confidence in an organization.*

Self-Centered Labeling

Labels can also expose an organization that, despite its best intentions, does not consider the importance of its customers' needs as important as its own goals. This is most common in web sites that use org-speak for their labels. You've probably seen such sites; their labels are crystal clear, obvious, and enlightening... as long as you're one of the .01 percent of the users who actually work for the sponsoring organization. A sure way to lose a sale is to label your site's product ordering system as an Order Processing and Fulfillment Facility. (Another way is to feature any label that includes the terms Total, Quality, and Management....)

Labeling Systems, Not Labels

It's important to remember that labels, like organization and navigation systems, are systems in their own right. So it follows that labeling systems, like any other, require planning to succeed. To illustrate, let's compare two labeling systems:

1. Unplanned Labeling System

        Faculty Skunkworks
        Office for Instructional Technology
        K12 PDN Projects Web Page
        Digital Libraries Project

---

* Counterpoint: the Web is a more insouciant, fun-loving medium than, for example, the buttoned-down stuffiness of annual reports. At least for now, that is. That's why investors were willing to pump millions into something called Yahoo! (which, incidentally, is an acronym for "Yet Another Hierarchical Officious Oracle"). A year before Yahoo! came out, we started something stuffily named "The Clearinghouse for Subject-Oriented Internet Resource Guides" (now called The Argus Clearinghouse: *http://www.clearinghouse.net/*); if only we'd gone with something cuter or hipper—for example, Dogwash!—we would now be worth zillions.

```
Office of Technology Management
Extension Services
The New Media Center
Project 1999
Institute for Information Technology
English Composition Board
Technology Dissemination Office
```

2. Planned Labeling System

```
Arts & Humanities
Business & Employment
Communication
Computers & Information Technology
Education
Engineering
Environment
Government & Law
Health & Medicine
Places & Peoples
Recreation
Science & Mathematics
Social Sciences & Social Issues
```

What is the difference between these two labeling systems?

If you were a first-time visitor, you'd have little sense of what the labels in the Unplanned System represent. They were created with the assumption that users would know these programs and acronyms. We can assume that this site deals with something academic, because of the labels Faculty, English Composition, and so forth. The list does seem somewhat consistent, as it includes many terms that seem to represent organizational units, such as Office, Services, Board, Project, and Institute. However, some terms are confounding, such as K12 PDN Web Page, Project 1999, Faculty Skunkworks, and The New Media Center. It's not clear if these represent web sites, organizational units, or something else altogether. So we scratch our heads and wonder what this is all about.

The Planned System, without context, might also make us wonder. What resources do these subjects cover? But at least we're clear that these indeed are subject areas. Also, the lack of exceptions indicates comprehensiveness: each is a subject area, so all possible subjects must be covered here. This is a useful trick: although there is no proof that this list is indeed comprehensive, users will often assume that consistent, systematic labeling systems do in fact cover the full extent of the domain that they represent. Most importantly, users have seen this type of system before, so the user only needs to learn the *labeling system*, not each individual label. After one quick look, the user understands how this system works: it's subject-oriented. Consistency breeds familiarity, and familiarity breeds content(ment).

Types of Labeling Systems

In web sites, labels come in two formats, textual and iconic. We typically find them used in two ways: as links to chunks of information on other pages (usually within the context of navigation systems, as index terms, or as labels for links), and as headings that break up and identify the chunks of information on the same page (much like the heading on this printed page). Of course, a single label can do double duty; for example, the link Contact Us could lead to a page that uses the title label Contact Us.

Labels Within Navigation Systems

Navigation system labels demand consistent application more than any other type of labeling system. Navigation systems, as we described in Chapter 4, *Designing Navigation Systems*, occur again and again within a web site. Just as users rely on navigational systems to be positioned on a page consistently and look the same throughout the site, they rely on their labels to work in a consistent, familiar way, as in Figure 5-1. Effectively applied labels are integral to building this sense of familiarity, so they'd better not change from page to page. That's why using the label Main, on one page, Main Page on another, and Home elsewhere will surely destroy the familiarity that the user needs when navigating a site.

Some conventions have emerged for navigation system labels. You should consider using these, as they are already familiar to most web users. Here is a non-exhaustive list:

- Main, Main Page, Home, Home Page
- Search, Find, Browse, Search/Browse, Site Map, Contents, Table of Contents, Index
- Contact , Contact Us, Contact Webmaster, Feedback
- Help, FAQ, Frequently Asked Questions
- News, What's New
- About, About Us, About <company name>, Who We Are

However, each example has two or more textual variants used to represent the same information. So these conventions aren't completely conventional; use them with care! At least use them consistently within your site, as in the example in Figure 5-1.

Conversely, the same label can often represent different kinds of information. For example, in one site News may link to an area in a site that includes announcements of new additions to the site. In another site News may link to an area of news stories describing national and world events. Obviously, if you use the same labels in different ways *within* your own site, your users will be very confused.

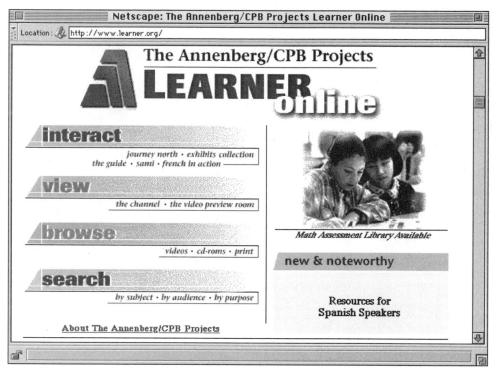

Figure 5-1. The labels Interact, View, Browse, and Search are part of a site-wide navigation system. This labeling system uses consistent verb-based terminology.

To address both problems, navigational labels can be augmented by brief descriptions (also known as *scope notes*) when initially introduced. For example, when a user first encounters these navigational labels on a site's main page, he or she will get a sense of their meaning from their accompanying descriptions:

Label	Scope Note
Search/Browse	Search this site by entering a query, or browse it via a comprehensive site map.
Contact Us	A direct line to our customer service department, with a 24-hour turn-around guaranteed.
News	Keep current with our up-to-the-minute stock prices and press releases.
Help	Our site's FAQ, and how to contact our webmaster.

After this initial introduction, the user should easily understand how to use the following navigation bar that appears on all the other pages in the site:

Search/Browse | Contact Us | News | Help

The labels are now familiar, and if used consistently, will work effectively. Usability tests run on many major sites have confirmed the contextual value of providing descriptions.* The Argus Clearinghouse provides a more extensive example of the use of scope notes (Figure 5-2).

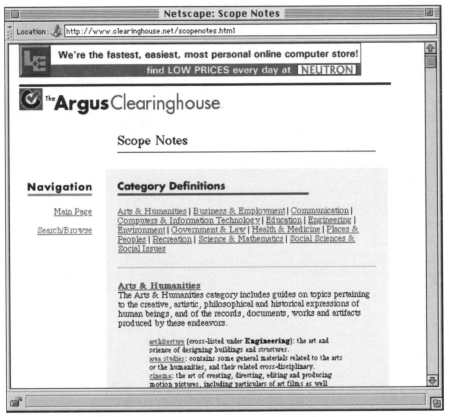

Figure 5-2. Each category and subcategory is described further by a scope note.

Labels as Indexing Terms

Labels are increasingly used as indexing terms for classifying the contents of large sites. They work in two ways: enhancing a document's chance of getting retrieved by a searching system, and supporting browsing within a site.

To support searching, keywords are assigned to a document, whether within the <META> tag or in an accompanying database record that describes the document's contents. These labels are usually heard but not seen; in other words, they aren't necessarily visible to the user, but instead work in the background to ensure a search engine appropriately indexes the document. For example, we

---

* Jared Spool et al., *Web Site Usability: A Designer's Guide.* (Andover, MA: User Interface Engineering, 1997.)

inserted the following code in the main page for International Furniture Rentals (*http://www.rent-ifr.com*):

```
<META name="keywords" content="IFR Furniture Rentals, International
Furniture Rentals, IFR Rentals, relocation, furniture rental, furniture
leasing, interim housing, furnished apartments, executive suites,
residential furniture, office furniture">
```

These indexing terms are keywords that describe the company's services and locations, as well as synonyms and name variants (e.g., IFR Rentals) that we anticipated might be searched by users. Search engines, whether Web-wide (e.g., Alta Vista, Hotbot) or specific to this site would then include these terms in their indexes, thereby improving user searching.

Indexing labels effectively within a page's <TITLE> tags can similarly improve a searcher's chances of retrieving the right pages in your site. In fact, we've found that Web-wide search engine relevance ranking algorithms seem to consider terms in a document's <TITLE> as very indicative of the document's content, and so these documents often end up ranked quite highly on result lists. In our own site, we included these descriptive labels within the <TITLE> tags:

```
<TITLE>Argus Associates. information architecture design, organization,
labeling, navigation, searching, indexing, intranets, Web sites</TITLE>
```

It's surprising that labels as indexing terms are not used more. Site sponsors do crazy things to get their sites noticed, including advertising their URL on banners flown over football stadiums, but they don't always bother to insert accurate, descriptive terms in their site's pages.

Besides enhancing searching, index labels can also improve browsing. By using keywords to manually index a site's content, you can provide additional means for accessing its content *beyond its main organization scheme*. For example, the Henry Ford Health System's site (shown in Figure 5-3) contains many records for each department, division, hospital, program, and so on. Because those are the major entities of the health system, they constitute the main organization system for that content. However, we also added topical keywords to each record (e.g., heart, kidney, liver, lung, skin graft, and transplantation) to allow users to access the site's content by topic. This approach allows users to cut across the grain of the site's main organization system and browse the content in a completely different mode.

Link Labels

Labels are also used as textual links within the body or text of a chunk of information. These aren't as difficult to create because, unlike navigation system labels, they are naturally used in the descriptive context of their surrounding text. See Figure 5-4 for an example of link labels.

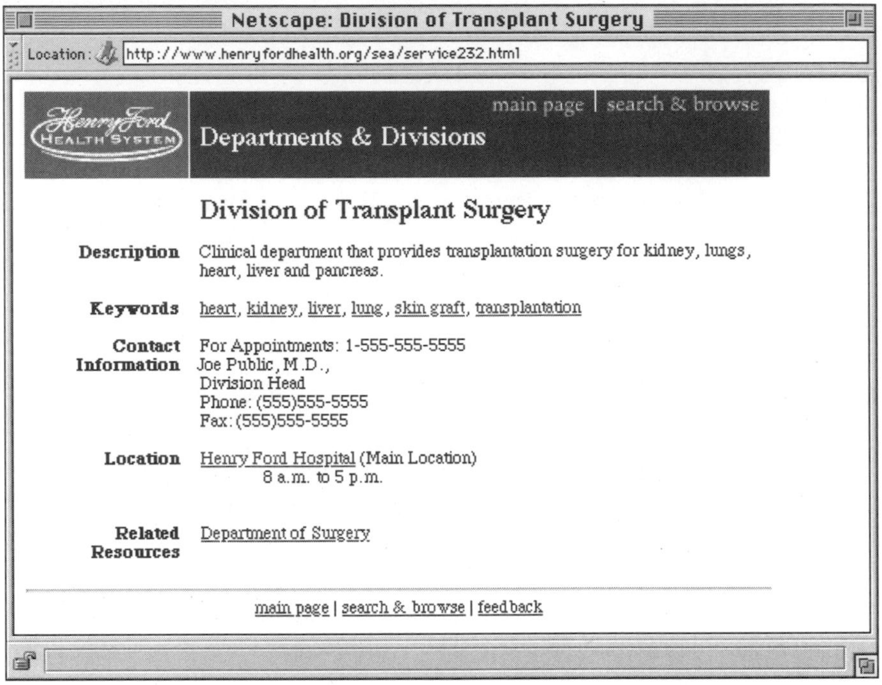

Figure 5-3. Content already accessible through a major organization system (e.g., organizational designations such as Departments & Divisions) can also be made accessible by indexing terms (e.g., keywords). In this case, each keyword serves as a link, allowing users to access other content indexed under the same keyword.

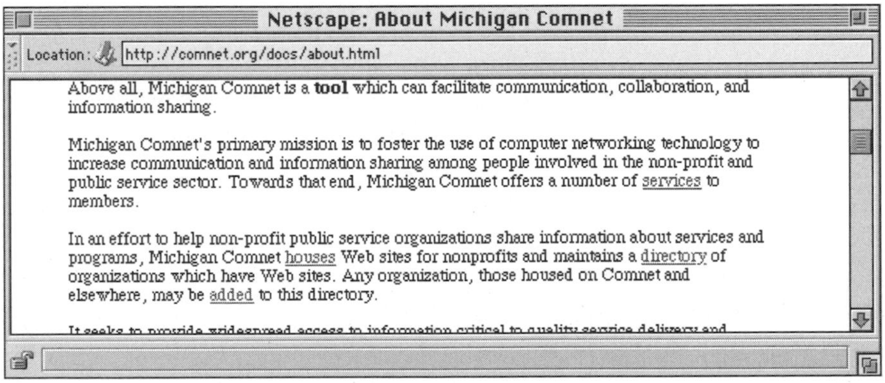

Figure 5-4. In this example, the link labels are services, houses, directory, *and* added. *When people describe hypertext, they're often thinking of link labels.*

Just because they're relatively easy to create doesn't mean they necessarily work well. For example, take the following list of link labels:

Amalgamated
annual report
Bob Pobjoy
ButtMaster 5000
forty percent

Here, we have no clue what these labels mean because there is no context. Without context, these aren't part of a system at all. Certainly, if they were being used as part of a navigation system, they'd never work.

However, as we see these labels as links within the context of the text, they start to make sense:

> ...<u>Amalgamated</u> employees believe in the products that they manufacture, market, and sell. For example, <u>forty percent</u> of the company's employees religiously work out on Amalgamated's <u>ButtMaster 5000</u> at least once per work day. According to <u>Bob Pobjoy</u>, Amalgamated's Chief Morale Officer, "It's a great stress reducer, healthful, and good clean fun. And if you read our <u>annual report</u>, you'll know that Amalgamated is firmly behind firm behinds" quips Pobjoy....

Systematic consistency isn't an issue for link labels. These labels are glued together by the copy, not by a particular system. However, consistency does become an issue between these labels and the chunks of information they link to.

For example, the link "annual report" may take the user to a page with the heading Financial Information. *Most* users won't have a problem with this, but at least a few will be confused. But if the link "Amalgamated" leads to a page labeled Acme Corporation, most users won't bother reading the copy far enough to learn that Amalgamated is really a division of Acme.

Avoiding the problems associated with inconsistencies between link labels and where they lead is difficult. We'll never be certain, for example, what we get if we select the link "Bob Pobjoy." A biography? A photo? A personal home page? A mailto:? An entry in a corporate directory? Will "forty percent" lead to a simple pie chart, or the results of a rigorous scientific study of Amalgamated employee exercise habits? These problems can be minimized by asking yourself, "What kind of information will the user expect to be taken to?" *before* creating and labeling a link. Then, apply your answer consistently. For example, consider having all references to personal names (e.g., Bob Pobjoy) lead to the same sort of destination (e.g., always to a mailto: link).

A note of caution about link labels: links embedded in text can be difficult for the eye to scan. They are fine for ad hoc links that cannot be easily separated from surrounding text, but don't rely on them for frequently used links such as navigational links.

Labels as Headings

Links are often used as headings that describe the chunk of information that follows the heading. For example, the label for this part of the page you are reading, "Labels as Headings," represents the chunk of information between it and the next heading, "Iconic Labeling Systems." To some degree, a heading label, like a link label, also relies on the text that follows to convey its meaning (see Figure 5-5). However, unlike link labels, there is no guarantee that the user will read the associated chunk of text. So there is extreme pressure on heading labels to draw the user's attention to the accompanying chunk of information.

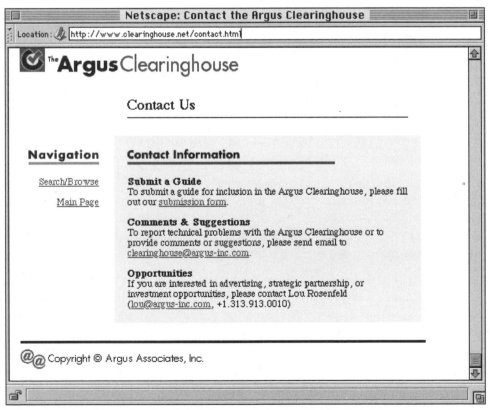

Figure 5-5. The obvious heading labels here are Submit a Guide, Comments & Suggestions, and Opportunities. These were designed so that users could understand what the labels represent without reading the actual copy. Navigation and Contact Information could also be considered heading labels, in this case for broader areas.

To ensure that your heading labels work well as a system, display the heading labels from each page in your site as a single outline. Look for two characteristics: *consistency in terminology* and *consistency in granularity*. Consistent terminology means that the wording used among labels is uniform and cohesive. Consistent granularity means two things: 1) that the chunks of information represented at each level of labels are roughly of equal importance, and 2) that the levels of labels don't vary greatly in how deeply they cover parts of a site.

In the following example, we see the outlines for a site's main page and two of its component pages:

Heading Labels from Main Page

```
GPSC: Global Psychic Services Corporation
    Call our Telephone Hotline
    GPSC Publications for Sale
    For Prospective Employees
    Search This Site
    Questions/Feedback
```

Heading Labels from "GPSC Publications for Sale" Page #1

```
GPSC Publications for Sale: The Bon Vivant's Guide to Nouvelle Psychic
                                       Cooking
    What is "Psychic Cooking"?
    Synopsis
    About the Author
    What People are Saying About The Bon Vivant's Guide to Nouvelle Psychic
                                       Cooking
        Testimonials
        Reviews
Ordering Information
        By Fax
        By Telephone
        Via the Internet
```

Heading Labels from "GPSC Publications for Sale" Page #2

```
    Publications for Sale-"Your Psychic Pet"
    How to Order This Book
```

The main page's problems with consistent terminology are due to a poor organization system. These labels are a mix of tasks (e.g., Call our Telephone Hotline, Search This Site), audiences (e.g., For Prospective Employees), and general topics (e.g., GPSC Publications for Sale, Questions/Feedback). Because the organization system is poorly designed, the labels that represent it are confusing.

The two GPSC Publications for Sale pages have inconsistent labels for the main heading and the ordering information:

GPSC Publications for Sale: *The Bon Vivant's Guide to Nouvelle Psychic Cooking* vs. Publications for Sale–"Living with Psychic Pets"

Ordering Information vs. How to Order This Book

One echoes the original heading on the main page, while the other omits the GPSC. One uses a colon, the other a dash to separate the generic label from the publication's title. One uses italics, while the other encloses the title in quotation marks. Also, these two pages have radically different sets of headings for no particularly good reason. Mightn't users also want a synopsis and author information for Your Psychic Pet?

Lastly, the first publication's page goes into much more detail than the second. The first has a much finer level of granularity than does the second. For example, on Page #1, there are heading labels for ordering By Fax, By Telephone, and Via the Internet, but on Page #2 the granularity is coarser: we only know How to Order This Book without mention of how it can be ordered. Is there any good reason for this? This sort of problem is caused by carelessness or, in other words, lack of planning.

Iconic Labeling Systems

It's true that a picture is worth a thousand words. But *which* thousand?

Icons can represent information in much the same way as text. We see them frequently used as navigation labels. Additionally, icons occasionally serve as heading labels and have even been known to show up as link labels, although this is rare.

The problem with iconic labels is that they constitute a much more limited language than text. Consider the concept *home page*. You'll find that there are icons that are commonly recognized as representing home pages. Here are a few examples:[*]

But what about when you want to represent something more complex? Like, for instance, a link to Press Releases? You may have occasionally seen a newspaper or cascaded trio of icons, like these:

Does it work? Would you automatically know that these icons represent press releases? Or would you have guessed that it represents a report? Or something that's already in print? Or something else altogether?

---

[*] These icons come from IconBAZAAR (*http://www.iconbazaar.com/*).

English has over 610,000 words.* Remarkably, English speakers have generally agreed to certain conventions about its syntax and semantics. In other words, there isn't much doubt what is meant by the textual label Main Page.

Iconic languages, however, are a bit more constrained. Because we're not all artistic, it's harder to convey a concept visually than it is in text (see Figure 5-6). For example, if I drew an image of a house for use as a main page icon, it's as likely that you'd interpret my drawing as representing a home page as you'd interpret it as a dog chasing its tail.

Even more than text labels, iconic labels rely on consistent positioning on a site's pages. Moving them around from page to page can sacrifice the user's ability to scan the page quickly and understand what the labels represent, thereby negating much of the benefit of using iconic labels.

Icons are fine for representing a few key concepts in a web site. We've all seen a few conventions, such as a house icon for a main page, a question mark for a help page, a magnifying glass for a search page, and so forth. But there aren't too many more that conform to convention, so using icons to represent a large, complex site is an approach that won't scale well. How large is the language of standard web icons? A dozen, perhaps? Certainly no comparison to its textual counterpart, English. In fact, you'll notice that very few web sites bother to use iconic labels *without* accompanying textual labels, if they use icons at all.

So why use iconic labels, especially if you can't use them without textual labels? Two reasons: 1) they can contribute to a consistent, attractive graphic identity for a site, and 2) they are familiar and easy for the user to find on a page (*if* they are drawn from the small group of concepts conventionally understood and are used consistently on all the site's pages).

Creating Effective Labeling Systems

Successful labeling systems mirror the thinking and language of a site's users, not its owners. If you've done your homework and created a sound organizational system for your site, the labeling system should follow its lead. So, for example,

---

* According to Nettie Lagace, Reference Librarian at the Internet Public Library (*http://www.ipl.org*), "If you take the *Oxford English Dictionary* as gospel, (English) contains half a million words in the CD-ROM edition (*http://www.oup-usa.org/oed/oed2cdfaq.html*) according to its own homepage, but 616,500 words according to Harvard's link (*http://hplus.harvard.edu/descriptions/oed.html*). The *Encyclopedia Britannica* says *Webster's Third New International Dictionary of the English Language* (1961), another authoritative unabridged source, contains 'more than 450,000' words, but in its entry for 'English Language' doesn't address the size of our collective vocabulary." Thanks Nettie!

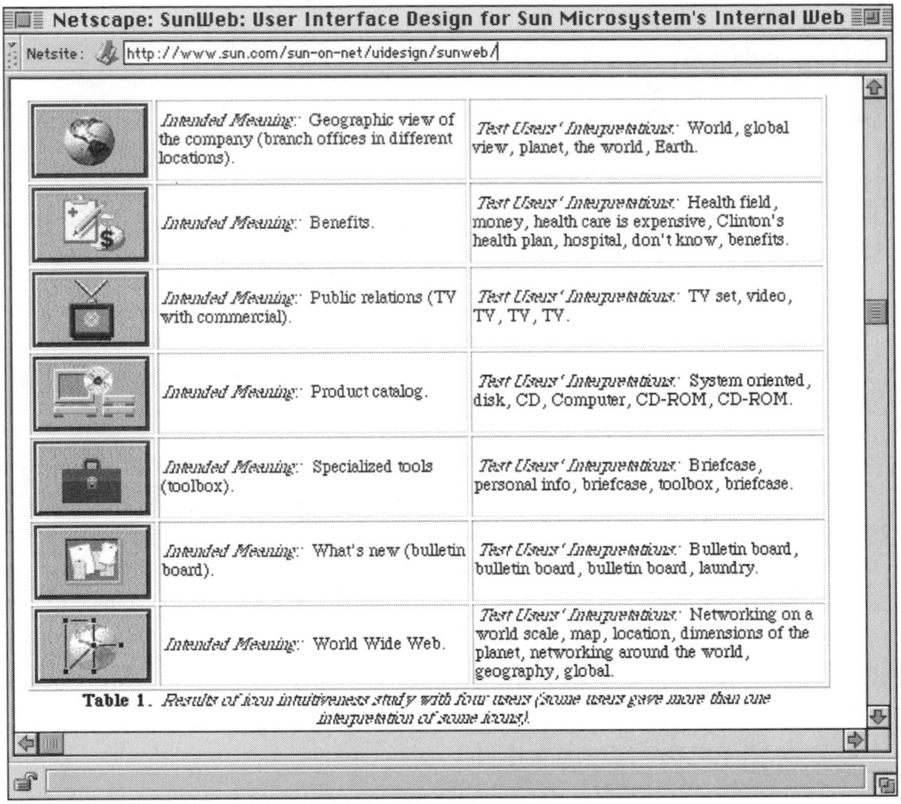

	Intended Meaning: Geographic view of the company (branch offices in different locations).	*Test Users' Interpretations:* World, global view, planet, the world, Earth.
	Intended Meaning: Benefits.	*Test Users' Interpretations:* Health field, money, health care is expensive, Clinton's health plan, hospital, don't know, benefits.
	Intended Meaning: Public relations (TV with commercial).	*Test Users' Interpretations:* TV set, video, TV, TV, TV.
	Intended Meaning: Product catalog.	*Test Users' Interpretations:* System oriented, disk, CD, Computer, CD-ROM, CD-ROM.
	Intended Meaning: Specialized tools (toolbox).	*Test Users' Interpretations:* Briefcase, personal info, briefcase, toolbox, briefcase.
	Intended Meaning: What's new (bulletin board).	*Test Users' Interpretations:* Bulletin board, bulletin board, bulletin board, laundry.
	Intended Meaning: World Wide Web.	*Test Users' Interpretations:* Networking on a world scale, map, location, dimensions of the planet, networking around the world, geography, global.

Table 1. *Results of icon intuitiveness study with four users (Some users gave more than one interpretation of some icons).*

Figure 5-6. Jakob Nielsen of Sun Microsystems and Darrell Sano of Netscape Communications conducted an interesting study of how users interpreted the icons Sun was considering using on its intranet. Our favorite results: the icon for "Benefits" interpreted as "Clinton's health plan," the icon for "What's New" interpreted as "Laundry," and the icon for "World Wide Web" interpreted as "dimensions of the planet."

the labeling system should be topical if the organization system is topical. But once you've established a general approach (e.g., topical, task-oriented), where should the actual labels, the words themselves, come from?

Sources for Labeling Systems

The labels currently in place

Your web site already has labels by default. As you made some decisions during the course of the site's creation, you probably won't want to throw those labels out and start over. Instead, use them as a starting point for developing a complete labeling system, taking into consideration the decisions you made while creating the original system (if you can still remember them).

Capture the existing labels in a single document. To do so, you'll have to walk the entire site, either manually or automatically, to gather the labels. You might consider assembling them as a simple label table. Here's an example:

Page Title (rendered as a graphic at top of page)	Page Title (rendered with <TITLE> tags)	URL	Headings on Page
Argus Associates, Inc.	Argus Associates, Inc.	*http://www.argus-inc.com/*	• Who We Are. • What We Do. • Clients • Contact Argus.
Who We Are	The Argus Team	*http://www.argus-inc.com/staff/index.html*	• Principals • Senior Staff • The Argus Team
What We Do	Web Site Design	*http://www.argus-inc.com/design/index.html*	• Information Architecture Critique • Mission and Vision Articulation • Audience and Content Analysis • Idea Generation • Web Site Architecture • Deliverables
Clients	Argus Clients	*http://www.argus-inc.com/clients/index.html*	• <client name A> • <client name B> • <client name N>
Contact Argus	Contacting Argus	*http://www.argus-inc.com/contact/index.html*	(none)

This label table is short because the site is small. Arranging these labels in a condensed form provides a more accurate and complete view as a system than if you looked at each label within the site page by page. Inconsistencies are easier to catch; for example, we learned that we were using three different labels for the same content (e.g., What We Do vs. What We Do. vs. Web Site Design, and Contact Argus. vs. Contact Argus vs. Contacting Argus). As you can see, both the wording and the use of periods was inconsistent, and possibly confusing. Shame on us! This proves the point that it's easy to create inconsistent labels even within a relatively small site.

Other web sites

If you don't have a site in place or are looking for new ideas, you'll want to look elsewhere for labeling systems. The open nature of the Web encourages an atmosphere of benevolent plagiarism, so, just as you might view the source of a wonderfully designed page, you can "borrow" from another site's great labeling system. Make sure you're in top critical consumer mode to ensure that your audiences' needs are well-represented. Then surf your competitors' sites, borrowing what works and noting what doesn't. Also look at academic sites that deal with your site's subject; colleges and universities often have the luxury of retaining label-happy librarians on their staffs to assist in site creation.

Controlled vocabularies and thesauri

If you're feeling more ambitious, other places have labeling systems from which to borrow. *Controlled vocabularies* and *thesauri* are often useful sources created by professionals with library or subject-specific backgrounds. A controlled vocabulary is simply a list of predetermined terms that describe a topic, such as art or computer science. They are controlled in that you must use the vocabulary's terms for a topic, and not an alternative term. A common example is the set of categories found in any yellow pages directory. When you're looking for movies or cinemas, you'll find them listed under "Theatres-Cinema" and nowhere else (why the Ann Arbor area directory uses the British spelling for "theaters" is beyond us).

A thesaurus is a controlled vocabulary that includes relationships between those terms, including:

- "See" or "Use" terms: Some thesauri include common terms that aren't part of the controlled vocabulary, with a reference to the appropriate controlled term to use. So, in Figure 5-7, if you're looking for the term *Draft*, you're instructed to use *Compulsory military service* instead.

- "See Also" or "Related" terms: These relationships help you find other terms that might be of interest; in Figure 5-8, the term *Domestic politics and foreign policy* is related to *Bipartisan foreign policy*, *Congress and foreign policy*, and so on.

- "Broader" or "Parent" terms: If a term is too specific (i.e., its level of granularity is too fine), you might look to see what topic it is a part of. In Figure 5-8, *Domestic politics and foreign policy* is part of the broader area of *foreign relations*.

- "Narrower" or "Child" terms: Conversely, a narrower term may provide the level of specificity you need. *Dog* is a narrower term of *Mammal*.

These additional relationships can be useful for determining the labeling of the different levels of your site. If you've ever used a library catalog, you are already familiar with a thesaurus: the subject keywords associated with each book come from the *Library of Congress Subject Headings* (LCSH).

You can use and adapt terms from controlled vocabularies and thesauri, but remember: the more narrow and specific the vocabulary or thesaurus, the better

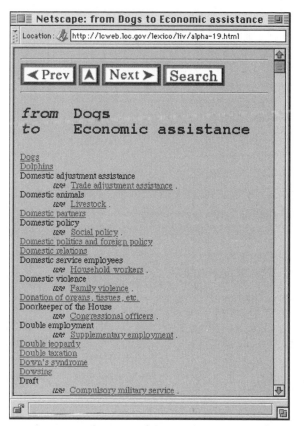

Figure 5-7. A subsection of the LIV *(Legislative Indexing Vocabulary) thesaurus. Note that some terms are not considered part of the controlled vocabulary; instead, they refer you to a similar term that is part of the controlled vocabulary (e.g., for the uncontrolled term* Draft, *use* Compulsory military service*).*

its terms will perform for your site. The *LCSH* is a thesaurus of terms intended to describe the whole universe of knowledge. This is an expansive and expensive task, and it's hard to keep up with all the changes going on in the world; *LCSH* still includes arcane terms like *water closet. LCSH* may often be out-of-date and is designed to be all things to all people; therefore, its terms may not be the best fit for your site, which probably doesn't deal with all aspects of human knowledge.

Instead, seek out vocabularies that are more narrowly focused and that help specific audiences to access specific types of content. For example, if your site's users are computer scientists, a computer science thesaurus "thinks" the same way the users do more than a general scheme like *LCSH* would. A good example of a specific controlled vocabulary is the *Legislative Indexing Vocabulary* (LIV), available at *http://lcweb.loc.gov/lexico/liv/brsearch.html,* which was designed by the Congressional Research Service to help users search in the Bill Summary & Status

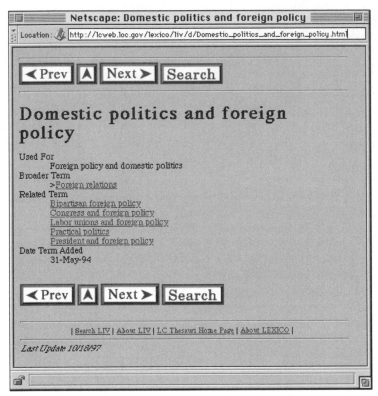

Figure 5-8. The value of a thesaurus is in the relationships it specifies between terms: selecting a term in the controlled vocabulary (e.g., Domestic politics and foreign policy) displays a broader term, related terms, and a similar term (Used For) that is not part of this controlled vocabulary.

files of THOMAS, the Library of Congress' web site for federal legislative information. If your site contains legislative information, or if your site's audience are legislative types, you might start with *LIV* as the basis of your site's labeling system.

Labels from content

Labels can come from the documents themselves. For example, if your site includes a number of technical reports created by a host of different authors, you can use the document's titles as part of an alphabetically sorted labeling system. Or, if you're creating a subject-oriented labeling system, you can learn a lot about these documents from the terms used in their titles and from their abstracts, if available. Perhaps you'll even read the reports themselves and come up with some terms that describe their content.

If you do use terms directly from the documents, be careful! A common (and wrong) assumption is that a document's author is the best candidate to label its content. For example, *Gone With the Wind* makes for an enticing title as we're sure Margaret Mitchell intended, but as a label it doesn't work at all. It has nothing to do with wind itself. Even if she had selected a representational title for her book, Ms. Mitchell wasn't concerned with how her book's title fit in with the titles of other books and how well the title would support users who were searching for it in an information system. If authors did have such concerns, they might select their titles from thesauri like *Library of Congress Subject Headings*! For various reasons (artistic, marketing-related, and more), authors' motives when they label their content may have absolutely nothing to do with ensuring that their information gets found. That's why it makes sense for *someone else* to take a close look at what's being labeled instead of relying upon the source to label the information accurately.

Labels from users and experts

Lastly, the users of a site may be telling you, directly or indirectly, what the labels should be. This isn't the easiest information to get your hands on, but if you can, it's the best source of labeling there is.

It would be great to simply ask them what terms they use, but this wouldn't be very practical. There is a less-intrusive source of useful information on what labels your site's audiences actually use: your search engine's query log (most search engines do log user queries). Query analysis is a great way to understand the types of labels your site's users typically use (see Figures 5-9 and 5-10). Besides shedding some light on user searching behavior, query analysis can also help you understand the content users are specifically asking for from your site. In the case of search queries that retrieve no results, consider these terms as candidates for inclusion in your labeling system, or consider adding relevant content to your site so that queries using these terms actually retrieve *something* in the future.

Another less technical approach is to determine if there are any advanced users or experts, such as librarians, switchboard operators, or other information specialists who are very familiar with the users' information needs, and who could therefore speak on the users' behalf.

We found this to be a useful exercise with one of our clients, a major health system. Working with their library staff, we set out to create two labeling systems, one with medical terms to help medical professionals browse the services offered by the health system, the other for the lay audience to access the same content. It wasn't difficult to come up with the medical terms, as there are many thesauri and controlled vocabularies geared toward labeling medical content. It was much more difficult to come up with a scheme for the layperson's list of terms. There

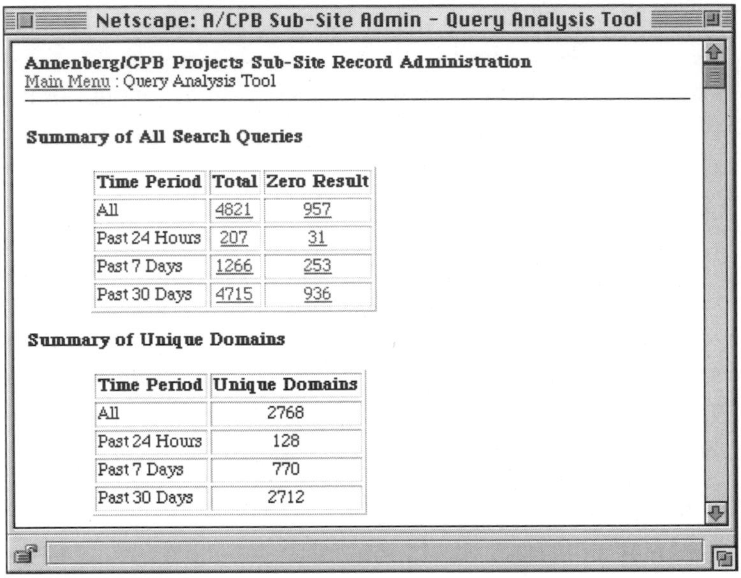

Netscape: A/CPB Sub-Site Admin - Query Analysis Tool

Annenberg/CPB Projects Sub-Site Record Administration
Main Menu : Query Analysis Tool

Summary of All Search Queries

Time Period	Total	Zero Result
All	4821	957
Past 24 Hours	207	31
Past 7 Days	1266	253
Past 30 Days	4715	936

Summary of Unique Domains

Time Period	Unique Domains
All	2768
Past 24 Hours	128
Past 7 Days	770
Past 30 Days	2712

Figure 5-9. Among other things, this custom-designed query analysis tool shows how many searches took place in total, as well as how many of those searches retrieved no results at all. It was developed by InterConnect of Ann Arbor.

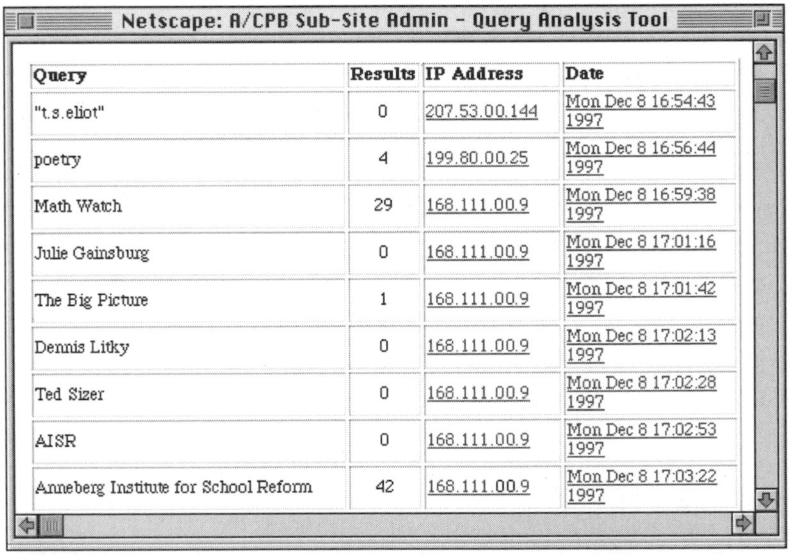

Netscape: A/CPB Sub-Site Admin - Query Analysis Tool

Query	Results	IP Address	Date
"t.s.eliot"	0	207.53.00.144	Mon Dec 8 16:54:43 1997
poetry	4	199.80.00.25	Mon Dec 8 16:56:44 1997
Math Watch	29	168.111.00.9	Mon Dec 8 16:59:38 1997
Julie Gainsburg	0	168.111.00.9	Mon Dec 8 17:01:16 1997
The Big Picture	1	168.111.00.9	Mon Dec 8 17:01:42 1997
Dennis Litky	0	168.111.00.9	Mon Dec 8 17:02:13 1997
Ted Sizer	0	168.111.00.9	Mon Dec 8 17:02:28 1997
AISR	0	168.111.00.9	Mon Dec 8 17:02:53 1997
Anneberg Institute for School Reform	42	168.111.00.9	Mon Dec 8 17:03:22 1997

Figure 5-10. Here the same query analysis tool helps us to view specific queries, how many results they retrieved, where they came from, and when they took place. The third through eighth came from the same IP address, and all took place within four minutes; this suggests that they were part of the same session by the same user.

didn't seem to be an ideal controlled vocabulary, and we couldn't draw labels from the site's content very easily, as it hadn't been created yet. So we were truly starting from scratch.

We solved this dilemma by asking ourselves what the users really wanted out of the site. We considered their general needs, and came up with a few major ones:

1. They need information about or a solution for a problem, illness, or condition.

2. The problem is with a particular organ or part of the body.

3. They want to know about the diagnostics or tests the health care professionals will perform to learn more about the problem.

4. They need information on the treatment, drug, or solution that will be provided by the health system.

5. They want to know how they can pay for the service.

6. They want to know how they can maintain their health.

We then could come up with basic terms to cover the majority of these six categories, taking care to use terms appropriate to this audience of laypersons. Here are some examples:

Category	Sample Labels
problem/illness/condition	HIV, fracture, arthritis, depression
organ/body part	heart, joints, mental health
diagnostics/test	blood pressure, X-ray
treatment/drug/solution	hospice, bifocals, joint replacement
payment	administrative services, health maintenance organization, medical records
health maintenance	exercise, vaccination

By starting with a few groupings, we were able to generate labels to support indexing the site. We knew a bit about the audience (who were laypersons), and so were able to generate the right kinds of terms to support their needs (e.g., *leg* instead of *femur*). The secret was working with people (in this case, staff librarians) who were knowledgeable about the kind of information the users want.

Fine-Tuning the Labeling System

The list of terms you are working with might be raw, coming straight from the content in your site, your site's users, or your own ideas of what should work best. Or, it may come straight from a polished controlled vocabulary. In either case, it'll need some work to become an effective labeling system.

The Basics

First, sort the list of terms alphabetically. If it's a long list (e.g., indexing labels), you might see some duplicates; remove these.

Then review the list for consistency of usage, punctuation, letter case, and so forth. For example, you'll remember that the label table drawn from the Argus web site had inconsistencies that became obvious right away. Sometimes we used periods after labels, sometimes we didn't. We also weren't consistent in our usage of link labels vs. the heading labels on the pages they referred to.

You might also find that the writing style varies too much from label to label. For example, one label might use an active verb (e.g., Order a Free Sample from Larry's Reptile Hut) while another may use more passive language (e.g., Larry's Reptile Hut Customer Service). This is a good time to resolve these inconsistencies and perhaps to establish conventions for usage in terms of punctuation, language, and so on.

Some terms will undoubtedly be synonyms (e.g., *cancer* and *oncology*), others will be variants on the same term (e.g., *microfiltration systems* and *microfiltration services*), and some will be related but not quite the same (e.g., *stationery* and *letterhead*). You'll need to make some tough decisions here. With synonyms, choose the term that best fits the language of your site's users. So, if they're medical professionals, use the medical term *oncology* rather than the more generic term *cancer.* If you encounter variants or synonyms, ask yourself if they are different or part of the same general concept. For example, do *microfiltration systems* and *microfiltration services* need to be distinguished, or could they be combined under *microfiltration*? Do you need very specific terms like *letterhead*, or will broader terms like *stationery* suffice?

All in all, strive to make your labels descriptive and differentiate them from one another. The studies by Jared Spool et al. demonstrate the confusion that can be wrought by putting similar terms such as *global* and *international* side by side, as was done in the Fidelity web site. If the site's designers had looked at these labels as part of a complete system, they'd likely have thought twice about using such similar labels.

Labeling System Scope and Size

Decisions about which terms to include need to be made in the context of how broad and how large a labeling system is required. First, determine if the labeling system has obvious gaps. Does it encompass all the possibilities that your site may eventually need to include? If, for example, your site is an online store that currently allows users to search a product database but does not support online ordering, ask yourself if eventually it might. Even if you're not certain, assume it will. Then devise a label for online ordering that fits within the rest of the labeling system. Or, if the site's labeling system is topical, anticipate the topics not yet covered by the site. In both cases, you might be surprised; you might learn that the addition of these phantom labels has a large impact on your labeling system, perhaps sufficiently enough for you to change its conventions in terms of wording, and so on. If you avoid this exercise, you might learn the hard way that future content doesn't fit well into your site because you're not sure how to label it, or it ends up in cop-out categories such as Miscellaneous, Other Info, and Stuff. Plan ahead so that labels you might add in the future don't throw off the current labeling system.

Balance this planning with an understanding of what your labeling system is there to accomplish. If you try to create a labeling system that encompasses the whole extent of human knowledge (instead of the current and anticipated content of your web site), you will encounter the sorts of nasty problems that the folks who created the *LCSH* have discovered. Keep your scope narrow and focused enough so that it can clearly address the requirements of your site's unique content and the special needs of its audiences, but be comprehensive within that well-defined scope.

Also consider the overall size of the labeling system. Obviously, if the goal is to label a navigation system, five or ten terms may be all you need. On the other hand, if you're creating a system for indexing the content of a large site, the labeling system may include hundreds of terms. What you'll want is the right level of *granularity* for your labeling system. Granularity, as mentioned before, refers to how specific you want to be in identifying and labeling your site's content. If you have ten thousand documents, can you use a labeling system of ten terms to label them? Sure, but under each label, you'd find hugely long and unusable lists of documents. On the other hand, if you use a three-tiered labeling system with hundreds of terms, users might shy away from its complexity. Is there a middle ground that makes sense in terms of labeling system size, a solution large enough to appropriately label the content, but not too overwhelming for users? If not, you might have to adjust the granularity that your labeling system is addressing. Perhaps instead of attempting to label every document, you'll have to address a coarser level of granularity by labeling logical groupings of documents (e.g., all the documents from the same department or by the same author) instead of each individual document.

Non-Representational Labeling Systems

This chapter emphasizes the need for labels to be familiar for users, and also that consistency and representation are the foundations for building that familiarity. Now that we have belabored that point, we'll counter it with another: labeling systems should not necessarily be representational.

What? Would you make up your mind already?

Well, let's put it this way: non-representational labeling is not something that we'd recommend using regularly. In fact, it's difficult to determine when it should be applied. Following are two examples where we think it succeeds.

Good Head-Scratching

Head-scratching is usually a Bad Thing. It means that some aspect of a site has confused a user and is in the way of achieving the site's main goal, namely, conveying a message. But, like everything else, even cognitive confusion has a good side: Mystery.

Consider the main page shown in Figure 5-11. What the heck is going on here? If you come to this site, you may already have a little context, knowing in advance that it's a personal site. If not, you might figure this out fairly quickly, as this text uses the first person and seems to describe a personal quest. Beyond that, this page tells nothing about what you'll find in this site.

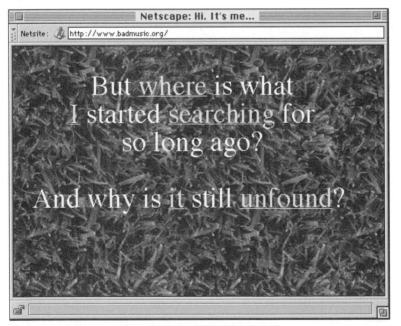

Figure 5-11. Is it obvious where these links lead you?

But you might want to know more. The radical aspect of this page involves its use of two brief sentences and five highly generic terms as labels to draw the user into a very personal experience. The labels are almost completely non-representational, and even in context they make you wonder and want to learn more.

If these link labels were accompanied by more information, such as scope notes, the effect would probably be lost:

Label	Scope Note
where	Descriptions of various places where the author has lived.
I	Basic information about the author.
searching	What the author has found while searching for meaning in his life.
it	Friends and meaning that the author found.
unfound	What the future may have in store.

There's no mystery if the site provided (gave away, really) this information on the main page. Without a little mystery, this site just wouldn't work.

When You Just Have To Use Icons

The same principle of mystery can apply with iconic labels. The site shown in Figure 5-12, Cool Central, showcases a different cool web site every few moments. It is geared toward web site developers and is a fun counterpart to the sponsor's other more informational site, *webreference.com*. The main page is distinguished by five holes, with miscellaneous pictures and activities (e.g., moving clouds, swimming fish) visible in each.

Each of the five holes links to a section of the site:

Iconic Label Position	Leads To
sky and floating clouds (top left)	About Cool Central
swimming fish	Nick's Picks
penguin	Cool Central Site of the [Moment, Hour, Day, Week]
sky and floating clouds (top right)	Advertising Information
smoking detective	Nick Click, Private Eye

Of course, none makes any sense at all, save for the detective icon, which leads to a private eye-themed area. Of course, you'll want to click on each just to learn what they lead to. Goofy, silly, and weird, but in a non-serious site that exists solely for the purpose of having fun, it works.

A Double Challenge

As with organization and navigation systems, labeling systems are much ignored and yet crucial to users understanding and being able to find information in your web site. Your challenge when working with labels is twofold. First, you want your site's labels to speak the same language as the site's users. We've discussed

Figure 5-12. These icons don't say much individually, but taken together they convey a sense of fun and invite the user to explore them further.

all sorts of sources for labels, from users to thesauri to analysis of users' queries to experts to the site's content itself. But human beings are fickle creatures; everyone is different, and everyone changes the way they think from moment to moment. Their use of language changes similarly. So the other half of your challenge is to use their language even more consistently than they do. That's why it's helpful to think of individual labels as parts of larger *systems*. Strive to design systems that are consistent in the labels that they use, the editorial style that colors those labels, and the granularity of content that those labels address.

6

Searching Systems

Searching and Your Web Site

The preceding three chapters were intended to help you create the best browsing system possible for your web site. This chapter describes when to use a search engine with your site and demonstrates techniques that will make searching work best for it.

Throughout this chapter, we use examples of searching systems from major sites which allow you to search the entire Web, as well as site-specific search engines. Although these Web-wide tools are different in that they index a much broader collection of content than your search system will, it is nonetheless very useful to study them. Of all searching systems, none has undergone the testing, usage, and investment that Web-wide search tools have, so why not benefit from their research?

When Not To Make Your Site Searchable

Before we delve into searching systems, we need to make a point: think twice before you make your site searchable.

What? What's the point of having a web site if people can't find information in it?

Your site should of course support the *finding* of its information. But don't assume a search engine alone will satisfy *all* users' information needs. While many users want to search a site, some just want to browse it.

Also, does your site have enough content to merit the use of a search engine? How much is enough? It's hard to say. It could be five resources or fifty; no specific number serves as a threshold. Perhaps a site with five long, dense documents deserves a search engine more than one with a collection of twenty brief, well-labeled documents. In any case, you'll want to balance the time necessary to set up and maintain a searching system with the payoff it brings to your site's users.

Because many site developers see search engines as *the* solution to the problems that users are experiencing when trying to find information in their sites, search engines become bandages for sites with poorly designed *browsing* systems. If you see yourself falling into this trap, you should probably suspend implementing your searching system until you fix your browsing system's problems.

Search engines are fairly easy to get up and running, but like much of the Web, they are difficult to set up effectively. As a user of the Web, you've certainly seen incomprehensible search interfaces, and we're sure that your queries have retrieved some pretty strange results. This often is the result of a lack of planning by the site developer, who probably installed the search engine with its default settings, pointed it at his or her site, and forgot about it. So, if you don't plan on putting some significant time into configuring your search engine properly, reconsider your decision to implement it.

Now that we've got our warnings and threats out of the way, we'll discuss when to implement searching systems, and how you can make them work better.

When To Make Your Site Searchable

Most web sites, as we know, aren't planned out in much detail before they're built. Instead, they grow organically. This may be all right for smaller web sites that aren't likely to expand much, but for ones that become popular, more and more content and functional features get added haphazardly, leading to a navigation nightmare.

There's a good analogy of physical architecture. Powell's Books (*http://www.powells.com*), which claims to be the largest bookstore in the world, covers an entire city block (43,000 square feet) in Portland, Oregon. We guess that it originally started as a single small storefront on that block, but as their business grew, they knocked a doorway through the wall into the next storefront, and so on, until they occupied the whole block. The result is a hodgepodge of chambers, halls with odd turns, and unexpected stairways. This chaotic labyrinth is a charming place to wander and browse, but if you're searching for a particular title, good luck. It will be difficult to find what you're looking for, although you might serendipitously stumble onto something better.

Yahoo! once was a Web version of Powell's. Everything was there, but fairly easy to find. Why? Because Yahoo!, like the Web, was relatively small. At its inception, Yahoo! pointed to a few hundred Internet resources, made accessible through an easily browsable subject hierarchy. No search option was available, something unimaginable to Yahoo! users today. But things soon changed. Yahoo! had an excellent technical architecture that allowed site owners to easily self-register their sites, but Yahoo!'s information architecture wasn't very well-planned, and couldn't keep up with the increasing volume of resources that were added daily. Eventually, the subject hierarchy became too cumbersome to navigate, and the Yahoo! people installed a search engine as an alternative way of finding information in the site. Nowadays it's a decent bet that more people use Yahoo!'s search engine instead of browsing through all those hierarchical subject categories, although the browsable categories remain useful as a supplement to the searching process (and, in fact, are included in search results).

Your site probably doesn't contain as much content as Yahoo! does, but if it's a substantial site, it probably merits a search engine. There are good reasons for this: users won't be willing to browse through your site's structure. Their time is limited, and their cognitive overload threshold is lower than you think. Interestingly, sometimes users won't browse for the *wrong* reasons; that is, they search when they don't necessarily know what to search for. Even though they would be better served by browsing, they search anyway.

You should also consider creating a searching system for your site if it contains highly dynamic content. For example, if your site is a Web-based newspaper, you could be adding dozens of story files daily. For this reason, you probably wouldn't have the time each day to maintain elaborate tables of contents, browsable indices, and other browsing systems. A search engine can help you by automatically indexing the contents of the site once or many times per day. Automating this process ensures that users have quality access to your site's content, and you can spend time doing things other than manually indexing and linking the story files.

Understanding How Users Search

Assuming you've decided to implement a searching system for your web site, it's important to understand how users really search before designing it. We'll try to condense decades of research and experience generated by the field of information retrieval into the next few paragraphs. But it really boils down to this point: searching systems can and should vary as much as browsing systems or any other components of web sites do, because all users aren't alike, and information retrieval is much harder than most people realize.

Users Have Different Kinds of Information Needs

Information scientists and librarians have been studying users' information finding habits for decades. Until recently, these studies usually pertained to traditional information systems, such as how to ask a library patron the right questions to learn their information needs, or how to make it easier to search for information in online library card catalogs or other databases.

Many studies indicated that users of information systems aren't members of a single-minded monolithic audience who want the same kinds of information delivered in the same ways. Some want just a little information, while others want detailed assessments of everything there is to know about a topic. Some want only the most accurate, highest quality information, while others don't care much about the reliability of the source. Some will wait for the results, while others need the information yesterday. Some are just plain happy to get any information at all, regardless of how much relevant stuff they're really missing. Users' needs and expectations vary widely, and so the information systems that serve them must recognize, distinguish, and accommodate these different needs.

To illustrate, let's look at one of these factors in greater detail: the variability in users' searching expectations.

Known-item searching

Some users' information needs are clearly defined and have a single, correct answer. When you check the newspaper to see how your stock in Amalgamated Shoelace and Aglet is doing (especially since the hostile Microsoft takeover attempt), you know exactly what you want, that the information exists, and where it can be found. This is the simplest type of information need. If it were the only type, the job of the web site architect would be much easier.

Existence searching

However, some users know what they want but don't know how to describe it or whether the answer exists at all. For example, you might want to buy shares in a particular type of mutual fund that invests in Moldovan high-tech start-ups and that carries no load. You are convinced that this sector is up-and-coming, but do Fidelity and Merrill Lynch know this as well? You might check their web sites, call a broker or two, or ask your in-the-know aunt. This kind of information need is more challenging: it might be hard to convey exactly what you're looking for ("Moldova? What's that?"), especially if it's a new and as-yet-unheard-of item. Rather than a clear question for which a right answer exists, you have an abstract idea or concept, and you don't know whether matching information exists. The success of your search depends as much upon the abilities of the brokers, the web sites, and your aunt to *understand* your idea and its context as whether the information (in this case, a particular mutual fund) exists.

Exploratory searching

Some users know how to phrase their question, but don't know exactly what they're hoping to find, and are really just exploring and trying to learn more. If you ever considered changing careers, you know what we mean: you're not sure that you definitely want to switch to a career in chinchilla farming, but you've heard it's the place to be, so you might informally ask a friend of a friend who has an uncle in the business. Or you call the public library to see if there's a book on the subject. Or you write to the Chinchilla Professionals' Association requesting more information. In any case, you are not sure exactly what you'll uncover, but you're willing to take the time to learn more. Like existence searching, you have not so much a question seeking an answer as much as an idea that you want to learn more about. Unlike the next type of searching, you don't need to know everything there is; a few pieces of good information will do fine for now.

Comprehensive searching (research)

Some users want everything available on a given topic. Scientific researchers, patent lawyers, doctoral students trying to find unique and original dissertation topics, and fans of any sort fit into this category. For example, if you idolize that late great music duo Milli Vanilli, you'll want to see everything that has anything to do with them—singles and records, bootlegs, concert tour posters, music videos, reviews, fan club information, paraphernalia, interviews, books, scholarly articles, and record-burning schedules. Even casual mentions of the band, such as someone's incoherent ramblings in a web page or Usenet newsgroup, are fair game if you're seeking all there is to know about Milli Vanilli. So you might turn to all sorts of information sources for help: friends, the library, bookstores, music stores, radio call-in shows, Ouija boards, and so on.

There are many other ways of classifying information needs, but the important thing to remember is that not all users are looking for the same thing. Ideally, you should anticipate the most common types of needs that your site's users will have and ensure that these needs are met. Minimally, you should give some thought to the variations and try to design a search interface that is flexible in responding to them.

Searching and Browsing Are Integrated

One drawback to the literature on information finding is that much of it deals with testing and improving a single information system (e.g., an online card catalog). But the truth is that most people, especially those with more involved information needs, use many information systems for a particular search. This often means jumping from Infoseek to Magellan to a specific site to Hotbot and so on, all in the context of one search. Even when using a single web site, users often alternate between browsing and searching. For example, when you use Yahoo!, you might first perform a search, find a useful site, and then, using its Yahoo! category, browse for similarly indexed sites.

Multiple Iterations Are Commonplace

Additionally, information searching generally doesn't take place within one clean pass, unless it's of the *known-item searching* variety. Information searching and browsing are by nature *iterative*: users will make a first attempt at finding information, learn something, refine their query, try finding some more, learn some more, refine again. This is commonly known as *associative learning*. Unfortunately, finding everything you need at once doesn't happen all that often, because you don't generally know enough about the topic to articulate your query the right way in the first place.

The Moving Target: A Likely Scenario

A typical example of a search for information might go something like this:

> Jan, a budding entrepreneur, wants to get business cards printed for her new company. She calls her pal Fred to see how he did it and what company he used. Unfortunately, Fred is not in, and, never one to dawdle, Jan leaves Fred voice mail and moves on to the yellow pages. She finds nothing under Business Cards, but does see a number of companies listed under Printers, and gets a few price quotes, which all seem to be in the same neighborhood. Not sure which to select, Jan contacts the local chapter of the Better Business Bureau for their recommendation. The BBB folks refer Jan to their web site, where she can search a database of companies with dubious histories. This provides Jan with useful information that helps whittle down her list of candidate printers. Meanwhile, Fred calls Jan back and tells her that she really shouldn't have just business cards printed, but that she should hire a graphic designer to create a full graphic identity package for Jan's new business, including letterhead, brochures, and so on. So, Jan realizes that she needs to find an affordable, reputable graphic design firm, and she returns to the yellow pages. She also goes to the library to do a catalog search to see if any books describe what it's like to work with a graphic design firm, and how much she ought to expect to pay. And so on...

As you can see, Jan's initially simple information need becomes a fully fledged associative learning process, changing at least twice (from a hunt for a printer to a hunt for a graphic design firm to information on negotiating and working with a graphic designer), and for all we know, it's not over yet. It also involves *multiple information sources* (Fred, the yellow pages, the library catalog, the bookstore), and utilizes *browsing* (the yellow pages directory), *searching* (the Web database, the library catalog), and even *asking* (Fred, the Better Business Bureau). Things aren't always as simple as they seem! Your challenge, of course, is to design your site's architecture to support the most common searching and browsing approaches in a smooth and integrated way.

Designing the Search Interface

With so much variation among users to account for, there can be no single ideal search interface. Although the literature of information retrieval includes many studies of search interface design, many variables preclude the emergence of the right way to design search interfaces. Here are a few of the variables on the table:

- The level of searching expertise users have: Are they comfortable with Boolean operators, or do they prefer natural language? Do they need a simple or high-powered interface? What about a help page?

- The kind of information the user wants: Do they want just a taste, or are they doing comprehensive research? Should the results be brief, or should they provide extensive detail for each document?

- The type of information being searched: Is it made up of structured fields or full text? Is it navigation pages, destination pages, or both? HTML or other formats?

- How much information is being searched: Will users be overwhelmed by the number of documents retrieved?

We can, however, provide basic advice that you should consider when designing a search interface.

Support Different Modes of Searching

Before diving into design, think hard about why users are searching your site, and what they want to get out of their search. Are they likely to search for certain types of information, such as specific product descriptions or staff directory entries? If so, support modes of searching that are delineated by content types— use the same interface to allow users to search the product catalog, or the staff directory, or other content areas (content-delineated indexing involves the creation of *search zones*, which we'll cover later in this chapter). Are non-English speakers important to your site? Then provide them with search interfaces in their native languages, including language-specific directions, search commands and operators, and help information. Does your site need to satisfy users with different levels of sophistication with online searching? Then consider making available both a basic search interface and an advanced one.

For example, one of our clients, UMI, sells dissertations to an audience that includes researchers, librarians, and others who have been using advanced online information systems for years. We needed an interface that would accommodate this important expert audience who were used to complex Boolean and proximity operators, and who were already very used to the arcane search languages of other commercial information services. However, a simple search interface was also required, because at times users wouldn't need all the firepower of an advanced search interface, especially when conducting simple, known-item searches. Additionally, because it had become available via the Web, a whole new audience of novices would encounter this product for the first time; we assumed that these newbies wouldn't be comfortable with a complex search interface.

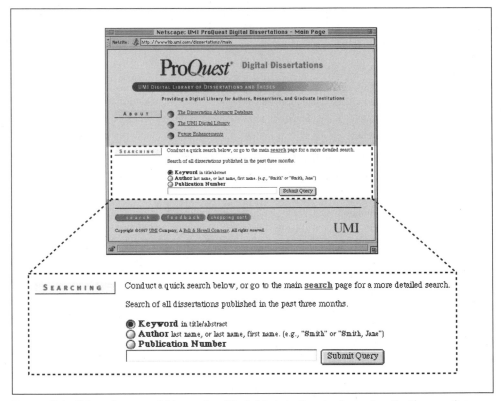

Figure 6-1. Although we could have simplified this interface by foregoing the three radio button selections, they add utility and let users know what they are searching without taking up too much screen space.

So we created a simple interface that almost anyone could figure out and use right away, shown above in Figure 6-1. A simple search box is ideal for the novice or for a user with a pretty good sense of what he or she is looking for. (We made sure to provide a single search query box; our experience shows that most users don't care for separate boxes, one for each query term, divided by Boolean operators.) Minimal filtering options are provided, including searching for keywords within title and abstract fields, searching within the author field, or searching within the publication number field. These filtering options provide the user with more power by allowing more specific searching. But because the labels Keyword, Author, and Publication Number are fairly self-explanatory, they don't force the user to think too much about these options.

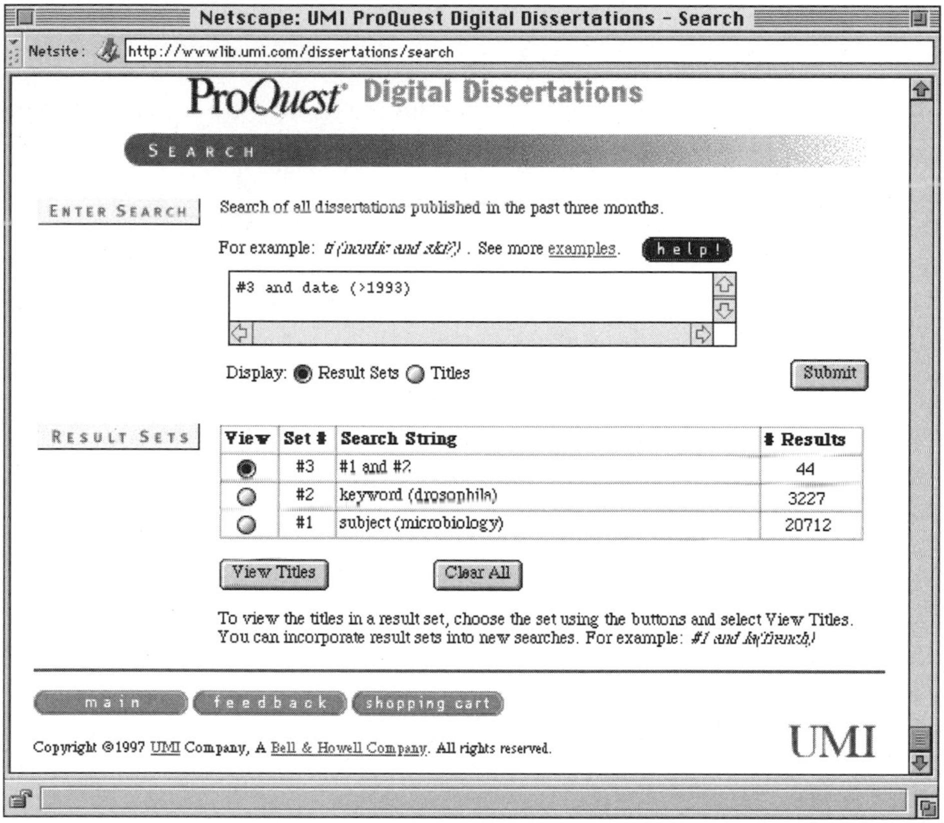

Figure 6-2. Because they present so much information, more complex search interfaces generally can't be embedded on other pages and instead require a dedicated page.

For the advanced users, a more powerful interface was created, shown above in Figure 6-2. This interface supports the following types of searching:

Fielded Searching

Author, Keyword, Title, Subject, and ten other fields are searchable. A researcher could, for example, find a dissertation related to his or her area of interest by searching the subject field, and learn who that doctoral student's advisor was by reading the abstract. To find other related dissertations, the researcher could then search the Advisor field to learn about other doctoral students who shared the same advisor.

Familiar Query Language

In Figure 6-2, the style "field(search term)" is used (e.g., "keyword(drosophila)"). Because many different query language conventions are supported by traditional online products, users may be used to an established convention. The effort to support these users is made by allowing variant terms. For the field Degree Date, the user can enter either "ddt," "da," "date," "yr," or "year."

Longer Queries

More complex queries often require more space than the single line entry box found in the simple search interface in Figure 6-1. The more complex interface supports a much longer query.

Reusable Result Sets

Many traditional online information products allow searchers to build sets of results that can be reused. In this example, we've ANDed together the two sets that we've already found, and could in turn combine this result with other sets during the iterative process of searching.

Because this advanced interface supports so many different types of searching, we provided a substantial help page to assist users. For users of common browsers, the help page shown in Figure 6-3 launches in a separate browser window so that users don't need to exit the search interface to get help.

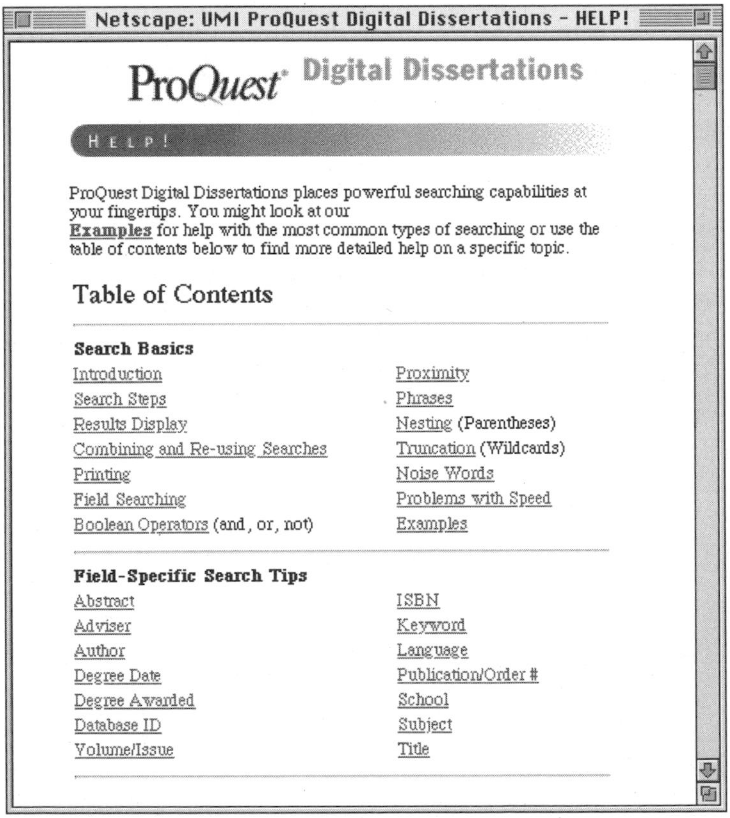

Figure 6-3. This help page serves as a ready reference to help users take advantage of the searching capability offered by this search engine and offers examples. It launches in a separate browser window.

Searching and Browsing Systems Should Be Closely Integrated

As we mentioned earlier, users typically need to switch back and forth between searching and browsing. In fact, users often don't know if they need to search or browse in the first place. Therefore, these respective systems shouldn't live in isolation from one another.

When we redesigned the Argus Clearinghouse, we integrated these two elements on a single page called Search/Browse, shown in Figure 6-4. This combined interface to searching and browsing makes it clear to the user what he or she can do there. The search/browse approach can be extended by making search and browse options available on the search results page as well, especially on null results pages, when a user might be at a dead end and needs to be gently led back into the process of iterative searching and browsing before frustration sets in.

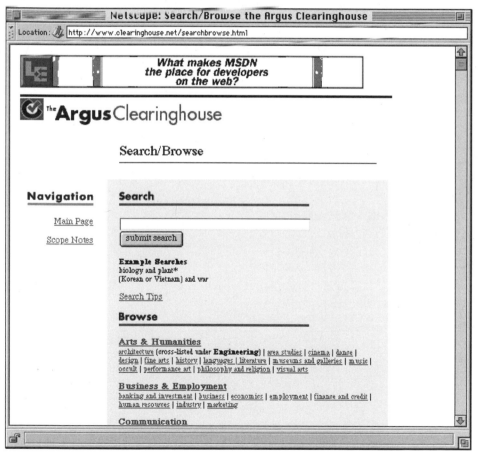

Figure 6-4. Because its vertical space requirements are relatively small, the simple search interface is located toward the top of the page. It is followed by a browsing scheme too long to be displayed in its entirety. But users get a sense of what they'll see if they scroll further.

Searching Should Conform to the Site's Look and Feel

Search engine interfaces, and more importantly, retrieval results, should look and behave like the rest of your site. This advice may seem painfully obvious, but because many search engines are packaged as ready-to-go add-ons to a site, site developers don't bother to customize them.* For example, the interface and results produced by the Excite search engine are easy to detect. In fact, they look and work so similarly from site to site that it's easy to forget that they are actually parts of individual sites. Figure 6-5 is a great example of a search interface which hasn't been customized, while Figure 6-6 shows how the search interface can be integrated with the rest of the site's look and feel.

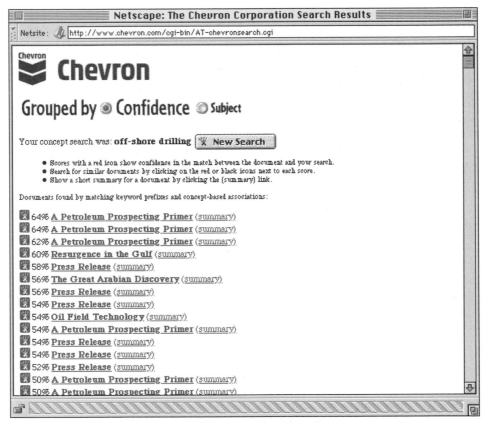

Figure 6-5. Search results from a search engine that hasn't been customized ...

---

* It should be mentioned that some search engines, like AltaVista, don't allow you to modify search and retrieval results pages.

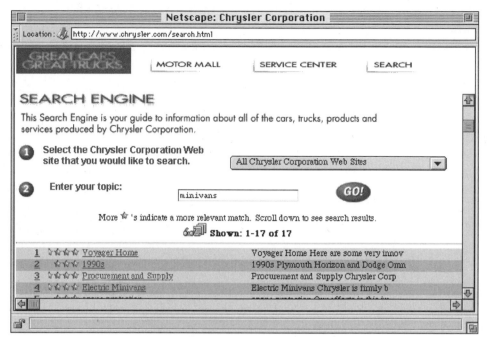

Figure 6-6. ... and from one that has. In Figure 6-5, the search results use Excite's standard images, and look more like they're part of Excite's site than Chevron's. The Chrysler site's searching system's look and feel is much more closely integrated with the rest of the site.

Search Options Should Be Clear

We all pay lip service to the need for user documentation, but with searching, it's really a must. Because so many different variables are involved with searching, there are many opportunities for things to go wrong. On a Help or Documentation page, consider letting the user know the following:

1. *What is being searched.* Users often assume that their search query is being run against the full text of every page in your site. Instead your site may support fielded searching (as in the UMI example above), or another type of selective searching (see "Indexing the Right Stuff" later in this chapter). If they're curious, users should be able to find out exactly what they are searching.

2. *How they can formulate search queries.* What good is it to build in advanced querying capabilities if the user never knows about them? Show off the power of your search engine with excellent real life examples. In other words, make sure your examples actually work and retrieve relevant documents if the user decides to test them.

3. *User options.* Can the user do other neat things such as changing the sorting order of retrieval results? Show them off as well!

4. *What to do if the user can't find the right information.* It's important to provide the user with some tricks to handle the following three situations:

   a. "I'm getting too much stuff."

   b. "I'm not getting anything."

   c. "The stuff I'm getting stinks!"

For case (a), you might suggest approaches that narrow the retrieval results. For example, if your system supports the Boolean operator AND, suggest that users combine multiple search terms with an AND between them (ANDing together terms reduces retrieval size).

If they are retrieving zero results, as in case (b), suggest the operator OR, the use of multiple search terms, the use of truncation (which will retrieve a term's variants), and so on.

If they are completely dissatisfied with their searches, case (c), you might suggest that they contact someone who knows the site's content directly for custom assistance. It may be a resource-intensive approach, but it's a far superior last resort to ditching the user without helping them at all.

Choose a Search Engine That Fits Users' Needs

At this point, you ideally will know something about the sorts of searching capabilities that your site's users will require (not to mention what your budget will allow!). So select a search engine that satisfies those needs as much as possible. For example, if you know that your site's users are already very familiar with a particular way of specifying a query, such as the use of Boolean operators, then the search engine you choose should also support using Boolean operators. Does the size of your site suggest that users will get huge retrieval results? Be sure that your engine supports techniques for whittling down retrieval sizes, such as the AND and NOT operators, or that it supports relevance-ranked results that list the most relevant results at the top. Will users have a problem with finding the right terms to use in their search queries? Consider building in a thesaurus capability (AltaVista's SearchWizard (*http://altavista.digital.com/av/lt/help.html*) is a common example) or synonym table so that a query for the term *car* may retrieve documents with the term *automobile*. As the market for search engines booms, more and more interesting options will be packaged with these tools; let your users' needs be the major factor that guides your choice.

Finding a Search Engine

Okay, you've decided you want to provide a search engine for your web site. Where do you get one?

There are several commercial solutions for web site indexing. Lycos licenses its search engine technology for individual web sites. So does Infoseek.

Excite for Web Servers, or EWS, is a free version of the Excite search engine. You can get it from *http://www.excite.com/navigate/*. The only requirement is that you include a link back to their web site.

Other freeware search engines include Glimpse (*http://glimpse.cs.arizona.edu:1994/*) and SWISH (Simple Web Indexing System for Humans) (*http://www.eit.com/software/swish/*).

Display Search Results Sensibly

You can configure how your search engine displays search results in many ways. There is no right way to do it. How you configure your search engine's results depends on two factors.

The first factor is the degree of structure your content has. What will your search engine be able to display besides just the titles of retrieved documents? Is your site's content sufficiently structured so that the engine can parse out and display such information as an author, a date, an abstract, and so on?

The other factor is what your site's users really want. What sorts of information do they need and expect to be provided as they review search results?

When you are configuring the way your search engine displays results, you should consider these issues:

1. How much information should be displayed for each retrieved document?

   A simple rule is to display less information per result when you anticipate large result sets. This will shorten the length of the results page, making it easier to read. Another rule is to display less information to users who know what they're looking for, and more information to users who aren't sure what they want. (Based on your initial research and assumptions about who will be using your site, you should be able to make at least an intelligent guess as to which types of users your site should support.)

   When it's hard to distinguish retrieved documents because of a commonly displayed field (such as the title), show more information to help the user differentiate the results. Consider allowing the user to choose how much information should be displayed. The Ann Arbor District Library, for example, allows users to display retrieval results in three different modes, thus allowing the same tool to serve users with varying information needs; see Figure 6-7.

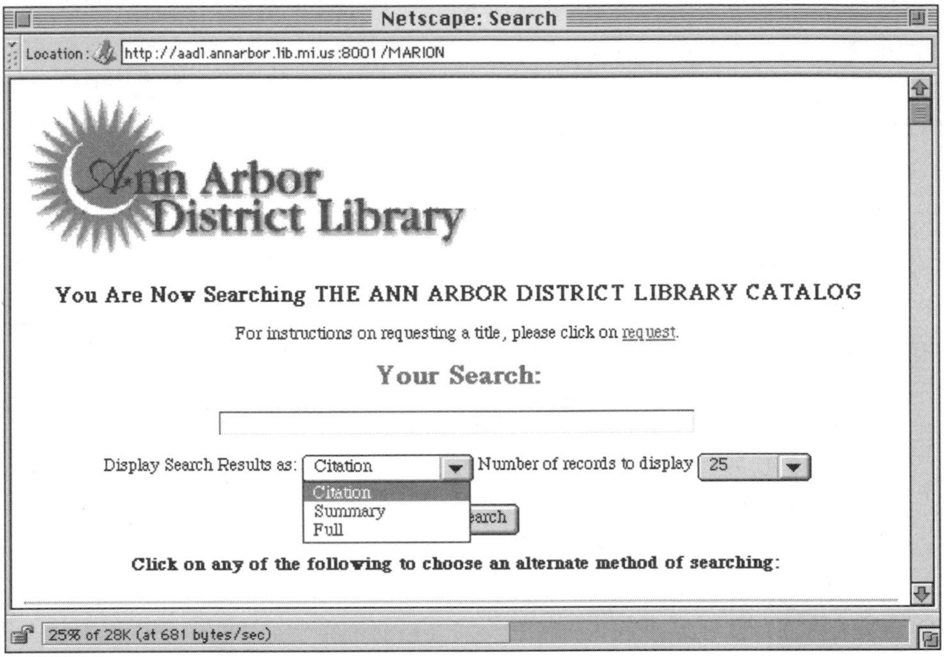

Figure 6-7. The Ann Arbor District Library provides three options (Citation, Summary, and Full) to help users control the amount of information they receive about each retrieved document.

2. What information should be displayed for each retrieved document?

   Which fields you show for each document obviously depends on which fields are available in each document (i.e., how structured your content is). What your engine displays also depends on how the content is to be used. Users of phone directories, for example, want phone numbers first and foremost. So it makes sense to show them the information from the *phone number* field on the results page (see Figures 6-8 and 6-9). Lastly, the amount of space available on a page is limited: you can't have each field displayed, so you should choose carefully, and use the space that is available wisely.

3. How many retrieved documents should be displayed?

   How many documents are displayed depends on the preceding two factors. If your engine displays a lot of information for each retrieved document, you'll want to consider a smaller size for the retrieval set, and vice versa. Additionally, the user's monitor resolution and browser settings will affect the amount of information that can be displayed individually. Your best bet is to provide

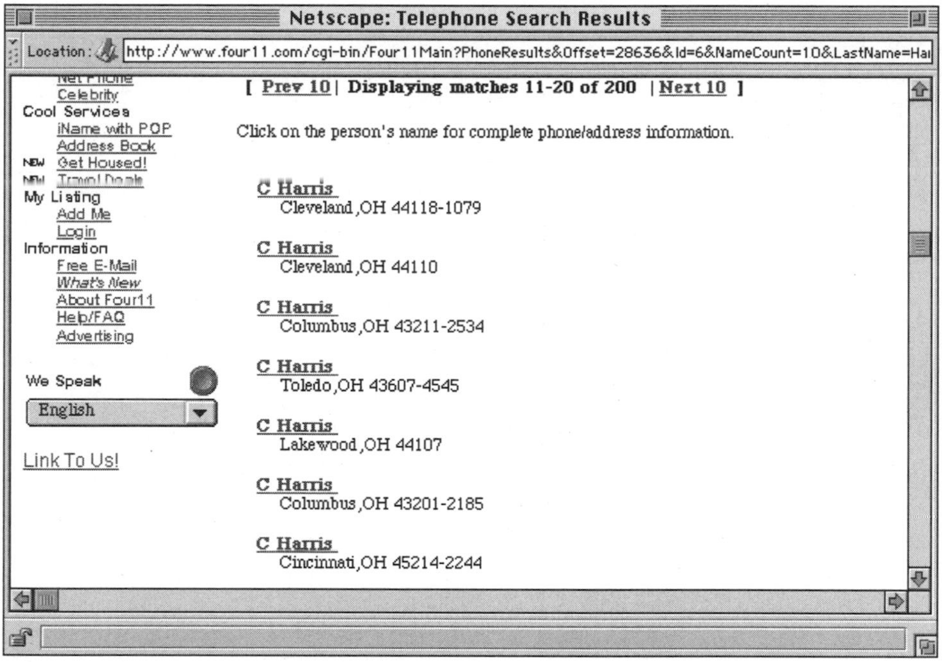

Figure 6-8. Although this page from the Four11 phone directory is visually uncluttered, it could be better; users need to click on a name to retrieve the actual phone number. City, state, and ZIP codes are useful in helping distinguish one C. Harris from the other, but there is no good reason not to display phone numbers on this page.

a variety of settings that the user can opt to select based on his or her own needs, and always let the user know the total number of retrieved documents.

4. How should retrieved documents be sorted?

Common options for sorting retrieval results include:

— in chronological order

— alphabetically by title, author, or other fields

— by an odd thing called relevance

Certainly, if your site is providing access to press releases or other news-oriented information, sorting by *reverse* chronological order makes good sense. Chronological order is less common, and can be useful for presenting historical data.

Alphabetical sorts are a good general purpose sorting approach (most users are familiar with the order of the alphabet!). Alphabetical sorting works best if initial articles such as *a* and *the* are omitted from the sort order (certain search engines provide this option). Users will find this helpful as they are more likely to look for *The Naked Bungee Jumping Guide* under *N* rather than *T.*

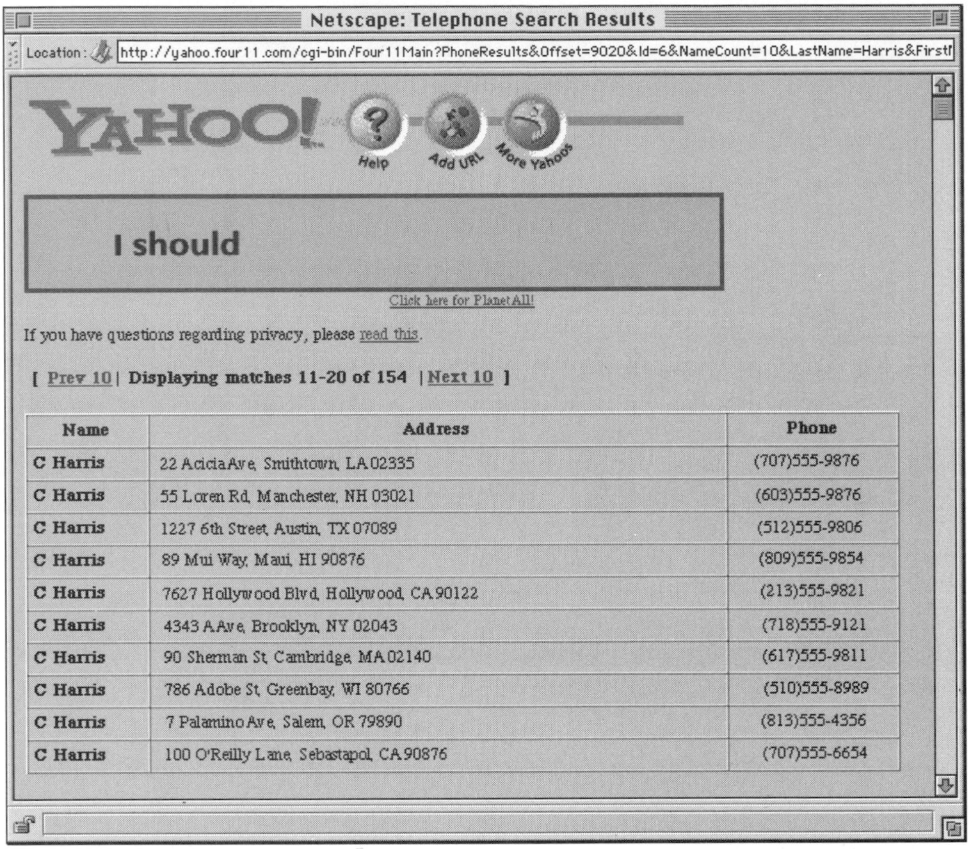

Figure 6-9. Yahoo!'s phone directory may not be as aesthetically appealing, but it gets the job done. Users can use the address information to determine the right C. Harris, and then can view the phone number without clicking further. The use of single lines for each entry also minimizes scrolling.

Relevance is an interesting concept; when a search engine retrieves 2,000 documents, isn't it great to have them sorted with the most relevant at the top, and the least relevant at the bottom? Well, certainly, if this actually would work. Relevance ranking algorithms (there are many flavors) are typically determined by some combination of the following: how many of the query's terms occur in the retrieved document; how many times those terms occur in that document; how close to each other those terms occur (e.g., are they adjacent, in the same sentence, or in the same paragraph?); and where the terms occur (e.g., a document with the query term in its title is more likely to be relevant than a document with the query term in its body).

It's confusing for certain if you're responsible for configuring the search engine, and probably more so for users. Different relevance ranking algorithms make sense for different types of content, but with most search engines, the content you're searching is apples and oranges. So, for example, a retrieval might rank Document A higher than Document B, but Document B is definitely more relevant. Why? Because Document B is a bibliographic citation to a really relevant work, but Document A is a long document that just happens to contain many instances of the terms in the search query.

Our advice is to use relevance with caution and consider doing something that few search tools do: *let the user know how your engine is calculating relevance*. Or, as with the Java implementation of Lycos Pro (Figure 6-10), let the user control the relevance algorithm.

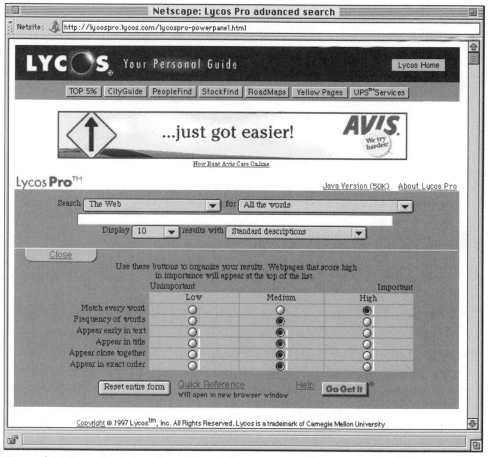

Figure 6-10. Lycos Pro's Java Power Panel allows users to determine which document characteristics are most relevant to their searches through adjusting their settings. Although it's not likely something you'll whip up in minutes for your own site, it is an interesting concept.

Many search engines use counterintuitive sorting approaches by default, including when the file was last updated or indexed (a variant of chronological ordering), or what physical directory the file resides in. Avoid these defaults; they are obtuse and will confuse the user. Whatever approach you use, make the ranking order clear to users by making the sort field a prominent part of each result. Consider shifting the decision on what sort is most useful by giving the user the option of selecting their own sorting option.

More About Relevance

Let's say you're interested in knowing what the New Jersey sales tax is. Maybe you're driving through on a trip, and want to know if you should stop at an outlet mall or wait until you get to Pennsylvania, where you know the sales tax. So you go to the State of New Jersey web site and search on *sales tax* (see Figure 6-11).

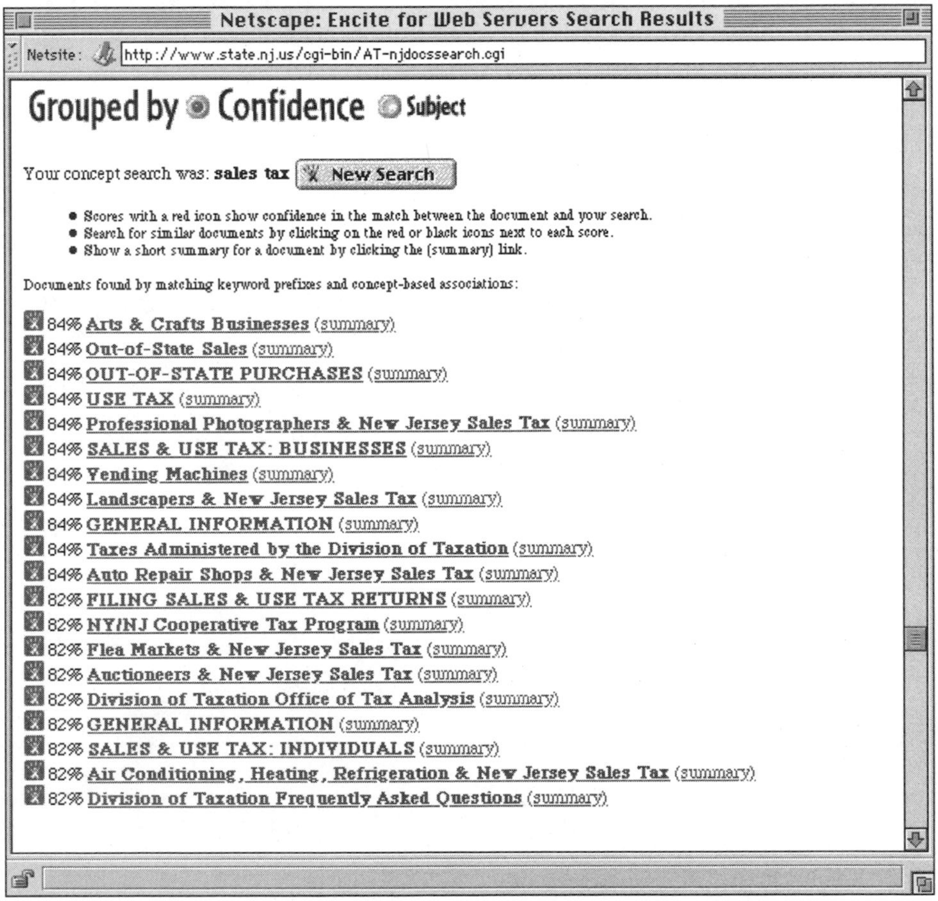

Figure 6-11. Results from the query "sales tax" in the State of New Jersey web site.

The 20 results are scored at either 84% or 82% relevant. Why does each document receive only one of two scores? Are the documents in each group so similar to each other? And what the heck makes a document 2% more relevant than another? Let's compare two retrieved documents, one which received an 84% relevancy score (Figure 6-12), the other 82% (Figure 6-13).

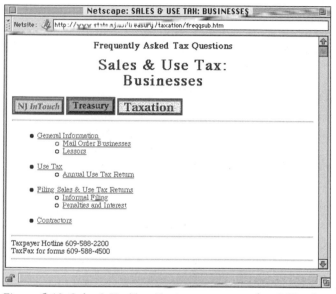

Figure 6-12. Sales & Use Tax: Business was scored at 84% relevancy...

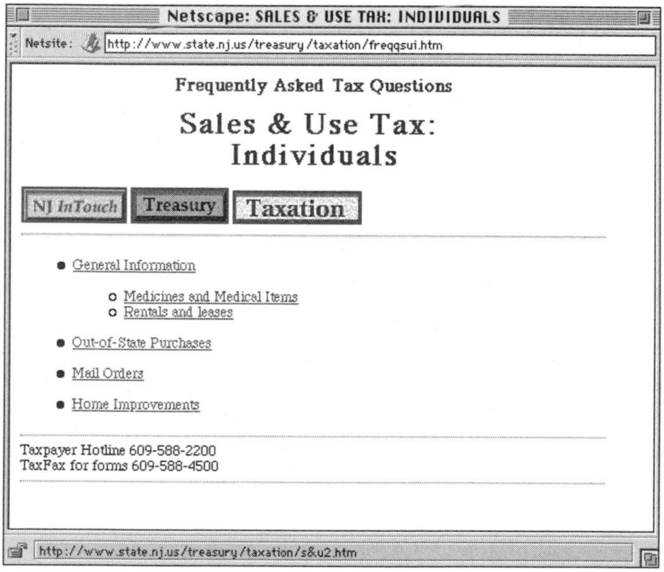

Figure 6-13. ...and Sales & Use Tax: Individuals received an 82% relevancy ranking. Can you tell the difference?

As you can see, these documents are almost exactly the same. Both have very similar titles, and neither uses hidden <META> tags to prejudice the ranking algorithm. Finally, both documents mean essentially the same thing, differing only in that one deals with businesses and the other with individual consumers. The only apparent difference? While *sales* and *tax* appear within <TITLE> and <H1> tags of both documents, they appear in the body of only the first document, not in the second. The search engine probably adds 2% to the score of the first document for this reason. *Probably,* because, as the algorithm isn't explained, we don't know for sure if this is the correct explanation.

Always Provide the User with Feedback

When a user executes a search, he or she expects results. Usually, a query will retrieve at least one document, so the user's expectation is fulfilled. But sometimes a search retrieves zero results. Let the user know by creating a different results page specially for these cases. This page should make it painfully clear that nothing was retrieved, and give an explanation as to why, tips for improving retrieval results, and links to both the Help area and to a new search interface so the user can try again (see Figure 6-14).

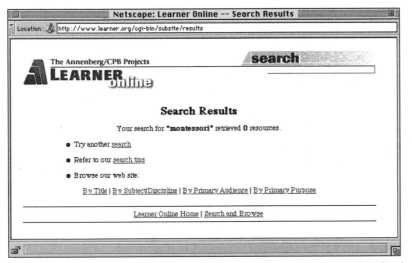

Figure 6-14. Although no results were retrieved, the user is presented with other options, such as trying another search, reviewing the search tips, or switching to browse mode. These options dissuade users from giving up on finding information in the site.

Other Considerations

You might also consider including a few easy-to-implement but very useful things in your engine's search results:

- Repeat back the original search query prominently on the results page.

  As users browse through search results, they may forget what they searched for in the first place. Remind them. Also include the query in the page's title; this will make it easier for users to find it in their browser's history lists.

- Let the user know how many documents in total were retrieved.

  Users want to know how many documents have been retrieved before they begin reviewing the results. Let them know; if the number is too large, they should have the option to refine their search.

- Let the user know where he or she is in the current retrieval set.

  It's helpful to let users know that they're viewing documents 31–40 of the 83 total that they've retrieved.

- Always make it easy for the user to revise a search or start a new one.

  Give them these options on every results page, and display the current search query on the Revise Search page so they can modify it without reentering it.

In an Ideal World: The Reference Interview

Obviously, searching can get pretty complex, and many pitfalls can prevent a user from achieving success. So how does it get done in the non-Web world, and can we learn anything from it?

In the real world, reference librarians and other information professionals often make the difference. In fact, without them, civilization would creak to a grinding halt. They are better than anyone else at finding information because they break up what seems to be a huge, complex information need into simpler, more digestible components by conducting a *reference interview* that is designed to learn more about the information need and its context (unless, of course, you're just looking for the bathroom or the copiers!).

Before you get spooked by the term *reference interview*, consider that you probably have been through quite a few of them yourself. When you go to the library and ask someone behind the reference desk a question, they'll probably respond with an open question, such as "Can you tell me a little more about how you'll be using this information?" The interview will often continue with more specific questions, such as "Do you need this information for business (or school, a dissertation, personal enjoyment, etc.)?" "Do you need it right away (or can we take some time to do some more involved searching or interlibrary loan for it)?" "Are you looking for something at no cost (or would you like us to do a literature search in some commercial databases like LEXIS/NEXIS or DIALOG)?" "Are you looking for a few items (or do you need all there is)?" and so on. These interactive iterations help both the librarian understand what you're looking for, and may also help you better understand your own needs by forcing you to articulate them. In effect, both you and the librarian engage in associative learning about the information need. Associative learning comes naturally to humans, but is extremely difficult for software systems to handle.

Can a web site do what a reference librarian does? Well, sort of, but not quite. We've already covered a sample of the variation found in users and their information needs, and we know that well-architected sites can largely address these needs. If we can determine the major needs of our sites' users and take steps to address them, then perhaps we'll cover 80% of all possible search queries. That would be wonderful, as most sites probably don't do half that well. But that other 20%, the really tricky stuff, can't be handled by automated means like a web site. You really do need humans to help out in those situations, because only humans are really good at figuring out context and knowing the right questions to ask. Don't hold your breath for this issue to be solved by an automated approach, such as with an intelligent agent. Instead, consider making someone in your organization (maybe the librarian, if your organization employs one) responsible for handling the tough queries, and make sure your site actively seeks feedback and directs it to those human information specialists.

Indexing the Right Stuff

So, let's get back to whether you need a search engine. Let's assume that you do intend to slap a search engine on top of your web site. Shouldn't be a problem right? Just point the indexer at the directory where all the pages live, and, voilà! Searchable site!

Of course, you knew it wasn't that simple. Searching only works well when the stuff that's being searched is the same as the stuff that users want. This means you may not want to index the entire site. We'll explain.

Indexing the Entire Site

Search engines are frequently used to index an entire site without regard for the content and how it might vary—every word of every page, whether it contains real content or help information, advertising, navigation menus, and so on.

However, searching works much better when the information space is defined narrowly and contains homogeneous content. In other words, the more you search through indices that combine *apples and oranges*, the worse your retrieval results will be. After all, when you search a site, you're probably looking for *apples* only, not *oranges*. As already discussed, a site's content is usually a mix of apples, oranges, kumquats, bell peppers, chainsaws, and Barbie dolls to begin with. So, when you tell your search engine to index your entire site, the site's users will be performing searches against all kinds of stuff—navigation, destination, and other kinds of pages—all at once. What they retrieve can often be ugly.

Let's try an example to see what happens. Searching Netscape's site for *plug-ins*, what do we find? Exactly 100 documents.* Of these:

- 58 documents are Welcome to Netscape Navigator version X.X pages for just about every version of Netscape Navigator and include information about plug-ins.

- 16 documents are in German (a language I don't read).

- 6 documents contain the potentially relevant term *application* in their titles, but 5 of these 6 have exactly the same title (*Netscape Handbook: Application Features*).

- 2 documents actually contain *plug-in* in their titles.

- 18 other assorted documents may be relevant, but are not labeled in a way that indicates whether this is the case.

Analyzing these search results, we find two common problems. First, we are presented with documents that clearly don't belong. If the site had been selectively indexed with audience differences in mind, 16% of the results would not have been displayed at all. Second, regarding relevant documents, it's not clear why we need 58 versions of the same type of document. It would have been useful to index pages more selectively, such as files relevant to Windows or Macintosh users, or recent versions versus older versions of the software. Are very many people still interested in old Netscape Beta versions? So, our search is less successful than it could have been; it gave us a lot of irrelevant documents, and too many that *could* be relevant.

Our search performed poorly because all the content in the site was indexed together. By doing so, the site's architects chose to ignore two very important things: that the information in their site isn't all the same, and that it makes good sense to respect the lines already drawn between different types of content. For example, it's clear that German and English content are vastly different and that

---

* Search done on February 2, 1997.

their audiences overlap very little (if at all), so why not create separately search-able indices along those divisions?

The site designers at Netscape are already doing this, in a limited way. They have put a lot of effort into helping you download the right version of the software from the nearest location. To download the software, you get asked several questions (not unlike those in a reference interview). Shown in Figure 6-15, the site asks the user:

- What operating system does your computer use?

- What language do you speak?

- Which of our products do you need?

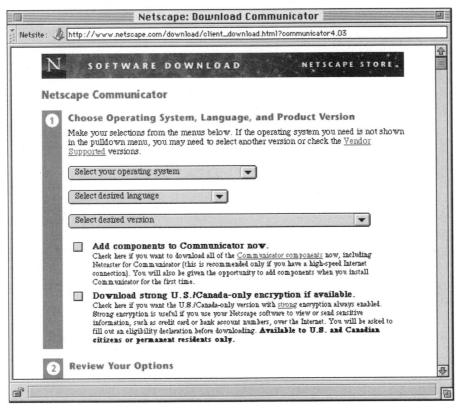

Figure 6-15. Three pull-down menus perform a brief reference interview sufficient to help users download the appropriate software product.

The result is a list of links to download sites that provide the user the right information (i.e., software appropriate to the user's platform), taking into account his or her geographic location and language. Why not apply this same careful approach to matching users with the right information to the entire site, instead of just to this specific situation?

Search Zones: Selectively Indexing the Right Content

Search zones are subsets of a web site that have been indexed separately from the rest of the site's content. When you search a search zone, you have, through interaction with the site, already identified yourself as a member of a particular audience or as someone searching for a particular type of information. The search zones in a site match those specific needs, and the result is improved retrieval performance. The user is simply less likely to retrieve irrelevant information.

The Microsoft site has a good example of search zone use. Although this site suffers from other searching problems, it compares favorably to the Netscape site when searching for our old stand-by, *plug-ins*. On the search page you're asked where you want to search in the Microsoft site, and are provided with the options on a pull-down menu (Figure 6-16).

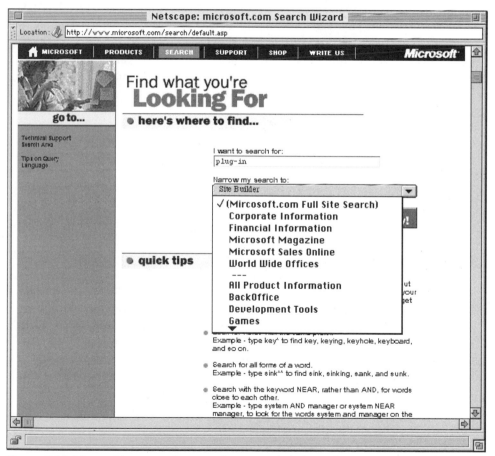

Figure 6-16. Microsoft's site employs search zones to help focus the user's search before submitting a query to the search engine.

You've got many options to review, but you can quickly find the *Internet Explorer* area of the site where you'd want to look for plug-ins. Consider how well the effort the user expends in reviewing and selecting from this menu compares to the much greater effort of searching the entire site and then sifting through a tremendously larger retrieval set. Also note the *Full Site Search* option; sometimes it does make sense to maintain an index of the entire site, especially for users who are unsure where to look, who are doing a comprehensive leave-no-stones-unturned search, or who just haven't had any luck searching the more narrowly defined indices.

How is search zone indexing set up? It depends on the search engine software used. Most support the creation of search zones, but some provide interfaces that make this process easier, while others require you to manually provide a list of pages to index. In either case, search zone indexing requires more work on your part than simply pointing the search engine at the entire site: you'll need to review and mark each page that should be indexed. To make this easier, you might design your site so that pages that should be indexed together are located in the same directory; that way, you would mark for indexing a directory (and, implicitly, its contents) instead of its individual pages. You may also be working with pages that are generated from a database. In this case, you could design the database to include a field for each record denoting which index the generated page should belong to.

You can create search zones in many ways. Examples of four common approaches are:

- by content type
- by audience
- by subject
- by date

Note that these approaches are similar to the organization schemes discussed in Chapter 3, *Organizing Information*. The decisions you made in selecting your site's organization scheme will often work for determining search zones as well. You could also try other ways; the most important consideration is to choose an approach appropriate to your site's audiences and their information needs.

Apples and apples: indexing similar content types

Most web sites contain, at minimum, two major and dissimilar types of pages: *navigation* and *destination*. Destination pages contain the actual information you want from a web site: sport scores, book reviews, software documentation, and so on. The primary purpose of a site's navigation pages is to *get you to the destination pages*. Navigation pages may include main pages, search pages, and pages that help you browse a site.

When a user searches a site, he or she is generally looking for destination pages. If navigation pages are part of the retrieval, they will just clutter up the retrieval results. In fact, the reason that the user is searching rather than browsing some other way could be because the navigation system is performing poorly in the first place. So why keep showing the user navigation pages that don't work and aren't relevant to the search?

Let's take a simple example. your company sells computer products via its web site. The destination pages consist of descriptions, pricing, and ordering information, one page for each product. Also, a number of navigation pages help users find products, such as listings of products for different platforms (e.g., Macintosh versus Windows), listings of products for different applications (e.g., word processing, bookkeeping), listings of business versus home products, and listings of hardware versus software products. If the user is searching for Intuit's Quicken, what's likely to happen? Instead of simply retrieving Quicken's product page, they might get all these pages:

> Financial Products Index Page
> Home Products Index Page
> Macintosh Products Index Page
> Quicken Product Page
> Software Products Index Page
> Windows Products Index Page

The user retrieves the right destination page (i.e., the Quicken Product Page), but also five more that are purely navigation pages. In other words, 83% of the retrieval is in the way. And keep in mind that this example is simple; what if the user had to ignore 83% of a much larger retrieval set, say, 200 documents?

Of course, indexing similar content isn't always easy, because "similar" is a highly relative term. It's not always clear where to draw the line between navigation and destination pages. In some cases, a page can be considered both. For example, we tried the approach described here for the SIGGRAPH 96 Conference web site.[*] We found that some pages didn't really fit the navigation/destination breakdown. For example, the Exhibition Hall Map page appears to be navigation. It links to pages for each of the five sections of the hall. These five pages appear to be destination, presenting detailed maps of their respective sections, including booth numbers and the names of exhibitors. But their parent page also provides important information, such as where the hall entrances are, and where the five sections are in relation to one another. So isn't the main Exhibition Hall Map page

---

[*] This site evolved greatly during the year leading up to SIGGRAPH 96, and then some after the conference was complete. The fullest version of this site is archived at *http://siggraph.anecdote.com/conferences/siggraph96.*

destination as well as navigation? The best solution, in this particular case, was to index these hybrid pages, but it wasn't ideal.

The more important lesson from this experience was to test out the navigation/ destination distinctions before actually applying them. The weakness of the navigation/destination approach is that it is essentially an exact organization scheme (discussed in Chapter 3) which requires the pages to be either one thing (in this case destination) or another (navigation). In the following three approaches, the organization approaches are ambiguous, and therefore more forgiving of pages that fit into multiple categories.

Who's going to care? Indexing for specific audiences

If you've already decided to create an architecture for your site that uses an audience-oriented organization scheme, it may make sense to create search zones by audience breakdown as well. We found this a useful approach for the original Library of Michigan web site.

The Library of Michigan has three primary audiences: members of the Michigan state legislature and their staffs, Michigan libraries and their librarians, and the citizens of Michigan. The information needed from this site is different for each of these audiences; for example, each has a very different circulation policy. Why would a state legislator care how long a citizen can check a book out for?

So we created four indices: one for the content relevant to each audience, and one unified index of the entire site in case the audience-specific indices didn't do the trick for a particular search. Here are the results from running a query on the word *circulation* against each of the four indices:

Index	Number of Documents Retrieved	Retrieval Reduced By
Unified	40	-
Legislature Area	18	55%
Libraries Area	24	40%
Citizens Area	9	78%

As with any search zone, less overlap between indices improves performance. If the sizes of retrieval results were reduced by a very small figure, let's say, 10% or 20%, it may not be worth the overhead of creating separate audience-oriented indices. But in this case, much of the site's content is specific to one of the audiences.

Drilling down: Indexing by subject

If your site uses a strong subject-oriented or topical organization scheme, you've already distinguished many of the site's search zones. Yahoo! is perhaps the most popular site to employ subject-oriented search zones. Every subject category and subcategory in Yahoo! can be searched individually. For example, let's say you're looking for sites that deal with science fiction movies. If you search for *science fiction* against the whole Yahoo! search index, you'll retrieve a lot of stuff: 35 category and subcategory matches and 816 site matches. But you're not looking for science fiction in general; you're looking for science fiction movies. So, instead you can run the same *science fiction* search against the index for the Yahoo! subcategory *Movies and Films*. This time you'll be happier with your retrieval: 2 category and subcategory matches and 19 site matches. This is another excellent example of how hierarchical search zones allow for increased specificity, and therefore improved retrieval results.

Yesterday's news: Indexing recent content

Chronologically organized content allows for perhaps the easiest implementation of search zones. (Not surprisingly, it's probably the most common example of search zones.) Because dated materials are generally not ambiguous, indexing them by date is staightforward.

News.Com is a great example (Figure 6-17); it supports highly flexible chronological searching by:

> Date Range (e.g., from 5/20/97 to 6/26/97)
> 3 Days Back
> 7 Days Back
> 14 Days Back
> 21 Days Back
> 30 Days Back
> 60 Days Back
> 90 Days Back

Regular users can return to the site and check up on the news depending on how regularly they use the site (e.g., every week, two weeks, three weeks). Users who are looking for news during a particular date range can essentially generate a custom search zone on the fly. The only negative in *News.Com*'s implementation is that they don't seem to support a search against all news articles, regardless of age.*

To Search or Not To Search?

It's becoming a moot question whether to apply a search engine in your site. Jared Spool's studies demonstrate how important searching systems are to users.

---

* There does seem to be a work-around to this problem: leave the pull-down menu on the default setting of Days back, and the resulting retrieval seems larger than 90 days. But this is simply a guess...

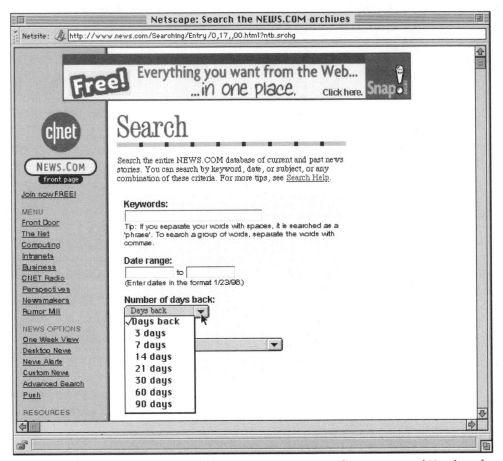

Figure 6-17. News.com's search interface uses two components (Date range and Number of days back) to allow for powerful chronological searching.

Although their subjects weren't told to use a site's search engine to find answers, "about one-third of the people we tested usually tried a search as their initial strategy, and others resorted to it when they couldn't find an answer by following links" (browsing).* Users generally expect searching to be available, certainly in larger sites. Yet, we all know how poorly many search engines actually work. They're easy to set up and easy to forget about. That's why it's important to understand how users' information needs can vary so much, and to plan and implement your searching system's interface and search zones accordingly.

---

* Spool et al., p. 47.

7

Research

So far, we've concentrated on the component parts and principles of information architecture design. Now, we're going to shift gears and explore the process that brings these components and principles together to form useful, elegant information architectures.

If it were just a matter of applying a few design principles to a web site, our jobs would be easy. However, as we discussed earlier, information architecture doesn't happen in a vacuum. The design of large sites requires an interdisciplinary team approach that involves graphic designers, programmers, information architects, and other experts. For everyone to collaborate effectively, you need to define and agree upon a relatively structured development process. Even for smaller projects when teams might be small and individuals might fill multiple roles, tackling the right challenges at the right time is critical to success.

The next few chapters provide an overview of the three major phases of site development. This chapter begins with a review of existing background materials and quickly moves into a series of meetings aimed at gathering and synthesizing information. In Chapter 8, *Conceptual Design*, we cover the creative brainstorming phase where you define the web site. Chapter 9, *Production and Operations*, shows how your ideas are put to the test as the site is built, tested, and launched.

Throughout these chapters, we'll sometimes refer to interactions with the *client*. This language betrays our consulting backgrounds but also raises an important point. As an architect, it's often useful to think like an outsider (even if you're really an insider) so you can escape preconceived notions and think outside the box.

Research is the first crucial step in the construction or renovation of any large web site. You won't get too far if you don't know what you're trying to do, and why.

Getting Started

If you want to create a successful web site, you first must understand the big picture. For that reason, the first step in the research process is to ask questions. You need to get everything out into the open: the individual visions for the site, the raw materials at your disposal, and any possible restrictions. Only then can you develop a solid architecture for your web site.

Questions you need to ask include:

- What are the short- and long-term goals?
- What can you afford?
- Who are the intended audiences?
- Why will people come to your site?
- What types of tasks should users be able to perform?
- What types of content should and should not be part of the site?

You'll find that everyone has different answers to these questions. Inevitably, we all bring personal, professional, and departmental biases to the table. The architect is no exception: both the architect and designer have their own biases and ambitions. To avoid wasted work and complications later on, you need to get these out in the open as soon as possible.

When you're architecting web sites, it's very important to get the project off to a good start. You want everyone to feel involved, enthusiastic, and confident that you know what you're doing. Let's explore ways to make this happen.

Face-to-Face Meetings

Because of the political objectives and the need to establish trust and respect, face-to-face meetings are essential during the research phase. Only in meetings will you learn about the real goals of the project and about the people you're working with. Only during face-to-face conversations will you reach a comfort level that allows both you and your colleagues to ask the difficult but necessary questions.

For example, a client once asked us to design a web site that supported the needs of the parent company and its primary subsidiary. Based upon telephone conversations with the client we believed that the (misguided) plan for a single point of entry to information about both organizations was already set in stone. We assumed the client had good reasons for this integrated approach. However, at an early face-to-face meeting, it became apparent that the client had not put a great deal of thought into this decision. Fortunately, we became comfortable enough with the client at that meeting to ask the obvious question. Within minutes, everyone agreed that two sites were needed rather than one. This decision at such an early stage of the project saved a great deal of potentially wasted time and money. It is often difficult to ask such questions over the phone, because it's difficult to establish a good comfort level without physical proximity and eye contact.

Information Architecture Meeting Agenda

I. Introductions

II. Web Site Critiques

What do you love and hate about the following sites?

III. Information Architecture Overview

What is information architecture?

Review of the process and deliverables.

Discussion of how both will fit into broader context of the project.

IV. Project Scope

Are we architecting just the umbrella site or the sub-sites as well?

What are the respective priorities, timelines, and budget considerations?

V. Centralization vs. Decentralization

Putting aside the web site for a second, to what extent do the separate affiliates, departments, and subsidiaries share organizational resources?

What is the strategy, goal, position, and target market for the holding company?

Will the parent company's brand be stronger/weaker than the subsidiary brands? Who will be responsible for collecting and maintaining content of the umbrella site? Is it correct to assume that the content that we will be classifying in the site is products and services, not individual subsidiaries? In the site, will there be a need to provide unified packaging (e.g., guides, indices) of products/services from separate subsidiaries?

VI. Metrics for Success

Discuss possible goals for the site and opportunities to measure success.

Potential to track leads, click throughs, media contacts, etc.

VII. Umbrella Information Architecture

What are the major questions that audience members will have upon arriving at the umbrella site?

What are the key ways they will want to navigate?

VIII. Discussion of Next Steps

The meeting agenda is an important tool for ensuring these sessions' productivity. By thinking through the key issues that you'd like to cover, you'll be much better prepared for the ensuing discussions. It's a good idea to involve clients and colleagues in the agenda setting process, so that everyone's needs are being addressed. Agendas will vary, depending on the project and the people involved; the sidebar on the following page will give you a sense of what you might expect to cover during an early meeting.

Web Site Critiques

One of the best ways to break the ice with clients and colleagues and move towards that important comfort level (while conducting research at the same time) involves the review and discussion of real-world web sites. It is much easier to express gut-level likes and dislikes about particular sites than to talk abstractly about aesthetic and functional preferences. It's also a lot more fun.

Show them web sites with a variety of architectures. Some might be competitors' sites. Others might come from a completely different industry. Invite them to suggest their own favorite sites for review. As we discussed in the "Consumer Sensitivity Boot Camp" exercise in Chapter 1, *What Makes a Web Site Work*, ask them what they love and hate and why. Point out features or approaches that you find particularly useful or useless. Don't be afraid to encourage or express strong feelings about specific sites. As we suggested in Chapter 1, passionate consumers become caring producers. A critique's transcript might look something like this:

Participant A:
> I hate this site because it's so difficult to find the information I need. It's like looking for a needle in a haystack.

Participant B:
> Yeah, and I can't stand their use of frames. The pages are so chopped up and take forever to load.

Architect:
> I agree. The graphic design and page layout are poorly done. What do you think about the organization scheme?

Participant B:
> There isn't one. There must be thirty links on the main page. Some point to major content areas and some go to a single page. It's horrible.

Architect:
> Yes, you're right. It looks like they could have used an audience-oriented architecture very successfully. Let's take a look at a site that shows what I mean.

Not only are critiques a great way to stimulate interesting and enthusiastic conversation while learning about people's preferences, they're also a sneaky way to educate them. Use the critique as an opportunity to explain and illustrate your ideas about what makes a web site good. Notice that we used this devious yet effective technique in the beginning of this book.

Be forewarned that participants may suggest the critique of existing web sites or intranets created within their organization. This is dangerous territory because some people in the room may have been directly responsible for the design of these sites or may be good friends with the site's designers. Proceed with caution to avoid hurting feelings and creating enemies. Stress the fact that it's easy to criticize in hindsight, try to encourage constructive criticism, and be sure to point out some positive aspects of the site. In general, the tone of these meetings should be kept light and cooperative.

The most obvious and common way to conduct web site critiques is via a connection to the Internet. Ideally, the presentation is conducted through a powerful computer with a reliable high-speed connection. The computer needs a sufficiently recent version of Web browsing software with all the necessary plug-in applications. Internet traffic congestion must not be too heavy. The web sites you visit must be up and running. And of course, when presenting on-site, the firewall must be negotiated.

As you quickly begin to see, many things can go wrong. Attempting to explore the Web live during a meeting often brings technology to the foreground in an intrusive way. There are better ways to solve this communication challenge.

You can use offline browsers such as Web Whacker* that quickly and easily download and package selected web sites on a floppy disk or hard drive, maintaining the integrity of links between offline and online pages. This allows for navigation of web sites without the problems associated with connectivity. However, keep in mind that these offline browsers may not handle enabling technologies such as Java and ActiveX. Also, note that even when using the safe approach of an offline browser, you should have a print-based backup plan. Murphy's Law (anything that can go wrong, will) is particularly applicable to technology-based presentations. You might even bring candles and matches in case of a power outage.

Alternatively, color prints of web sites mounted on cards can be an attractive, portable way of presenting sites for review. Multiple areas and levels of each site can be selected to show the ways in which people can navigate and explore. It may seem silly to present web sites on paper, but it works. By sending technology to the background where it belongs, you can focus on communicating your ideas.

Whatever technology you choose to use, it's often a good idea to assign site reviews as homework to be done before the meeting. This will give people the

---

* Learn about Web Whacker at *http://www.ffg.com/* or read about other offline browsers at *http://www.yahoo.com/Computers_and_Internet/Software/Reviews/Titles/Internet/Browsers/Offline_Browsers/.*

time to think more deeply about what they do and don't like. If you take this approach, you'll be rewarded with a more detailed discussion, though perhaps at the expense of some spontaneity. Try it both ways and see what you prefer.

Information Architecture Critiques

Another way to get even more specific feedback about architectural likes and dislikes is to have people critique the information architectures of a few existing sites. To make them focus solely on the architecture, provide them with a text-only view of the hierarchy of each site, as shown in Figure 7-1.

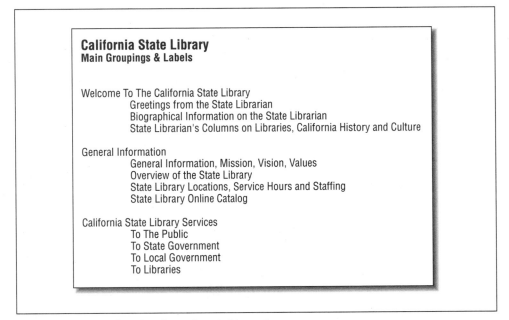

California State Library
Main Groupings & Labels

Welcome To The California State Library
        Greetings from the State Librarian
        Biographical Information on the State Librarian
        State Librarian's Columns on Libraries, California History and Culture

General Information
        General Information, Mission, Vision, Values
        Overview of the State Library
        State Library Locations, Service Hours and Staffing
        State Library Online Catalog

California State Library Services
        To The Public
        To State Government
        To Local Government
        To Libraries

Figure 7-1. Text-only view of a web site's hierarchy

You'll want to accompany the sample architectures with specific exercises that tell people what you'd like them to focus on. The sample exercise in the sidebar on the next page shows the types of questions you might ask.

Defining Goals

In early meetings, it's always easy to jump the gun and dive right into juicy discussions about possible information architectures. Sometimes you will need to ask everyone to step back and spend some time exploring bigger picture issues like mission and vision first.

Sample Exercise: Information Architecture Critiques

The following pages contain representations of the organization systems of three web sites. Please review each organization scheme and answer the following questions:

1. A site's organization scheme involves the placement of content into categories. Which organization scheme do you like best? Why?

2. The labels used for the groupings of content make a difference in a user's understanding of the site and their ability to navigate its content. Which labels stand out in your mind as particularly good ones? What makes them good? Which labels stand out in your mind as weaker ones? Why?

3. Overall, which architecture do you like best of these three? Why?

It's good to begin by brainstorming on mission and vision. To get these sessions going, you might ask some of the following questions:

- What is the mission of the organization?

- How does the web site support that organizational mission?

- Does the new medium of the Web force you to reconsider the organization's mission?

- What are the short-term goals with respect to the web site?

- What are the long-term goals?

- How do you envision the web site one to two years from now?

Once you've had a good opportunity to brainstorm, you can lead your colleagues through the exercise of writing a web site mission statement, which might look something like this:

> The mission of our web site is to create new customer relationships and strengthen existing customer loyalty. We see our web site not only as a promotional tool, but as a customer service tool.

Of course, it's easy to make fun of these touchy-feely mission statements, and they may soon be forgotten. However, the exercise of writing a mission statement can help a group to focus on the goals behind the site.

Towards that end, it's often useful to probe for goals not currently included in the mission statement. If the mission statement emphasizes sales and marketing, ask about customer support or the provision of new, innovative services. Use this exercise to explore the full range of possibilities before moving on to more practical matters.

Measuring Success

While it's definitely a good idea to address ideas like mission and vision directly, it can also be useful to take a more subtle tack by exploring opportunities for measuring the success of the web site. In these early meetings, an interesting and informative exercise involves challenging everyone to think into the future, about how you're going to evaluate whether the web site is a success or failure. The following worksheet presents possible goals and measurement opportunities.

Goals and Measurement Opportunities	Rank on a scale of 1 to 4
Lower Costs	
reductions in costs of distributing sales materials	
reductions in costs of distributing press releases	
reductions in number of phone calls taken at switchboards	
Business Development	
number of leads generated from existing target markets (and growth over time)	
number of leads generated from new target markets (and growth over time)	
number of sales that come from leads generated by the site (and growth over time)	
dollar amount of sales from leads generated by the site (and growth over time)	
Improved Customer Service	
usage of content and applications (growth over time)	
interactions via email	
customer feedback/testimonials	
Improved Public Perception	
user comments and testimonials	
positive comparisons with competitors	
mention of web site in mainstream press	
mention of web site in trade press	
number of links to the site from other web sites	
Site Performance	
number of site hits and growth of hits over time	
number of new users	

Goals and Measurement Opportunities	Rank on a scale of 1 to 4
number of repeat users	
usability testing	
Other Goals and Measurement Opportunities	

You can ask people to rank these goals and measurement opportunities in several ways. For example, you might ask how important each factor will be in obtaining additional funding from senior management after the site's launch. You might also ask how difficult each measurement opportunity will be to implement.

You can pass out this type of document and then encourage the group to brainstorm about these and other ways they might measure the site's success. How important are hard measurements that show return on investment compared to soft measurements that demonstrate customer satisfaction and public perception? In performing this exercise, it's important to realize that many of these ideas for measurement might not be practical and that decisions regarding measurement don't need to be made at this time. It's really just an exercise to get people thinking about these issues early in the process.

Learning About the Intended Audiences

If you want to design an architecture that supports the needs of the company and the needs of the users, you've got to get everyone thinking about the primary audiences for the web site right at the beginning. With information architecture, one size does not fit all, so your approach should be determined by the needs and characteristics of the major audiences.

You can start gathering this information during early meetings by getting everyone to brainstorm on the topic. You might ask some of the following questions:

- Who are the most important audiences for the web site?

- Are there other audiences we're not thinking about? How about the media, investors, competitors, and current and potential employees?

- Is there a difference between the most important audiences (e.g., those who influence funding) and the audiences who will use the web site most frequently? What are the implications?

- How do these audiences currently interact with your company? By phone, mail, email, fax, or in person?

- What will these audiences want to do when they visit the web site? Why will they come and what will make them return?

Once you've generated an initial list of possible audiences, ask the group to rank the relative importance of these audiences, and list their most important needs, as we've done in the following example:

Audiences	Rank audience in order of importance (#1 is most important)	List the three most important information needs of this audience with respect to the State Library
Librarians (members of cooperative)		
Librarians (non-members)		
Patrons of Public Libraries		
Patrons of State Library		
State Legislature		
State Government Employees		
Federal Government		
Media		
Medical Community		
Legal Community		
z39.50 Community		
Other Audiences (specify):		

We asked staff at the State Library of Iowa to rank their key audiences and list the major information needs of each audience. This structured approach to research enabled us to gather valuable information quickly and efficiently.

The results of this audience prioritization exercise will prove useful in considering possible information architectures for the web site. They can also be interesting to analyze and discuss.

This chart shows the varying degrees of consensus regarding the relative importance of each audience. The discrepancy factor is calculated by subtracting the lowest assigned ranking from the highest for each audience. While we can't vouch for the statistical validity of this calculation, we can assure you it provides for a lively (and ultimately useful) discussion.

Audience	Rankings Assigned by Each Respondent											Discrepancy Factor
Librarians (members of cooperative)	1	1	1	1	1	1	1	4	1	1	1	3
Librarians (non-members)	2	2	1	6	1	1	2	10	2	2	2	9
State Government Employees	5	3	4	1	3	1	6	3	6	4	4	5
State Legislature	6	4	4	1	3	1	3	6	8	3	5	7
Legal Community	3	5	4	1	3	7	4	7	6	6	9	8
Medical Community	4	6	4	8	3	1	5	8	5	7	8	7
Patrons of Public Libraries	8	8	3	8	8	10	8	5	3	5	3	7
Patrons of State Library	7	7	8	8	8	7	7	2	9	8	6	7
z39.50 Community	9	10	11	1	10	10	11	9	7	11	11	10
Media	11	9	9	6	11	10	9	11	4	10	10	7
Federal Government	10	11	9	8	3	10	10	12	12	9	7	8

Obviously, opinions regarding the importance of the z39.50 community as an audience for this Web site ranged wildly. These results uncovered this diversity of opinion about this particular audience and enabled us to explore the reasons each person had for choosing his or her audience priorities.

Identifying Content and Function Requirements

One of the biggest challenges in information architecture design is that of trying to get your arms around the intended content and functionality of the web site.

For a large site, this can be absolutely daunting. The first step to success is realizing that you can't do it all at once. The identification of content and function
requirements may involve several iterations. So just roll up your sleeves and get
started.

Identifying Content in Existing Web Sites

As the Web matures, more and more projects involve rearchitecting existing web
sites rather than creating new ones from scratch. In such cases, you're granted the
opportunity to stand on the shoulders of those who came before you. You can
examine the contents of the existing web site and use that content inventory as a
place to begin.

Rather than pointing and clicking your way through hundreds or thousands of
web pages, you should consider using an automated site mapping tool such as
SiteMap (see Figure 7-2).* These tools generate a text-only view of the hierarchy
of the web site. If the original architects structured the hierarchy and labeled page
titles reasonably well, you should get a bird's-eye view of the existing architecture
and a nicely organized inventory of the site's content. At this point, you're way
ahead of the game. However, it's almost certain that the site redesign will involve
the addition of new content and the integration of new applications, so don't
think you get to escape from the challenge of identifying content and function
requirements.

Wish Lists and Content Inventory Forms

Many clients come to us with completely unrealistic timelines in mind. It is not
unusual for a client to approach us in November stating that they want a world-
class web site by the end of the year. In the early days, this would send us into a
world-class panic. "How can we possibly build this site in 6 weeks?" we'd ask
ourselves. "We'll have to work 36 hours a day each." However, we soon learned
this panic to be unnecessary. Why? Because the greatest time-sink in Web and
intranet design projects involves the identification and collection of content,
meaning that the client, not us, quickly becomes the bottleneck.

Collecting content from people in multiple departments takes time and effort. This
is particularly true of large, geographically distributed organizations. Some people
and departments may care about the project and respond quickly to requests for
content. Others may not. Content will reside in a multitude of formats ranging

---

* To use SiteMap, go to *http://www.sitemap.com/* and enter the URL of the site you'd like to map. If that
web site is in the SiteMap database, you'll see the map right away. Otherwise, SiteMap will ask for your
email address and send you a message when the map is ready. Many offline browsers also offer a site
mapping capability.

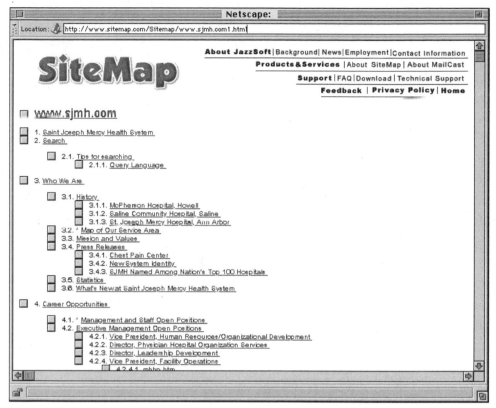

Figure 7-2. SiteMap provides a quick and easy way to generate a bird's-eye view of an existing web site's hierarchy. We typically print the complete map for detailed review, especially if we're dealing with a large site that has hundreds or thousands of pages.

from Microsoft Word to VAX/VMS databases to paper. Content may be limited for viewing by internal authorized audiences or subject to copyright restrictions. Since it is impossible to design an effective information architecture without a good feel for the desired content, you can rest easy knowing that the client's organization will soon become the bottleneck in the research phase.

However, that is not to say that the architect is not responsible for guiding this content collection process. On the contrary, your job is to help develop a process that efficiently and effectively collects all content and information about content that you will need to design and build the site. Wish lists and content inventory forms are invaluable tools for such a process.

Your most immediate goal is to gather enough information about the desired content to begin discussing possible architectural approaches. In the early stages, you do not need or even want the content itself. What you want is an understanding of the breadth and depth of content that might be integrated into the site over time. You want the top of the mountain, long-term view. Remember that you are trying to design for growth. You don't want your vision to be limited by short-term format or availability or copyright issues.

Wish lists are an excellent tool for this information gathering task (see Figure 7-3). Invite all relevant parties to create wish lists that describe the types of content they would like to see on the web site. Make sure you include people who deal with others' information needs on a regular basis (e.g., technical support staff, librarians). Ask them to take a first stab at organizing that content into categories. Involve senior managers and sales representatives, information systems specialists and secretaries. If appropriate and practical, involve representatives from the intended audiences as well. With these relatively unstructured wish lists you can expect a fast turnaround time. Within a week or so you can solicit, gather, and organize responses and begin moving ahead with conceptual design. You will find that this process helps you to define and prioritize the content for the web site.

Portion of a Sample Content Wish List

What's New

Advertisements
New Books List / New Journal Subscriptions
Seminars
Announcements: People, Product, and Services
Newsletter
Datasheets on Products and Services

Technical Information

Patent Data
Manufacturing Processes
Molecular Weight Calculator
Internal Research Reports
Chemical Abstracts Database
Online Catalog

Figure 7-3. As you can see, wish lists not only define the scope of content, but also provide you with a good start at organizing the content into categories.

Once people have taken a first pass at the wish list, you can compile the complete set of content requirements and ask the same group to rank that content according to importance and urgency, as in the example below. This type of structured form allows you to quickly learn about the desired content and associated priorities.

New Content Suggestions

Please complete the following form. For each content item, indicate its importance by assigning a priority of 1 to 4 (1 being most important and urgent). When appropriate, also provide a description, indicating how much content is involved and noting any important issues. You may use the blank rows for additional content items to be included in the Web Site Re-Launch.

Content Name	Priority	Description
Key Contact Departments		
Key Phone Numbers		
Maps and Directories		
Outpatient Buildings and Services		
Residency Programs (Expand)		
Orthopedics		
Cardiology		
OB/Women's Health		
Physician Database (Expand, Photos)		
Home Care and Hospice		
Annual Reports		

At this time, it is also important to begin a parallel process of content collection, not because you need the content yet, but because the process of collection takes a long time and can happen independently of your architecture efforts. The efficient collection of content in a large, distributed organization requires a highly structured process. A content inventory form is a useful tool for bringing structure to this process.

The sample content inventory form in Figure 7-4 provides an idea of the types of questions you might need to ask. You'll want descriptive information that includes a name and unique identification number (used to connect the content inventory form with print and electronic versions of the actual content). A brief content description and an indication of the intended audience will often prove more useful at this stage than seeing the content itself (which might really slow things down).

Sample Content Inventory Form

Instructions (please read carefully)

A Content Inventory Form must be filled out for each content area. These areas correspond to the "content chunks" listed on the attached document. Please provide a paper and electronic copy of all content when appropriate.

All content and completed forms must be provided to Anne Smith by December 2nd at the latest. We strongly encourage submission of content and completed forms as early as possible. If you have any questions about this form, please contact Anne Smith (asmith@company.com, 313.555.1234).

Content Area Name:
Content Area ID:

Description of Content Area:

Intended Audience: (please check one or both)

☐   Clients   ☐   Media

Original Source Format(s): (please check all that apply)

☐   Microsoft Word   ☐   ASCII Text
☐   Desktop Database (e.g. Filemaker)   ☐   Paper Copy Only

Expected Format Changes:

Do you expect the content delivery format to change in the future? If so, please describe the format change and the time frame. (e.g., change from VAX/VMS database to Oracle database)

Update Frequency of Content: (i.e., how often will content be changed or added to?)

Information Owner: (i.e., who is responsible for creating and maintaining this content?)

Name:
Dept. / Location:
Phone Number:
Email Address:

Figure 7-4. Sample content inventory form

This form should be accompanied by instructions that explain how to submit the response and by both print and electronic versions of the content. Ideally, you will design a simple data entry form that allows online submission of responses. You might use the Web as the medium for distributing the form. We've also used common database applications such as Microsoft Access.

In this way you can use a database as the repository of all completed content inventory forms. This facilitates tracking progress and content analysis. For

example, you will be able to generate a report that shows how much content is intended for a particular audience.

Grouping Content

As we explained in Chapter 3, *Organizing Information*, grouping content into the top-level categories of an information hierarchy is typically the most important and challenging process you will face. How should the content be organized? By audience or format or function? How do users currently navigate this information? How do the clients want users to navigate? Which content items should be included in which major categories?

The design of information architectures should be determined by research involving members of the team and representatives from each of the major audiences. Fortunately, you don't need the latest technology to conduct this research. Index cards, the 3 x 5-inch kind you can fit in your pocket and find in any stationery store, will help you get the job done. For lack of a better name, we call this index card-based approach *content chunking*. To try content chunking, buy a few packages of index cards and follow these steps:

1. Invite the team to generate a content wish list for the web site on a set of index cards.

2. Instruct them to write down one content item per card.

3. Ask each member of the group or the group as a whole to organize the cards into piles of related content items and assign labels to each pile.

4. Record the results of each, and then move on to the next.

5. Repeat this exercise with representative members and groups of the organization and intended audiences.

6. Compare and contrast the results of each.

7. Analysis of the results should influence the information architecture of the web site.

This card-based content chunking process can be performed collaboratively where people must reach consensus on the organization of information. Alternatively, individuals can sort the cards alone and record the results.

The biggest problem with shuffling index cards is that it can be time consuming. Involving clients, colleagues, and future users in the exercise and analyzing the sometimes confusing results takes time. Some of this content chunking can be accomplished through the wish list process as noted earlier. However, the major burden of content chunking responsibility often falls to the information architect in the conceptual design phase.

8

Conceptual Design

In this chapter:
- *Brainstorming with White Boards and Flip Charts*
- *Metaphor Exploration*
- *Scenarios*
- *High-Level Architecture Blueprints*
- *Architectural Page Mockups*
- *Design Sketches*
- *Web-Based Prototypes*

Based upon information gathered during the research phase, you must now create order out of chaos. Is there a metaphor that will drive the organization of the site? How should the information be organized and labeled at the highest levels of the hierarchy? What types of navigation systems will be applied? How will searching work? This is where the fun begins.

Early conceptual design meetings focus on metaphor and high-level organization. You need to present possible organization schemes, balancing the desire to reach consensus and move forward with the need to remain open-minded about alternate approaches. White boards and flip charts, high-level architecture blueprints, and scenarios are key tools at this stage. After the major issues have been worked out, later meetings involve the consideration of more detailed organization, labeling, indexing, and navigation systems. Detailed blueprints and Web-based prototypes will serve you well in these discussions.

Brainstorming with White Boards and Flip Charts

For collaborative purposes, white boards are unparalleled. The ephemeral nature of white board scribblings permits a creative freedom not found in other media. The technology disappears and inhibitions fall away.

In early research-oriented meetings, white boards support collaboration around the definition and refinement of the mission, vision, and goals of the project. When working with several people from the organization, each with a different

set of experiences, perspectives, and goals, you can use the white board to help identify issues, resolve differences, and achieve consensus.

White boards are also useful for considering possible information architectures. Presenting ideas on the white board triggers new understanding and further brainstorming (see Figure 8-1). The white board, the architect, and colleagues become connected in a feedback cycle that moves towards the articulation of an information architecture.

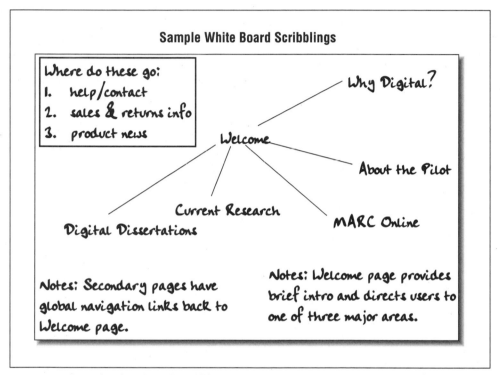

Figure 8-1. Sample white board scribblings

At face level, a major problem of white boards revolves around the difficulty of recording a white-boarding session. White board scribblings do not leave a permanent record. Ideas flow. The board fills up. The board is erased. Eventually, everyone leaves and the scribblings remain trapped on the surface of the white board, soon to be erased by the participants of the next meeting.

In reality, you can use this problem to your advantage. Each time consensus is reached, record the relevant white board scribblings. Differences of opinion and dead-end discussions are quickly forgotten and only the agreements remain. Alternatively, if you're not comfortable with this level of sneakiness, you can assign a designated notetaker to record agreements and disagreements alike.

We are aware of high-tech white boards that allow you to print or save your scribbles. While we don't have much direct experience, we're guessing many of these gadgets are more trouble than they're worth. Sorry for the skepticism, but what do you expect from librarians?

While the flip chart is a close relative of the white board, several characteristics distinguish the two. Advantages of using the flip chart during the research phase include its high portability and intrinsic record-generating nature. Flip charts are portable. Their tearaway sheets can be taken back to the office for study and transcription. White boards are often anchored to walls and won't fit in your car.

However, flip charts don't really support iteration and collaboration. Due to the difficulty of erasing ink on paper and the ugliness of extensively marked-up pages, flip charts invoke in people a higher fear of error and greater resistance to change. When working with flip charts, people try to get it right the first time. Whether or not they succeed, they tend to live with the results rather than mark up the page. This limits the freedom and creativity of group collaboration.

While the visible differences between white boards and flip charts are fairly subtle and seemingly innocent, the ultimate impact upon the collaborative process can be significant. For collaborative brainstorming, give us a white board any day.

Metaphor Exploration

Metaphor can be a powerful tool for communicating complex ideas and generating enthusiasm. By suggesting creative relationships or by mapping the familiar onto the new, metaphor can be used to explain, excite, and persuade. In 1992, vice-presidential candidate Al Gore popularized the term *information superhighway*. This term mapped the familiar and respected metaphor of the physical highway infrastructure of the United States onto the new and unfamiliar concept of a national information infrastructure. Gore used this term to excite the voters about his vision for the future. While the term did oversimplify and has since been horribly overused, it succeeded in helping people to begin learning about and discussing the importance and direction of the global Internet.

Three types of metaphor can be applied in the design of web sites. These are organizational, functional, and visual metaphors:

- *Organizational metaphors* leverage familiarity with one system's organization to convey quick understanding of a new system's organization. For example, when you visit an automobile dealership, you must choose to enter one of the following departments: new car sales, used car sales, repair and service, or parts and supplies. People have a mental model of how dealerships are organized. If you're creating a web site for an automobile dealership, it may make sense to employ an organizational metaphor that draws from this model.

- *Functional metaphors* make a connection between the tasks you can perform in a traditional environment and those you can perform in a new environment. For example, when you enter a traditional library, you can browse the shelves, search the catalog, or ask a librarian for help. Many library web sites present these tasks as options for users, thereby employing a functional metaphor.

- *Visual metaphors* leverage familiar graphic elements such as images, icons, and colors to create a connection to the new. For example, an online directory of business addresses and phone numbers might use a yellow background and telephone icons to invoke a connection with the more familiar print-based yellow pages.

The process of metaphor exploration can get the creative juices flowing. Working with your clients or colleagues, begin to brainstorm ideas for metaphors that might apply to your project. Think about how those metaphors might apply in organizational, functional, and visual ways. How would you organize a virtual bookstore or library or museum? Is your site more like a bookstore or a library or a museum? What are the differences? What tasks should users be able to perform? What should it look like? You and your colleagues should cut loose and have fun with this exercise. You'll be surprised by the ideas you come up with.

After this brainstorming session, you'll want to subject everyone's brilliant ideas to a more critical review. Start populating the rough metaphor-based architecture with random items from the expected content to see if they fit. Try one or two user scenarios to see if the metaphor holds up. While metaphor exploration is a useful process, you should not feel obligated to carry all or any of the ideas forward into the information architecture. The reality is that metaphors are great for getting ideas flowing during the conceptual design process, but can be problematic when carried forward into the site itself.

For example, the metaphor of a virtual community has been taken too far in many cases. Some of these online communities have post offices, town halls, shopping centers, libraries, schools, and police stations. Figuring out what types of activities take place in which "buildings" can be a real challenge for the user. In such cases, the metaphor hampers usability. As an architect, you should ensure that any use of metaphor is empowering and not limiting (see Figure 8-2).

You should also go into this exercise understanding that people tend to fall in love with their own metaphors. Make sure everyone knows that this is just an exercise and that it rarely makes sense to carry the metaphor into the information architecture design.

Figure 8-2. The Internet Public Library uses visual and organizational metaphors to provide access to the reference area. Users can browse the shelves or ask a question. However, the traditional library metaphor did not support integration of a multi-user, object-oriented environment, or MOO. Applied in such a strong way, metaphors can quickly become limiting factors in site architecture and design.

Scenarios

While architecture blueprints are excellent tools for capturing an approach to information organization in a detailed and structured way, they do not tend to excite people. As an architect who wants to convince your colleagues of the wisdom of your approach, you need to help them envision the site as you see it in your mind's eye. Scenarios are great tools for helping people to understand how the user will navigate and experience the site you design. They will also help you think through the experience your site will provide and may generate new ideas for the architecture and navigation system.

To provide a multidimensional experience that shows the true potential for the site, it is best to write a few scenarios that show how people with different needs and behaviors would navigate your site. Before beginning the scenario, you should think about the primary intended audiences. Who are the people that will use your site? Why and how will they want to use it? Will they be in a rush or will they want to explore? Try to select three or four major user types who will use the site in very different ways. Create a character who represents each type. Give them a name, a profession, and a reason for visiting your site, as demonstrated in the sidebar. Then, begin to flesh out a sample session in which that person uses your site. Try to highlight the best features of the site through your scenario. If you've designed for a new customization feature, show how someone would use it.

This is a great opportunity to be creative. You'll probably find these scenarios to be easy and fun to write. Hopefully, they'll help convince your colleagues to invest in your ideas.

Sample Scenario

Rosalind, a tenth grader in San Francisco, regularly visits the LiveFun Web site because she enjoys the interactive learning experience. She uses the site in both *investigative mode* and *serendipity mode*.

For example, when her anatomy class was studying skeletal structure, she used the investigative mode to search for resources about the skeleton. She found the interactive human skeleton that let her test her knowledge of the correct names and functions of each bone. She bookmarked this page so she could return for a refresher the night before final exams.

When she's done with homework, Rosalind sometimes surfs through the site in serendipity mode. Her interest in poisonous snakes led her to articles about how certain types of venom affect the human nervous system. One of these articles led her into an interactive game that taught her about other chemicals (such as alcohol) that are able to cross the blood-brain barrier. This game piqued her interest in chemistry and she switched into investigative mode to learn more.

This simple scenario shows why and how users may employ both searching and browsing within the web site. More complex scenarios can be used to flesh out the possible needs of users from multiple audiences.

High-Level Architecture Blueprints

The collaborative brainstorming process is exciting, chaotic, and fun. However, sooner or later, you must hole up away from the crowd and transform this chaos into order. Blueprints are the architect's tool of choice for performing this transformation.

The very act of shaping ideas into the more formal structure of a blueprint forces you to become realistic and practical. If brainstorming takes you to the top of the mountain, blueprinting brings you back down to reality. Ideas that seemed brilliant on the white board may not pan out when you attempt to organize them in a practical manner. It's easy to throw around concepts such as *audience-specific gateways* and *adaptive information architectures*. It's not so easy to define on paper exactly how these concepts will be applied to a specific web site.

During the conceptual design phase, high-level blueprints are most useful for exploring primary organization schemes and approaches. High-level blueprints map out the organization and labeling of major areas, usually beginning with a bird's-eye view from the main page of the web site. This exploration may involve several iterations as you further define the information architecture. High-level blueprints are great for stimulating discussions focused on the organization and management of content as well as the desired access pathways for users. These blueprints can be created by hand, but we prefer to use diagramming software such as Visio or NetObjects Fusion. These products not only help you to quickly layout your architecture blueprints, but can also help with site production and maintenance.

Let's walk through the blueprint in Figure 8-3, as we would when presenting it to clients or colleagues. The building block of this architecture is the sub-site. Within this company, the ownership and management of content is distributed among many individuals in different departments. There are already dozens of small and large web sites, each with its own graphic identity and information architecture. Rather than try to enforce one standard across this collection of sites, this blueprint suggests an umbrella architecture approach that allows for the existence of lots of heterogeneous sub-sites.

Moving up from the sub-sites, we see a directory of sub-site records. This directory serves as a card catalog that provides easy access to the sub-sites. There is a sub-site record for each sub-site. Each record consists of fields such as *title*, *description, keywords, audience, format*, and *topic* that describe the contents of that sub-site.

By creating a standardized record for each sub-site, we are actually creating a database of sub-site records. This database approach enables powerful known-

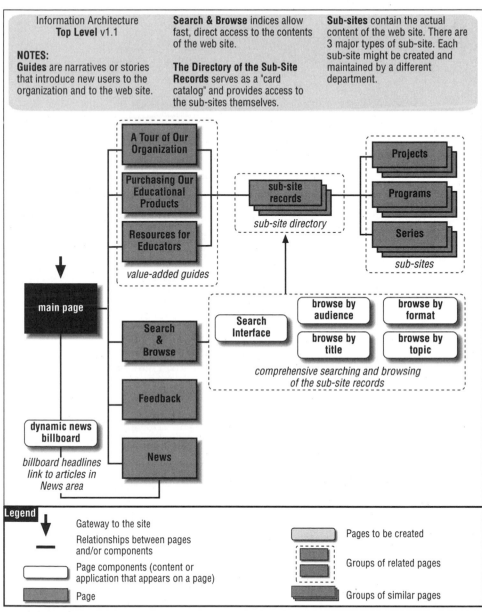

Figure 8-3. *This high-level blueprint shows pages, components within pages, groups of pages, and relationships between pages. The grouping of pages can inform page layout. For example, the three value-added guides should be presented together, whereas Search & Browse, Feedback, and News should be presented separately.*

item searching and more exploratory browsing. As you can see from the Search & Browse page, users can search and browse by title, audience, format, and topic.

We also see three value-added guides. These guides take the form of simple narratives or stories that introduce new users to the organization and to the web site. Interwoven throughout the text of these narratives are in-context links to selected sub-sites. They guide users through the site in an interesting and friendly way.

Finally, we see a dynamic news billboard (perhaps implemented through Java or JavaScript) that rotates the display of featured news headlines and announcements. In addition to bringing some action to the main page, this billboard provides yet another way to access important content that might otherwise be buried within a sub-site.

At this point in the discussion of the high-level blueprint, you are sure to have questions. As you can see, the blueprints don't completely speak for themselves. This is why it's ideal to present these blueprints in person, so you can answer questions and explore new ideas.

In addition, your architectural ideas may need selling. Now, we're not suggesting that you buy a polyester suit, but an element of sales is involved. You need to excite your clients and colleagues about your approach and vision for the site. You need to explain the ideas behind your labeling and organization schemes and describe how this model will support growth over time. These challenges are difficult to address without a meeting (or at least a telephone conference call).

However, if a meeting is simply not possible, you can accompany blueprints with descriptive text-based documents that anticipate and answer the most likely questions. You can then follow up with a conference call to answer the questions you didn't anticipate and move the process along.

You should note that these high-level blueprints leave out quite a bit of information. They focus on the major *areas* of the site, ignoring navigation elements and page-level details. These omissions are by design, not by accident. Shaping the information architecture of a complex web site is a challenging intellectual exercise. You and your colleagues must be able to focus on the big picture issues at hand. For these blueprints, as with the web sites you design, remember the rule of thumb that *less is more*. Detailed page-level blueprints come later in the process.

Architectural Page Mockups

Information architecture blueprints are most useful for presenting a bird's-eye view of the web site. However, they do not work well for helping people to envision the contents of any particular page. They are also not straightforward enough for most graphic designers to work from. In fact, no single format does a perfect job of conveying all aspects of an information architecture to all audiences. Because information architectures are multi-dimensional, it's important to show them in multiple ways.

For these reasons, architectural page mockups are useful tools during conceptual design for complementing the blueprint view of the site. Mockups are quick and dirty textual documents that show the content and links of major pages on the web site. They enable you to clearly (yet inexpensively) communicate the implications of the architecture at the page level. They are also extremely useful when used in conjunction with scenarios. They help people to see the site in action before any code is written. Finally, they can be employed in some basic usability tests to see if users actually follow the scenarios as you expect. Keep in mind that you only need to mockup major pages of the web site. These mockups and the designs that derive from them can serve as templates for the design of subsidiary pages.

In the example in Figure 8-4, you see that mockups are easier to read than blueprints. By integrating aspects of the organization, labeling, and navigation systems into one view, they will help your colleagues to understand the architecture. In laying out the content on a page mockup, you should try to show the logical visual grouping of content items. In this example, the search interface and the browsing options are two separate content groups. You can also indicate prominence in these mockups. Placing a content group at the top of the page or using a larger font size indicate the relative importance of that content. While the graphic designer will make the final and more detailed layout decisions, you can make a good start with these mockups.

Design Sketches

Once you've developed high-level blueprints and architectural page mockups, you're ready to collaborate with your graphic designer to create design sketches on paper of major pages in the web site. In the research phase, the design team has begun to develop a sense of the desired graphic identity or look and feel. The technical team has assessed the information technology infrastructure of the organization and the platform limitations of the intended audiences. They understand what's possible with respect to features such as dynamic content management and interactivity. And, of course, the architect has designed the high-level information structure for the site. Design sketches are a great way to pool the collective knowledge of these three teams in a first attempt at interface design for the top level pages of the site. This is a wonderful opportunity for interdisciplinary user interface design.

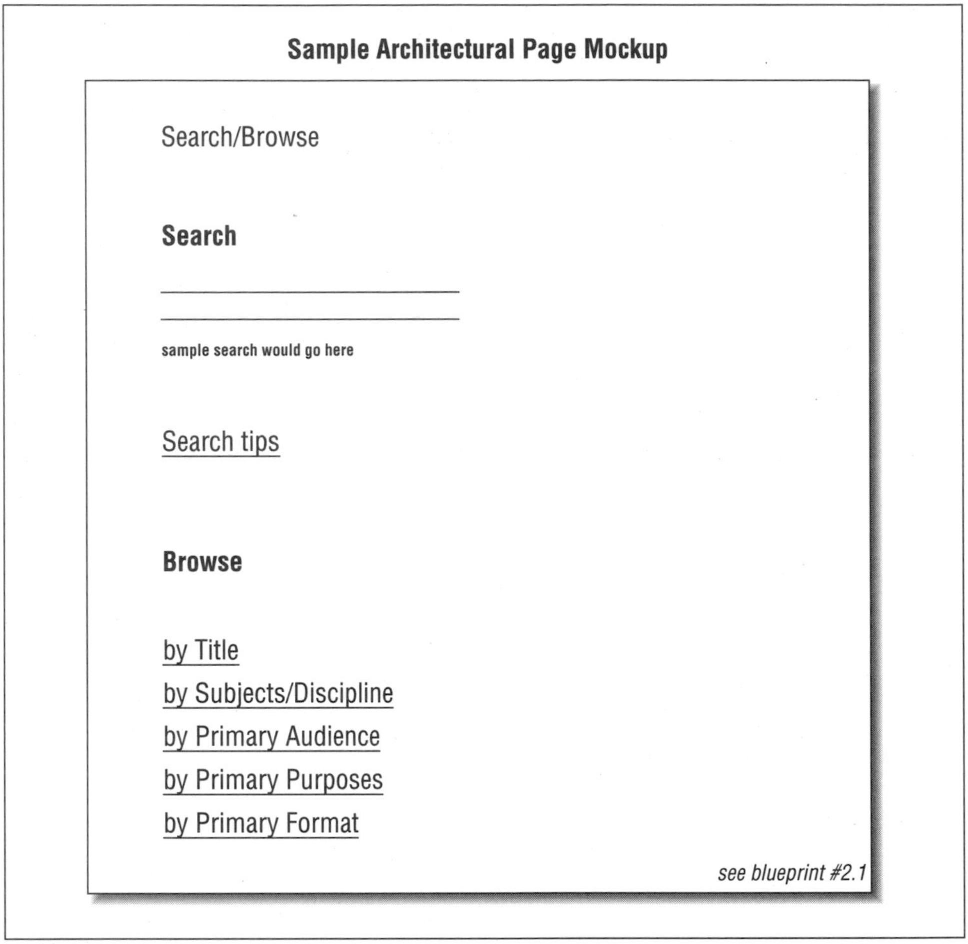

Sample Architectural Page Mockup

Search/Browse

Search

_____
_____

sample search would go here

Search tips

Browse

by Title
by Subjects/Discipline
by Primary Audience
by Primary Purposes
by Primary Format

see blueprint #2.1

Figure 8-4. In this architectural mockup of a combination search/browse page, we show an area for entering queries and an area for browsing. We typically use a word processor like Microsoft Word to create these mockups quickly. However, you can also create quick and dirty HTML mockups, and even work quite interactively with the graphic designer.

Using the architectural mockups as a guide, the designer begins sketching pages of the site on sheets of paper. As the designer sketches each page, questions arise that must be discussed. Here is a sample sketching session dialog:

Programmer:

I like what you're doing with the layout of the main page, but I'd like to do something more interesting with the navigation system.

Designer:

Can we implement the navigation system using pull-down menus? Does that make sense architecturally?

Architect:

> That might work, but it would be difficult to show context in the hierarchy. How about a tear-away table of contents feature? We've had pretty good reactions to that type of approach from users in the past.

Programmer:

> We can certainly go with that approach from a purely technical perspective. How would a tear-away table of contents look? Can you sketch it for us? I'd like to do a quick-and-dirty prototype.

As you can see, the design of these sketches requires the involvement of people from all three teams. It is much cheaper and easier for the group to work with the designer on these rough sketches than to begin with actual HTML page layouts and graphics. These sketches allow rapid iteration and intense collaboration. The final product of a sketching session might look something like that in Figure 8-5.

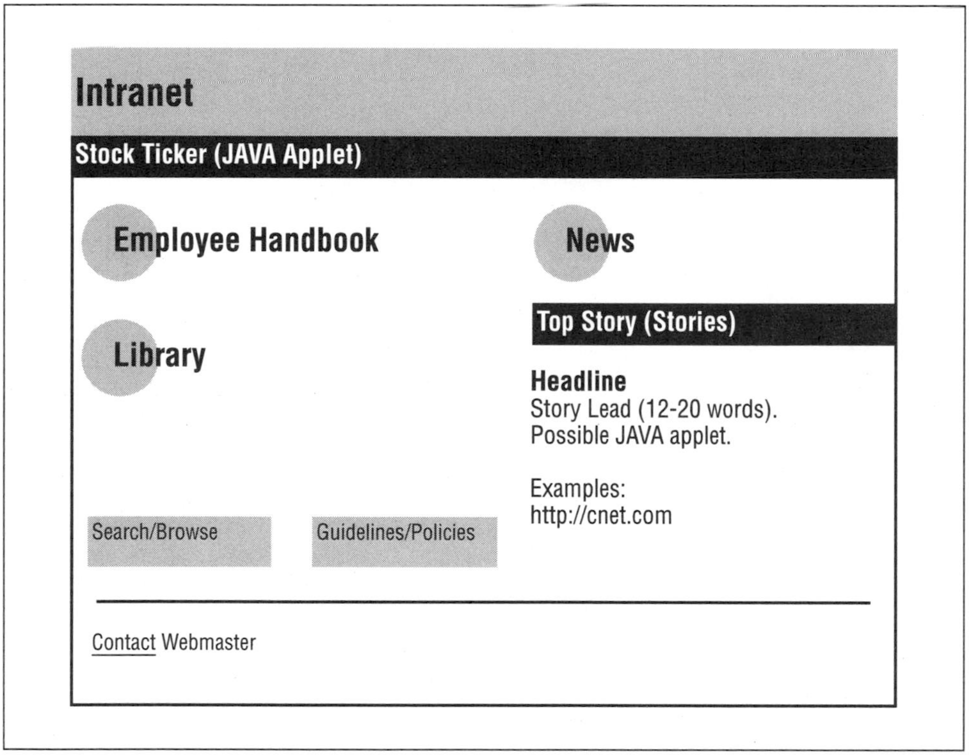

Figure 8-5. In this example, Employee Handbook, Library, and News are grouped together as the major areas of the web site. Search/Browse and Guidelines/Policies make up the bottom of the page navigation bar. A news area defines space for a dynamic Java-based news panel.

Web-Based Prototypes

For the architect, a high point of conceptual design comes when a highly skilled graphic designer creates beautiful Web-based prototypes. More than sketches or scenarios, these digital renditions show how the site will look and function. While the balance of attention shifts with these prototypes towards the aesthetic considerations such as page layout and graphic identity, the prototypes frequently identify previously unseen problems or opportunities related to the information architecture. Once your architecture and navigation system are embodied in actual web pages, it becomes much easier for you and your colleagues to see whether they are working.

The designer may begin with two concepts based upon a single information architecture. After getting feedback from the client, the designer and architect may work together to adapt and extend the preferred concept. At this point, conceptual design ends and planning for production begins. The most exciting challenges for the architect have been met and the days of detail begin.

9

Production and Operations

Before actual production of the web site can begin, you enter an intense period of planning or pre-production, during which the project manager must coordinate the architecture, design, and technical components. For the architect, this is where the blueprints meet the content. You'll want to create detailed page-level architecture blueprints and start mapping the content.

With a production plan in place, the actual construction of the web site can begin. At this point, you may find yourself engaged in the delicate art of point-of-production architecture, trying to resolve minor or major problems that arise as the production team charges forward. Why are these items grouped together? Shouldn't we break this long page into several pages? What was the architect thinking?

The final stages of production are marked by extensive testing and revision, leading up to the web site launch with the requisite marketing extravaganza and smashing of champagne bottles on computer screens.

Don't drink too much champagne, however, because an architect's work is never done. A web site keeps growing and changing. The information architecture can easily get out of hand, and you must actively guide its continued development. Unfortunately, you can't always be there as the web site grows. Architects sometimes have little hands-on control over the site during production, and even less after its launch. An information architecture style guide can serve as a useful tool for maintaining the integrity of the architecture over time, even in the absence of the original architect. In more ideal situations where you are involved with the site after launch, tools for tracking and analyzing usage can help you to identify opportunities for improving the architecture.

Detailed Architecture Blueprints

During the transition from conceptual design to production, the focus shifts from external to internal. Rather than communicating high-level architectural concepts to the client, your job is now to communicate detailed organization, labeling, and navigation decisions to your colleagues on the site development team. This shift is similar to that in the traditional world of architecture and construction. The architect may work closely with the client to make big picture decisions about the layout of rooms and location of windows. However, decisions regarding the size of nails or routing of the plumbing typically do not involve the client. Often neither sufficient time nor interest justifies close client involvement in these minutiae.

The detailed architecture blueprints serve a very practical purpose. They must map out the entire site so that the production team can implement your plans to the letter without requiring your physical presence during production. The blueprints must present the complete information hierarchy from the main page to the destination pages. They must also detail the labeling and navigation systems to be implemented in each area of the site.

The blueprints will vary from project to project, depending upon the scope. On smaller projects, the primary audience for your blueprints may be one or two graphic designers responsible for integrating the architecture, design, and content. On larger projects, the primary audience may be a technical team responsible for integrating the architecture, design, and content through a database-driven process. Let's consider a few examples to see what they communicate and how they vary.

As the legend suggests in Figure 9-1, there is a distinction between a local and a remote page. A local page is a child of the main page on that blueprint. The local page inherits characteristics such as graphic identity and navigation elements from its parent. In this example, the Papers Committee page inherits its color scheme and navigation system from the Papers main page. On the other hand, a remote page belongs to another branch of the information hierarchy. The Session Room Layout page will show a graphic identity and navigation system unique to the Maps area of the web site.

Another important concept is that of the *content chunk*. To meet the needs of the content mapping process and to allow for flexibility during the production process, it is often necessary to separate the content from its container. Content chunks such as location information and papers video proceedings are sections of content composed of one or more paragraphs that can stand alone as independent packages of information. The rectangle that surrounds these content chunks indicates that they are closely related. By taking this approach, the architect provides the designer with flexibility in defining the layout. Depending upon the space each content chunk requires, the designer may choose to present all of these chunks on one page or create a closely knit collection of pages.

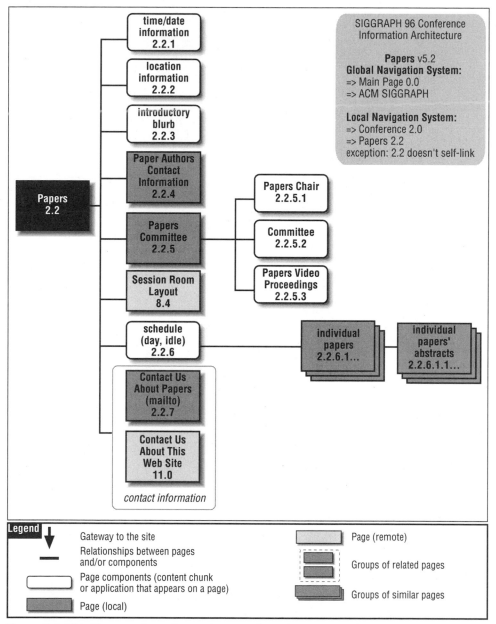

Figure 9-1. This blueprint from the SIGGRAPH 96 Conference introduces several concepts. By assigning a unique identification number (e.g., 2.2.3.1) to each component (pages and content chunks), the architect lays the groundwork for an organized production process, ideally involving the use of a database system to manage the population of the web site structure with content.

You may decide to also communicate the navigation system using these detailed blueprints. In some cases, one- and two-way arrows can be used to show navigation. However, arrows can become confusing and are easily missed by the production staff. A sidebar is often the best way of communicating both global and local navigation systems (see Figure 9-2).

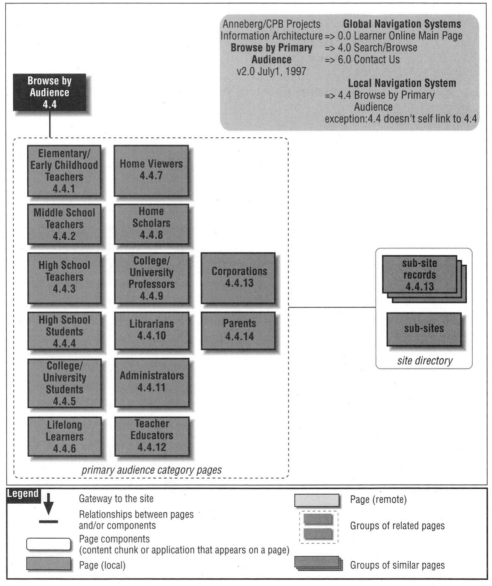

Figure 9-2. The sidebar in the upper right of this blueprint explains how the global and local navigation systems apply to this area of the web site.

Content Mapping

During research and conceptual design, you are focused on the top-down approach of defining an information structure that will accommodate the mission, vision, audiences, and content. As you move into production, you complete the bottom-up process of collecting and analyzing the content. Content mapping is where top-down meets bottom-up.

The process of content mapping involves breaking down or combining existing documents into logical content components or *chunks*, thereby separating the content from its container. A content chunk is not a sentence or a paragraph or a page. Rather, it is the most finely grained portion of content that merits or requires individual treatment.

The content, often received from a variety of sources and in a multitude of formats, must be mapped onto the information architecture. Because of differences between formats, you cannot count on a one-to-one mapping of source page to destination page. One page from a print brochure does not necessarily map onto one page on the Web. For this reason, it is important to separate content from container, at both the source and destination. In addition, when combined with a database-driven approach to content management, the separation of content and container facilitates the reuse of content chunks across multiple pages. For example, contact information for the customer service department might be presented in context within a variety of pages throughout the web site. If the contact information changes, modification can be made once to the database record for that content chunk and then propagated throughout the web site at the push of a button.

In some cases, you will need to create original content for a web site. However, content mapping may still be necessary. It often makes sense to create content in a word processing application rather than an HTML editor, since tools like Microsoft Word tend to have more powerful editing, layout, and spell checking capabilities. In such cases, you'll still need to map the Word documents to HTML pages.

The subjective process of defining chunks should be determined by answers to the following questions:

- Can this document be segmented into multiple chunks that users might want to access separately?

- What is the smallest section of content that needs to be individually indexed?

- Will this content need to be repurposed across multiple documents or as part of multiple processes?

Once the content chunks have been defined, they can be mapped onto destination web pages. You will need a systematic means of documenting the source and destination of all content, so that the production team can carry out your instructions. As discussed earlier, one approach involves the assignment of unique identification codes to each content chunk.

For example, creation of the SIGGRAPH 96 Conference web site required the translation of print-based content to the online environment. In such cases, content mapping involves the specification of how chunks of content in the print materials map to pages on the web site. For SIGGRAPH 96, we had to map the contents of elaborately designed brochures, announcements, and programs onto web pages. It would have been difficult and silly to attempt a one-to-one mapping of printed pages to web pages. Therefore, we needed to go through a process of content chunking and mapping with the content editor. First, we broke each page of the brochure into logical chunks or atoms of information. We devised a simple scheme tied to page numbers for labeling each chunk (see Figures 9-3 and 9-4).

As you saw in Figure 9-1, we had already created a detailed information architecture blueprint with its own content chunk identification scheme. We then had to create a content mapping table that explained how each content chunk from the print brochure should be presented in the web site.

Armed with the original print documents, architecture blueprints, and the content mapping table, the production staff created and populated the SIGGRAPH 96 Conference web site. As you can see in Figure 9-5, the contents of the web page are quite different from the original print page.

Web Page Inventory

The content mapping process should result in the creation of an inventory of all web pages to be created. Depending upon the size and complexity of the web site and the process and technology in place for production, you can choose many ways to present this inventory. For larger sites, you can require a document management solution that leverages database technology to produce a workflow process that can determine a team approach to page-level design and editing. For simpler sites, you may create a Web-based inventory that presents the titles and unique identification numbers of each page for the site, such as that shown in Figure 9-6.

You can create a web page inventory as soon as you have completed the content mapping process. Over time, it can serve as an inventory of pages that need to be created, an inventory of architectural page mockups that need to be designed, and an inventory of designed pages that need to be reviewed before integration into the web site.

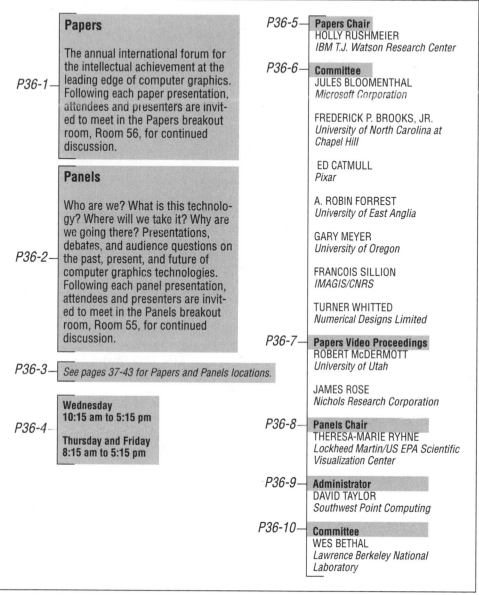

Figure 9-3. Print chunks, to be mapped out as shown in Figure 9-4.

Point-of-Production Architecture

Ideally, with the detailed architecture blueprints and content mapping complete, the production process would proceed smoothly in a paint-by-numbers manner, and the architect could sit back and relax. In reality, you must be actively

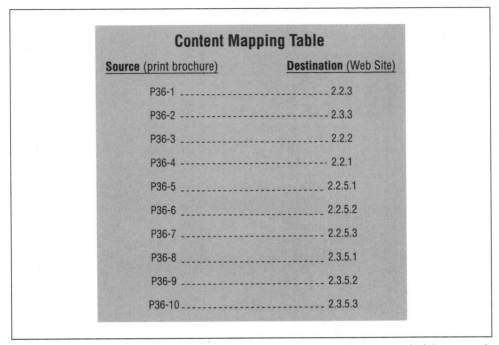

Figure 9-4. In this example, P36-1 refers to the first content chunk on page 36 of the original print brochure (Figure 9-3). This source content chunk maps onto the destination content chunk labeled 2.2.3, which belongs in the Papers (2.0) area of the web site.

involved to make sure the architecture is implemented according to plan and to address any problems that arise. Why? Because you're human. No architect can anticipate everything.

Many decisions must be made during production. Are these content chunks small enough that we can group them together on one page, or should they remain on separate pages? Should we add local navigation to this section of the site? Can we shorten the label of this page? During this phase, be aware that the answers to these questions may impact the burden on the production team as well as the usability of the web site. You need to balance the requests of your client, the sanity of the production team, the budget and time-line, and your vision for the information architecture of the web site.

You should not need to make major decisions about the architecture during production. A significant investment has already been made in a particular direction. Discovery of a major flaw in the architecture at this point is an information architect's nightmare. Fortunately, if you've followed the process of research and conceptual design before production, this is unlikely. You have worked hard to define the mission, vision, audiences, and content for the web site. You have

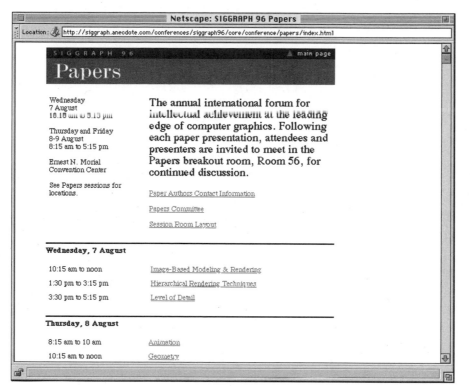

Figure 9-5. Because of the differences between the print and online media, the translation from print brochure to web site involved significant changes.

documented the decisions made along the way. You have resolved the top-down and bottom-up approaches through content mapping and detailed blueprints. Through careful planning, you've created a solid information architecture that should stand the test of time.

Architecture Style Guides

As we mentioned earlier, a web site keeps growing and changing. As an information architect, you must guide its development or risk architectural drift. It's frustrating to see your carefully designed organization, navigation, labeling, and indexing systems become mangled as site maintainers add content without heeding the architectural implications. While it may be impossible to completely prevent this disfigurement, an architecture style guide can steer content maintainers in the right direction.

An architecture style guide is a document that explains how the site is organized, why it is organized that way, and how the architecture should be extended as the site grows. The guide should begin with documentation of the mission and vision

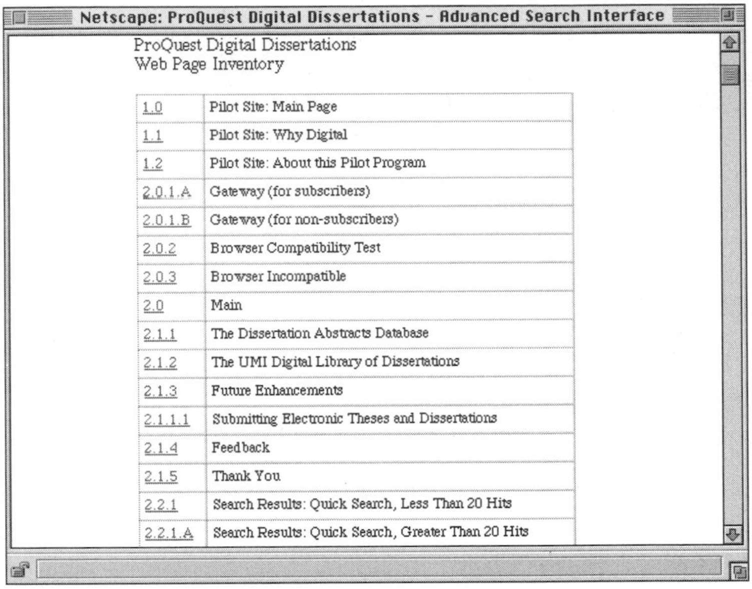

```
┌─────────────────────────────────────────────────────────────┐
│▣ ═══ Netscape: ProQuest Digital Dissertations – Advanced Search Interface ═══ ▣│
├─────────────────────────────────────────────────────────────┤
│   ProQuest Digital Dissertations                          ⬆│
│   Web Page Inventory                                       ▓│
│                                                            │
│   ┌─────────┬─────────────────────────────────────────┐    │
│   │ 1.0     │ Pilot Site: Main Page                   │    │
│   ├─────────┼─────────────────────────────────────────┤    │
│   │ 1.1     │ Pilot Site: Why Digital                 │    │
│   ├─────────┼─────────────────────────────────────────┤    │
│   │ 1.2     │ Pilot Site: About this Pilot Program    │    │
│   ├─────────┼─────────────────────────────────────────┤    │
│   │ 2.0.1.A │ Gateway (for subscribers)               │    │
│   ├─────────┼─────────────────────────────────────────┤    │
│   │ 2.0.1.B │ Gateway (for non-subscribers)           │    │
│   ├─────────┼─────────────────────────────────────────┤    │
│   │ 2.0.2   │ Browser Compatibility Test              │    │
│   ├─────────┼─────────────────────────────────────────┤    │
│   │ 2.0.3   │ Browser Incompatible                    │    │
│   ├─────────┼─────────────────────────────────────────┤    │
│   │ 2.0     │ Main                                    │    │
│   ├─────────┼─────────────────────────────────────────┤    │
│   │ 2.1.1   │ The Dissertation Abstracts Database     │    │
│   ├─────────┼─────────────────────────────────────────┤    │
│   │ 2.1.2   │ The UMI Digital Library of Dissertations│    │
│   ├─────────┼─────────────────────────────────────────┤    │
│   │ 2.1.3   │ Future Enhancements                     │    │
│   ├─────────┼─────────────────────────────────────────┤    │
│   │ 2.1.1.1 │ Submitting Electronic Theses and Dissertations│ │
│   ├─────────┼─────────────────────────────────────────┤    │
│   │ 2.1.4   │ Feedback                                │    │
│   ├─────────┼─────────────────────────────────────────┤    │
│   │ 2.1.5   │ Thank You                               │    │
│   ├─────────┼─────────────────────────────────────────┤    │
│   │ 2.2.1   │ Search Results: Quick Search, Less Than 20 Hits│ │
│   ├─────────┼─────────────────────────────────────────┤    │
│   │ 2.2.1.A │ Search Results: Quick Search, Greater Than 20 Hits│⬇│
│   └─────────┴─────────────────────────────────────────┘    │
└─────────────────────────────────────────────────────────────┘
```

Figure 9-6. This Web Page Inventory presents the names and identification numbers of all pages to be created for the site. Selecting the hypertext linked numbers pops up another browser window that shows the appropriate web page.

for the site. It's important to understand the original goals of the site. Continue with information about the intended audiences. Who was the site designed for? What assumptions were made about their information needs? Then, follow up with a description of the content policy. What types of content will and won't be included and why? This documentation of lessons learned and decisions made during the research phase is very important. These underlying philosophies drove the design of the architecture. Any future modifications to the architecture should be determined by this early work. Also, if the goals change or the assumptions prove incorrect, corresponding architectural modifications may be required.

Next, you should present both the high-level and detailed information architecture blueprints. Since you won't always be there to explain them, it may be necessary to explain the blueprints with narrative text. You also need to create guidelines for adding content to ensure the continued integrity of the organization, labeling, navigation, and indexing systems. Keep in mind that this can be a challenge. When should a new level in the hierarchy be added? Under what conditions can new indexing terms be introduced? How should local navigation systems be extended as the web site grows? By thinking ahead and documenting decisions, you can provide much needed guidance to the site maintainers.

Ideally, a graphic design style guide and perhaps a suite of HTML templates will complement your architecture style guide. In combination, and assuming the site maintainers don't ignore them, these style guides and templates can ensure that the integrity of the information architecture and graphic identity of the web site is maintained.

Learning from Users

Unfortunately, many sites fall victim to the launch 'em and leave 'em attitude of site owners, who turn their attention to more urgent or interesting projects, allowing the content or the architecture to become obsolete quickly. Even for those sites kept current with respect to content, the information architectures are rarely refined and extended.

This is too bad, because it is after the launch of a web site that you have the best opportunity to learn about what does and doesn't work. If you are fortunate enough to be given the time, budget, and mandate to learn from users and improve your web site, a number of tools and techniques can help you do so.

As you read this section, please understand that high-quality testing of site architectures requires experts in usability engineering. For pointers to expert coverage of tools and techniques specific to usability engineering, please review the usability area of our bibliography.

Focus Groups

Focus groups are one of the most common and most abused tools for learning from users. When conducting focus groups, you gather together groups of people who are actual or potential users of your site. In a typical focus group session, you may ask a series of scripted questions about what users would like to see on the site, demonstrate a prototype or show the site itself, ask questions about the users' perception of the site, and get their recommendations for improvement.

Focus groups are great for generating ideas about possible content and function for the site. By getting several people from your target audiences together and facilitating a brainstorming session, you can quickly find yourself with a laundry list of suggestions.

However, focus groups are very poor vehicles for testing the usability of a site. A public demonstration does not come close to replicating the actual environment of a user navigating a web site. Consequently, the suggestions of people in focus groups do not necessarily carry much weight. Sadly, focus groups are often used to prove that a particular approach does or doesn't work. Through the skillful selection and phrasing of questions, focus groups can easily be influenced in one direction or another. To learn more about when and how to conduct focus groups, see the usability section of our bibliography.

Individual User Testing

A much more appropriate way to study the usability of a prototype or post-launch web site is to conduct individual user testing. This method involves bringing in some real users, giving them some typical test tasks, and asking them to think out loud while they perform the tasks. The statements and actions of the user can be recorded several ways, ranging from the high-tech videotape and usage tracking approach to the low-tech notes-on-paper approach. Either way, it's important to try this exercise with several different users, ideally from different audience groups. As Jakob Nielsen suggests in "Guerrilla HCI" (*http://www.useit.com/papers/ guerilla_hci.html*), you can learn a great deal about what does and doesn't work very quickly and inexpensively using this approach.

Questions and Suggestions

One of the simplest ways to collect information about the usability of your site is to ask users to tell you what does and doesn't work. Build a Questions and Suggestions area in your site, and make it available from every page in the site.

In addition, you should adopt a No Dead-Ends policy, always giving the user a way to move towards the information they need. One technique involves using the following context-sensitive suggestion at the bottom of a search results page.:

> Not finding what you're looking for with search? Try browsing our web site or tell us what you're looking for and we'll try to help.

Whether employing a generic or context-sensitive approach, make it easy for users to provide feedback. Instead of using a *mailto:* tag that requires proper browser customization, use a form-based approach that integrates online documentation with the opportunity to interact. In this way, you might answer the user's question faster and avoid spending staff time on producing the answer.

Avoid the temptation of creating a feedback form that is long, since most users will never fill it out. Ask only the most important and necessary questions. If your site is blessed with an active audience willing to provide feedback, wonderful. If not, you might combine an online survey with a contest involving free gifts.

Finally, if you're going to make it easy for users to ask questions and make suggestions, you also need to establish procedures that allow you to respond quickly and effectively.

It's important to respond to users who take the time to provide feedback. This is common courtesy. It also makes sense since a user may be a customer or investor, or perhaps a senior executive in virtual disguise.

To facilitate prompt responses and promote efficiency at the back-end, build triage into your site's feedback system. Provide users with the option to contact the webmaster for technical problems and the content specialist for questions about the site's content.

You'll also need to create a system for reviewing and acting upon questions and suggestions. In a large organization, you may need to form a site review and design committee to meet once per month, review the questions and suggestions, and identify opportunities for improvement.

Usage Tracking

Basic usage logs and statistics reports are of little value. They do tell you roughly how many times your site is visited and which pages are viewed. However, this information does not tell you how to improve your site.

If you want more useful information, you can use more complex approaches to tracking users. The most complex approach involves the tracking of user's paths as they search and browse a web site. You can trace where a user comes from (originating site) to reach your site; the path they take through your organization, navigation, and searching systems; and where they go next (destination site). Along the way, you can learn how long they spend on each page. This creates a tremendously rich data stream, which can be fascinating to review, but difficult to act upon. What you need to make this information valuable is feedback from users explaining why they came to the site, what they found, and why they left. If you combine technology that pops up a questionnaire when users are about to leave the site with an incentive for completing your questionnaire, you might be able to capture this information. Just be careful not to irritate the users with this kind of approach. It may be something you do for a short period of time in conjunction with a special promotion.

A simpler approach involves the tracking and analysis of queries entered into the search engine, like that shown in Figure 9-7. By studying these queries, you can identify what users are looking for and the words and phrases they use. You can isolate the queries that retrieve zero results. Are users employing different labels or looking for information that doesn't exist on your site? Are they failing to use Boolean operators the way you intended? Based upon the answers, you can take immediate and concrete steps to fix the problems. You may change labels, improve search tips, or even add content to the site.

In considering these approaches, it's important to realize that the data is useful only if you and your organization are committed to acting upon what you learn. Gigabytes upon gigabytes of usage statistics are ignored every day by well-meaning but very busy site architects and designers who fail to close the feedback loop.

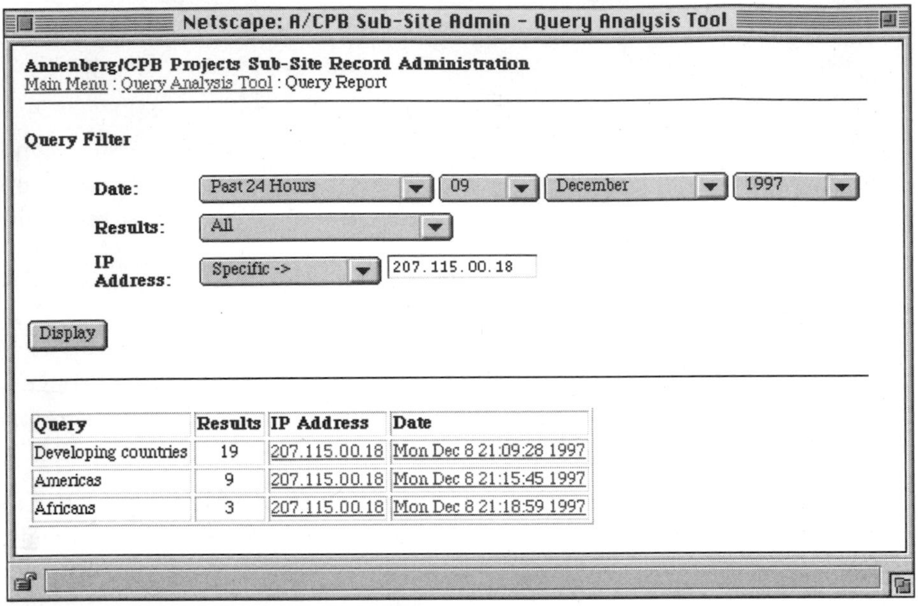

Figure 9-7. This query analysis tool allows you to filter by date and IP address. You can also isolate queries that resulted in zero hits. By leveraging the IP address and date/time information, the software enables you to see an individual user's progress (or lack thereof) as he or she tries one search after another.

However, if you can commit to continuous user-centric improvement, your site will soon reach a level of quality and usability beyond what could have ever been achieved through good architectural design alone. And it will only get better, as it is subjected to the contant evolutionary pressures of time, competition, and increasingly demanding users.

Similarly, if you maintain that personal feedback loop between your experiences as a consumer and your sensibilities as a producer, your information architectures will continue to improve over time.

10

Information Architecture in Action

In Chapters 3 through 6, we covered the basic principles of information architecture and illustrated those principles with examples and practical advice. Chapters 7 through 9 explained the role of both information architecture and architect in context of a web site's development and described the architect's tools and deliverables.

This chapter provides you with a case study that illustrates how an information architecture can solve some of the most common and irritating problems faced by web designers and developers. The architecture described here is *not* a silver bullet; it certainly doesn't work for all possible types of sites. Use this chapter instead to get a sense of the decision making that goes into creating an information architecture that fulfills specific needs.

Archipelagoes of Information

As do most of his books, James Michener's *Hawaii* starts at the dawn of time. He describes how the lovely Hawaiian archipelago grows over millions of years from humble, organic beginnings, each island birthing and dying in explosions of lava emanating from beneath the Earth's crust.

Large, complex web sites and intranets have similarly organic beginnings. These sites are loosely connected archipelagoes of information, starting slowly with one island, coming from sources often unseen, exploding with change and growth, out of control. It often goes like this: someone in the MIS department gets a web server, sets it up, builds a small, experimental web site, and starts having fun. Other early adopters check out this unofficial site and get ideas of their own. The MIS boss finds out and, horrified by his or her lack of control over the situation, forces the free-thinker to terminate the maverick site, while enlisting someone from Graphics to help start up the official intranet. The MIS boss later learns (to her dismay) that the pesky Marketing Department has already decided to contract their advertising firm to build an external site, and the Human Resources people aren't far behind. And there are rumors that both the Hong Kong and Hoboken divisions are setting up their own sites....

Sites that grow this way within an organization are really a collection of sub-sites. Their complexity runs deeper than you may think. Indeed, the biggest challenge is often the degree to which organizational politics intrude into the process. This isn't surprising if we consider the differences between the ways modern corporations and the World Wide Web work.

Corporations and other large organizations are traditionally modeled hierarchically, structured as single entities with clear chains of command. The power of a corporation lies in its ability to leverage the sum of its independently working parts while laboring to keep those parts from completely splitting apart. The Web, on the other hand, goes completely against the grain of centralization, serving instead as an agent of organizational chaos. Because web sites are cheap and easy to create, corporations have a difficult time controlling them.

As some poor souls try to bring all these separate efforts together under the venue of a single corporate web site or intranet, the politics can get especially ugly. Marketing wants links to its news releases to go on the main page. Human Resources is convinced that most of the users are going to be employees, and wants the employee handbook front and center. And MIS's content already blankets the main page. Meanwhile the Information Center has trashed the look and feel of the site because they don't have the budget to pay for professional graphic design. Have we left anyone out?

Oh, yes. The user.

The user, as we know, doesn't care about organizational politics. The user wants information to be made accessible the way he or she thinks, not the way the corporation thinks. Instead, the user is often confronted with corporate jargon and organization schemes based on corporate organization charts, and the site's value to users and to the sponsoring organization plummet.

Unfortunately, this is a common situation. Fortunately, the principles of information architecture can address and solve many of these problems.

A Case Study: Henry Ford Health System

The Henry Ford Health System (HFHS) is one of the largest health care providers in Michigan, with over 17,000 employees and almost $2 billion in annual revenues. They approached Argus and its strategic partners, Q LTD (which provides graphic design and editorial services) and InterConnect of Ann Arbor (which provides programming and technical design consulting) to create an external corporate web site from scratch. Needless to say, we were delighted to take on the project. We also realized that we would need to avoid the usual problems of main page crowding, political jockeying, poor navigation, and inconsistent look and feel that were abundant in many other health care organizations' sites. Although the HFHS internal Internet committee was very sensitive to these problems, we all faced a huge challenge of creating a useful, user-centered site for such a large corporation.

Org Chart as Default Architecture

We began with the assumption that we could not force the 90 or so HFHS hospitals, medical centers, departments, units, and programs to halt their own web development efforts and comply with the look and feel of the site we were about to create. In fact, it would be better to accept the reality that sites grow organically within an organization, and build a strong umbrella site around these local islands of corporate information. So, we began visualizing an architecture that looked like the one in Figure 10-1.

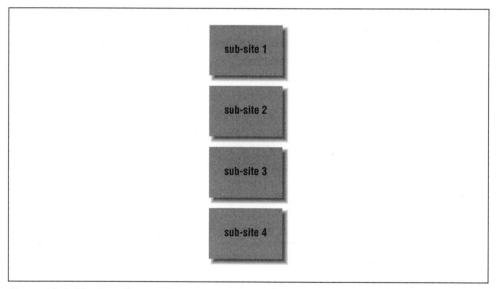

Figure 10-1. The Org Chart architecture. It obviously won't scale well for most large organizations. Imagine a main page with links to 90 sub-sites... on second thought, we're sure you've seen quite a few of those!

Each sub-site represented an *organizational entity*: a department, unit, division, medical center, hospital, or program sponsored by HFHS. We learned from our initial research that many of these entities did not yet have their own sub-sites, although they would over time. Some entities might never create their own sub-sites. So the reality of their web environment really looked a bit more like Figure 10-2.

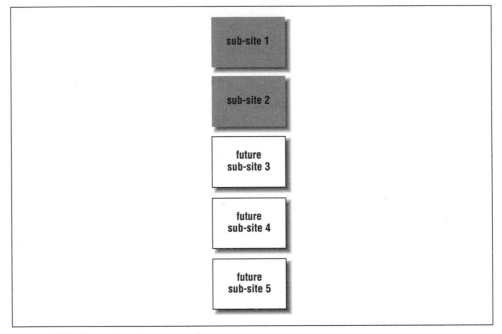

Figure 10-2. Expecting future growth

The organization scheme at this point very closely mirrored the political boundaries of the HFHS org chart. Users might come to the main page of such a site and find prominent links to the Department of Gynecology next to the Office of the President. Also, as HFHS is a large organization, there would be many more links than the five represented here. So how could we leave these default organic partitions of information in place, and yet provide a more usable, user-centered view? We had to find a way to cut across the grain of the org chart, yet leave it in place (see Figure 10-3).

Sub-Site Record Pages

Our solution was to create a database of records or meta-information pages to represent each sub-site. These sub-site record pages include information *about* each sub-site, and are centrally created and controlled by HFHS. Together, they serve as a catalog for the site's sub-sites; using database technology, they are easy to maintain and content duplication is minimized. The fields in these records and the relationships between each type of record were determined through a fairly conventional process of data modeling. The use of fielded information supports

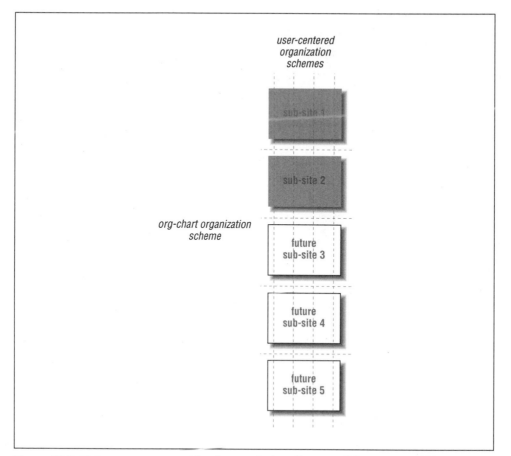

Figure 10-3. Unless we come up with a better solution, the site will be organized like an "org chart" (the horizontal dotted lines). Can we cut "across the grain" of the org chart (the vertical dotted lines) for a more user-centered approach?

improved information retrieval, as described in Chapter 6, *Searching Systems*. Also, the whole structure of sub-site records can be bypassed if need be, with users bookmarking an individual sub-site's main page if they so desire.

The sub-site record approach allows the sub-sites themselves to be controlled autonomously and anticipates sub-site growth well. If a sub-site existed, a sub-site record page would also link to the sub-site. If no sub-site existed yet (e.g., sub-site records 4 through 6 in Figure 10-4), the sub-site record would serve as a placeholder until it could be linked to a new sub-site. If a particular department wasn't likely to ever create a sub-site, the sub-site records would at least provide useful information about that department (e.g., sub-site record 3).

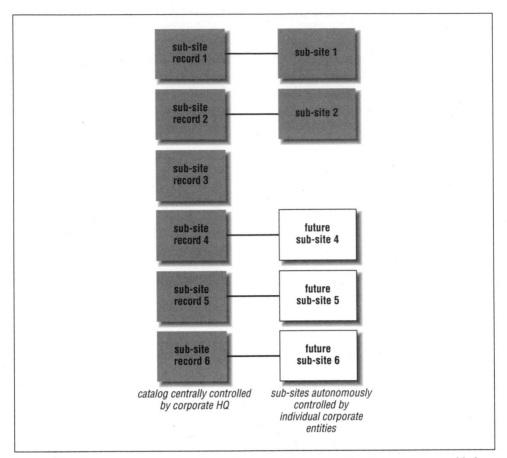

Figure 10-4. Sub-site record pages allow other ways of accessing the site's content, and help delineate responsibility for content ownership and management.

Labeling Systems for Sub-Site Record Pages

To address the need to cut across the grain of the default org chart-centered organization scheme, the sub-site record pages include manually created keyword indexing to support various user-centered means of accessing the sub-sites. In this case, we worked with HFHS' staff librarians to index each sub-site using medical terms in schemes that matched their two primary audiences: one controlled vocabulary for medical professionals and another for regular people. On each sub-site record page, these terms were shown together in one keywords field. Within that field, the keywords served as links to other sub-site record pages which had been similarly indexed, which can greatly enhance user navigation (for example, users can find other HFHS resources that are related to cancer—see Figure 10-5).

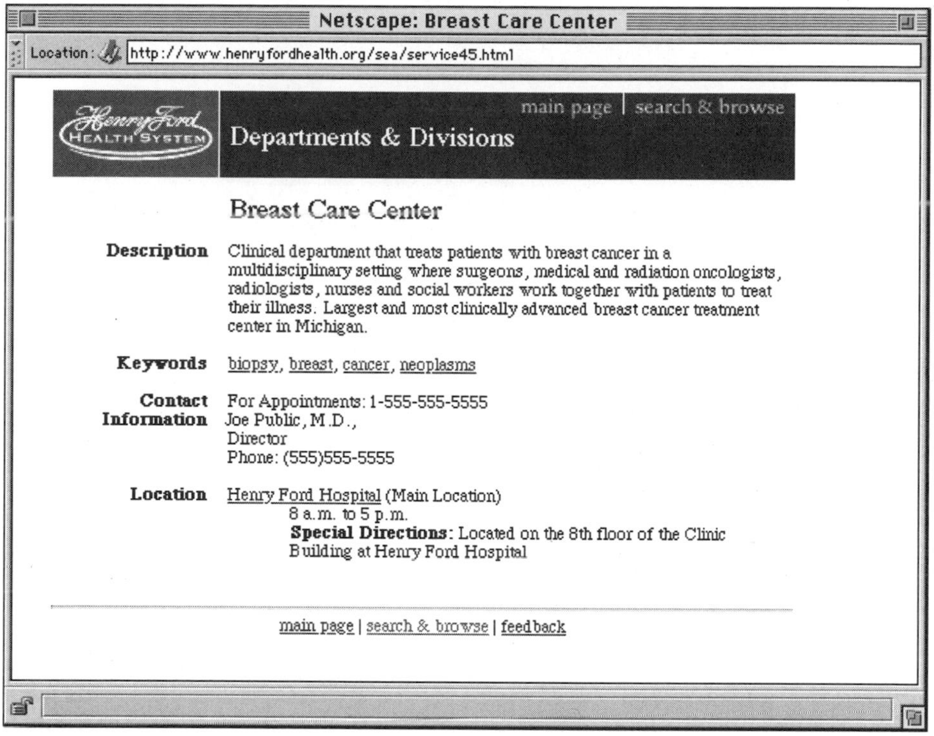

Figure 10-5. A sample sub-site record page can work as a placeholder or as a link to the actual sub-site. It also helps maintain a look and feel consistent with the remainder of the umbrella site.

These topical keywords provide access to the HFHS sub-sites' content in a more user-centered manner than the org chart approach did. We also provided other ways of navigating the sub-sites, leveraging the sub-site records to allow browsing by Organizational Resource (e.g., hospital vs. program vs. department and so on), and by location (City). And we did maintain a browsable org-chart index (Browse By Organizational Resources); browsing the site in this way remains useful in certain cases, especially for internal audiences.

Searching System

We also included a searching facility to allow for fast known-item searching (and, as you can see in Figure 10-6, we integrated it with the browsing options). Queries are run against a set of fields that we selected from the sub-site record pages, including document titles, descriptions, and keywords. Such selective indexing supports improved searching results because queries are run against homogeneous information created and maintained by the same central authority. The results are far more consistent than if a single index of all the content in all of the sub-sites could be created. Creating such an index could also be challenging if the owners of certain sub-sites disallowed spiders to crawl their sites.

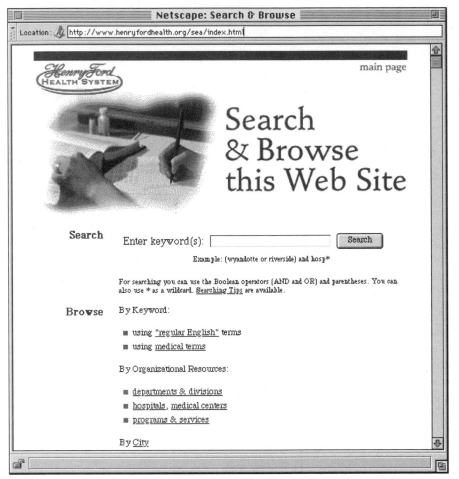

Figure 10-6. Multiple means of searching and browsing the sub-site record pages' content.

The architecture now looked something like that in Figure 10-7.

This architecture provides quick and easy access to content in sub-sites, especially for users who already know what they're looking for or who understand a bit about the nature of HFHS. Users can get straightforward lists of all that HFHS has to offer by city, by keywords, by searching, and so on. But what about users who don't really know what they're looking for? Or those who need a warm, fuzzy introduction to the Henry Ford Health System in general?

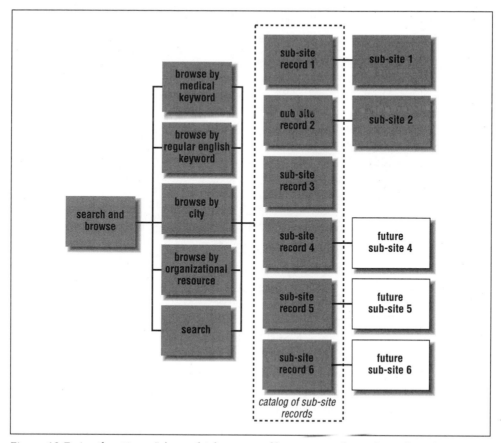

Figure 10-7. Another view of the multiple means of browsing and searching the sub-site record collection.

Guides

To give users, especially first-timers, a view of the HFHS web environment that goes beyond raw lists of sub-sites, we worked with HFHS staff to create guides[*] to HFHS and its information. Guides add value to the user's experience by telling a story about the site; in effect, they come as close as the Web can to serving as friendly tour guides. They wrap narrative text around featured links to sub-site record pages (or, for that matter, actual sub-site content) in a way that educates users about the site and its sponsor (in this way, they can allow marketing goals to be met). They can stand alone: guides provide value for users even if they

---

[*] In this book, we mention the Argus Clearinghouse (*http://www.clearinghouse.net*) on a number of occasions. The mission of the site is to serve as a central access point for guides to the Internet. If you're interested in seeing hundreds of examples of guides, try the Argus Clearinghouse.

don't wish to pursue the links. Guides also can be customized for different audiences or needs, and they can exist somewhat independently of the changes that might happen in the sub-sites themselves.

For HFHS, we identified major information needs that users might have when they reached the HFHS main page. Besides wanting to find a sub-site (which we'd already covered with the architecture we've shown so far), users might be members of four primary audiences:

- *Medical students* who were considering doing their residencies at HFHS.

- *Researchers*, both internal and external, who want to keep abreast of the role that HFHS plays in medical research.

- *Patients* who want to know about the care they could receive at HFHS.

- *Generic users* who want to know about HFHS in general.

We knew other audiences could be served by guides, and that there were other ways to define guides, such as by topic or task. But, after much discussion, we felt that these four guides would address the needs of perhaps 80% of first-time users of the site. What about the additional 20%? We hoped that they would be served by the Help Yourself search and browse features. Realistically, our feeling is that most sites' main pages probably don't address even 50% of their users' needs, so we felt that 80% was a pretty good goal. (In fact, the 80/20 Rule is good for web developers in general; use it to remind yourself that you can't always satisfy 100% of all possible users of your site, but that if you can assist 80%, your site will do better than the majority of its competitors.)

Each of the four guides would describe HFHS's offerings in a style that best fit the needs of each audience. Also, each guide would link to the subset of HFHS sub-sites that was relevant to that particular audience (see Figure 10-8).

Multiple Pathways to Content

Now our architecture supported different ways to get users to information in the HFHS Web environment. Users doing exploratory searching could easily move back and forth between browsing and searching a catalog of sub-site records. Known-item searchers and repeat users could go right to the search engine or quickly scan the browsable indices. New users who wanted a better sense of what HFHS offers could get a taste through any of the four guides to selected HFHS sub-sites. The top-level information architecture was nearing completion (see Figure 10-9).

There were still some other areas we'd not yet dealt with. One area was the news announcements and press releases that HFHS would naturally want to make available. We created a news area in the site and augmented it with a dynamic

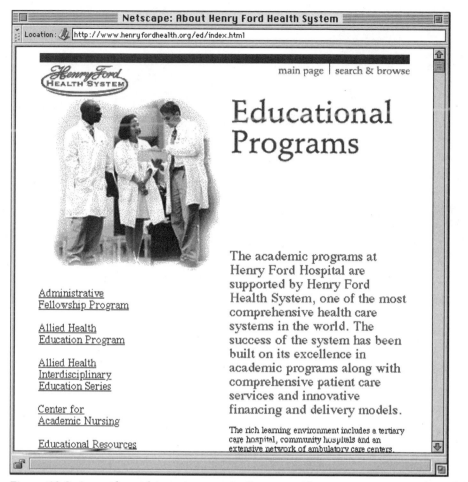

Figure 10-8. A sample guide's main page. Audience-specific narrative text is on the right and links to sub-site records and other useful resources on the left.

billboard that showed news headlines and, when clicked, would take users to the story that it had introduced. The billboard adds nice visual splash to the main page. It also helps defuse potentially sticky political situations by unburying sub-site content that deserves occasional exposure on the main page. At this point, we also added the de rigeur "About HFHS" section. So the final top-level architecture looked like Figure 10-10.

Pretty confusing, eh? Certainly the blueprint diagram is overwhelming; that's why we always use mock-up pages at this point in the conceptual design phase. However, when you look at the final product, the main page for this site (Figure 10-11), you will note its simplicity.

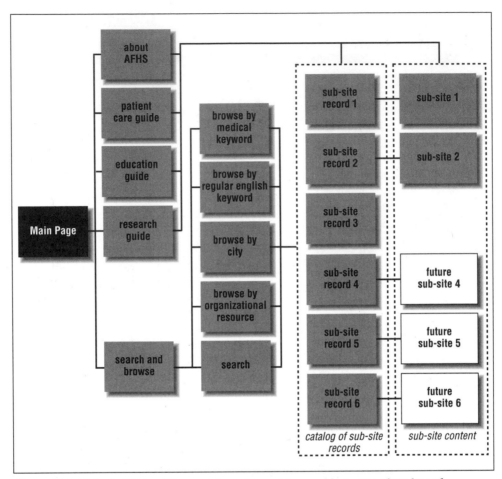

Figure 10-9. Value-added guides complement searching and browsing plain lists of resources.

The HFHS main page has few links, a balance between static and dynamic information (e.g., the dynamic billboard at the top of the page), and no names of departments, units, or other political entities that might typically sneak their way there due to political infighting. Yet it provides users with *ten* ways to reach information in the HFHS Web environment:

1. Browse by Keyword (both medical and lay)

2. Browse by Organizational Resource

3. Browse by City

4. Search

5. Patient Care Guide

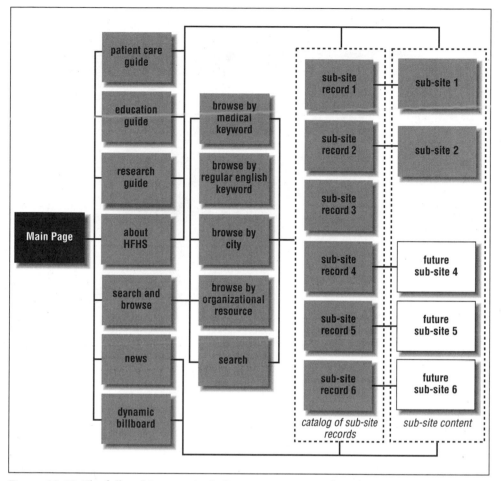

Figure 10-10. The full architecture, including two new ways of reaching content (news and the dynamic billboard).

6. Research Guide

7. Education Guide

8. About HFHS Guide

9. News Area

10. Dynamic Billboard

Conclusion

We addressed the issues of politics and main page cluttering by creating additional real estate, in the form of guides, just off that most prime real estate, the

Figure 10-11. The HFHS site's main page—a concise gateway to a complex information environment

main page. We moved mention of and links to individual sub-sites from that main page to these guides, thus reducing the clutter of the main page. This approach could be embodied as a policy that would stand up to any unit or department demanding to be linked to from the main page.

We also architected and created a catalog of the entire HFHS Web environment. This alone was a first for the organization: there had never been a comprehensive, up-to-date publicly accessible catalog of HFHS and its offerings. This represented a huge value-add for users. From a maintenance perspective, the sub-site record pages, as well as the various browsable indices, could all be generated by a database. New records could be added without affecting the overall architecture.

We addressed navigation challenges by creating many different ways for users to browse information, and applying these navigation systems consistently on the site's pages (thanks in part to generating these pages from a database with easily configurable templates). We believe that searching performs better thanks to the use of search zones and controlled vocabularies.

Lastly, we allowed sub-sites to maintain their own personalities independently of the umbrella site. We also provided a style guide for others at HFHS to create sub-sites that match the umbrella site's look and feel. Better a carrot than a stick!

All of this was accomplished by considering *before production* the needs of the site's users and fitting the organization, navigation, labeling, and searching systems around those needs. What we've covered here is an illustration of what information architecture is all about.

We don't intend to portray the architecture depicted in this case study as one-size-fits-all. We feel that it works well as an external site for a large, distributed institution. There are bits and pieces of it that you might apply to your situation, but your site might benefit from a completely different architecture. Your mileage will certainly vary. But as long as you ask the questions, plan ahead, and consider the user, your information architecture should succeed.

Selected Bibliography

This bibliography is intended to provide a few suggestions for further reading and to credit some of the people from whom we have drawn ideas and inspiration. For a more current and comprehensive bibliography of resources related to information architecture, please see our online "Guide to Information Architecture" at *http://argus-inc.com/iaguide/*.

Information Architecture

Argus Associates. "Web Architect" (column). *Web Review Magazine*. *http://webreview.com/universal/previous/arch/index.html* or *http://argus-inc.com/design/webarch.html*.

Benedikt, Michael, ed. *Cyberspace: First Steps*. Cambridge, MA: MIT Press, 1991.

Cook, Melissa A. *Building Enterprise Information Architectures: Reengineering Information Systems*. Upper Saddle River, NJ: Prentice Hall, 1996.

Instone, Keith. "Usable Web: Guide to Web Usability Resources" (updated monthly). *http://usableweb.com/*.

Kahn, Paul and Krzysztof Lenk. *Website Information Architecture*. Indianapolis, IN: New Riders, 1998.

Mok, Clement. *Designing Business: Multiple Media, Multiple Disciplines*. San Jose, CA: Adobe Press, 1996.

Nielsen, Jakob. *Designing Websites With Authority: Secrets of an Information Architect*. Indianapolis, IN: New Riders, 1998.

Sano, Darrell. *Designing Large-Scale Web Sites: A Visual Design Methodology*. New York: Wiley, 1996.

Tufte, Edward R. *Envisioning Information*, 3rd Edition. Cheshire, CT: Graphics Press, 1990.

Tufte, Edward R. *The Visual Display of Quantitative Information*. Cheshire, CT: Graphics Press, 1992.

Tufte, Edward R. *Visual Explanations: Images and Quantities, Evidence and Narrative*. Cheshire, CT: Graphics Press, 1997.

Wurman, Richard Saul. *Information Architects*. Zurich, Switzerland: Graphis Press Corp, 1996.

Organization

Blair, David C. *Language and Representation in Information Retrieval*. New York: Elsevier Science Publishers, 1990.

"Cataloging Policy and Support Office Home Page." Library of Congress. *http://lcweb.loc.gov/catdir/cpso/*.

"Dewey Decimal System Home Page." OCLC Forest Press. 1997. *http://www.oclc.org/oclc/fp/ddchome.htm*.

Friedlander, Amy, ed. *D-Lib Magazine: The Magazine of Digital Library Research*. Reston, VA: Corporation for National Research Initiatives. *http://www.dlib.org/*.

Gorman, Michael and Paul W. Winkler, eds. *Anglo-American Cataloging Rules*, 2nd Edition, 1998 Revision ed. Chicago, IL: American Library Association, 1988.

"Hypertext Now: Archives." Eastgate Systems. *http://www.eastgate.com/HypertextNow/*.

Lakoff, George and Mark Johnson. *Metaphors We Live By*. Chicago: University of Chicago Press, 1983.

Meadow, Charles T. *Text Information Retrieval Systems*. San Diego: Academic Press, 1992.

Richmond, Alan and Lucy Richmond. "The WDVL: Resource Location." Web Developer's Virtual Library, Cyberweb Software. *http://Stars.com/Location/*.

Rosenfeld, Louis. "Particles, Waves, and Site Visualization," Web Architect. *Web Review Magazine*. July, 1997. *http://www.webreview.com/97/07/11/arch/index.html*.

Rowley, Jennifer E. *Organizing Knowledge*, 2nd Edition. Brookfield, VT: Ashgate Publishing, 1992.

Navigation

Fleming, Jennifer. *Web Navigation: Designing the User Experience.* Sebastopol, CA: Songline Studios, 1998.

Gloor, Peter A. *Elements of Hypermedia Design: Techniques for Navigation and Visualization in Cyberspace.* Boston: Birkhauser, 1997.

Hoffman, Michael. "Information Structuring for Rapid Knowledge Transfer." 1997. *http://www.well.com/user/hoff/index.htm.*

"Hypertext Now: Archives." Eastgate Systems. *http://www.eastgate.com/HypertextNow/.*

Instone Keith. "Usability Matters" (column). *Web Review. http://www.webreview.com/universal/previous/usability/.*

Instone, Keith. "Usable Web: Guide to Web Usability Resources" (updated monthly). *http://usableweb.com/.*

Laurel, Brenda. *The Art of Human-Computer Interface Design.* Reading, MA: Addison-Wesley Publishing, 1990.

Morville, Peter. "Dynamic Dueling," Web Architect. *Web Review.* May, 1997. *http://www.webreview.com/97/05/16/arch/index.html.*

Nielsen, Jakob. *Multimedia and Hypertext: The Internet and Beyond.* Boston, MA: AP Professional, Academic Press, 1995.

Nielsen, Jakob. "The Rise of the Sub-Site." *The Alertbox: Current Issues in Web Usability.* September, 1996. *http://www.useit.com/alertbox/9609.html.*

Vroomen, Louis C. "Graphical User Interfaces for Hierarchies: A Workshop." Centre de recherche informatique de Montréal. *http://www.crim.ca/~vroomen/workshop/workshop.htm.*

Labeling

Bailey, Samantha. "Love Your Labels," Web Architect. *Web Review.* February, 1997. *http://www.webreview.com/97/02/21/arch/index.html.*

"Cataloging Policy and Support Office Home Page." Library of Congress. *http://lcweb.loc.gov/catdir/cpso/.*

"Dewey Decimal System Home Page." OCLC Forest Press. 1997. *http://www.oclc.org/oclc/fp/ddchome.htm.*

"Library of Congress Thesauri Home Page." Library of Congress. *http://lcweb.loc.gov/lexico/.*

McKiernan, Gerry. "Beyond Bookmarks: Schemes for Organizing the Web." Iowa State University Library. *http://www.public.iastate.edu/~CYBERSTACKS/CTW.htm.*

Meadow, Charles T. *Text Information Retrieval Systems.* San Diego: Academic Press, 1992.

Nielsen, Jakob and Darrell Sano. "User Interface Design for Sun Microsystem's Internal Web." 1997. *http://www.sun.com:80/sun-on-net/uidesign/sunweb/.*

Pao, Miranda L. *Concepts of Information Retrieval.* Englewood, CO: Libraries Unlimited, 1989.

Rosenfeld, Louis. "Label Laws," Web Architect. *Web Review.* March, 1996. *http://www.webreview.com/96/03/29/webarch/index.html.*

Rowley, Jennifer E. *Organizing Knowledge*, 2nd Edition. Brookfield, VT: Ashgate Publishing, 1992.

Searching

Blair, David C. *Language and Representation in Information Retrieval.* New York: Elsevier Science Publishers, 1990.

Friedlander, Amy, ed. *D-Lib Magazine: The Magazine of Digital Library Research.* Reston, VA: Corporation for National Research Initiatives. *http://www.dlib.org/.*

Morville, Peter, Louis Rosenfeld, and Joseph Janes. *The Internet Searcher's Handbook: Locating Information, People, and Software.* New York: Neil-Schuman Publishers, 1996.

Nielsen, Jakob. "Search and You May Find." *The Alertbox: Current Issues in Web Usability.* July, 1997. *http://www.useit.com/alertbox/9707b.html.*

Pao, Miranda L. *Concepts of Information Retrieval.* Englewood, CO: Libraries Unlimited, 1989.

Sullivan, Danny. Mecklermedia. "Search Engine Watch: News, Tips and More About Search Engines." *http://www.searchenginewatch.com/.*

Walker, Geraldine and Joseph Janes. *Online Retrieval: A Dialogue of Theory and Practice.* Englewood, CO: Libraries Unlimited, 1993.

Strategy and Process

Brigman, Linda. *Web Site Management Excellence.* Que Education & Training, 1996.

Buchanan, Robert W., Charles Lukaszewski, and Robert W. Buchanan, Jr. *Measuring the Impact of Your Web Site.* New York: John Wiley and Sons, 1997.

DeMarco, Tom. *The Deadline: A Novel About Project Management.* New York: Dorset House Publishing, 1997.

Harrel, Clayton. "Heuristic Planning Makes the Past Current." *Electronic Design* 44, no. 8. April, 1996: 83.

Kelly, Kevin. *Out of Control: The New Biology of Machines, Social Systems, and the Economic World.* Reading, MA: Addison-Wesley Publishing, 1994.

Lewis, James P. *Fundamentals of Project Management.* WorkSmart Series. New York: AMACOM, 1995.

Morville, Peter. "Calculating the Cost of a Large-Scale Web Site," Web Architect. *Web Review Magazine.* August, 1997. *http://www.webreview.com/97/08/08/ arch/index.html.*

Morville, Peter. "Design for Change: Looking Beyond Opening Day," Web Architect. *Web Review Magazine.* April, 1996. *http://www.webreview.com/96/04/12/ webarch/index.html.*

Nielsen, Jakob. "Guerrilla HCI: Using Discount Usability Engineering to Penetrate the Intimidation Barrier." *Cost-Justifying Usability.* 1994. *http://www.useit.com/ papers/guerrilla_hci.html.*

Schwartz, Peter. *The Art of the Long View.* New York: Currency, Doubleday, 1996.

Siegel, David S. *Secrets of Successful Web Sites: Project Management on the World Wide Web.* Indianapolis, IN: Hayden Books, 1997.

Zuboff, Shoshana. *In the Age of the Smart Machine: The Future of Work and Power.* New York: Basic Books, 1988.

Usability

Cooper, Alan. *About Face: The Essentials of User Interface Design.* Foster City, CA: IDG Books Worldwide, 1995.

Instone Keith. "Usability Matters" (column). *Web Review.* *http://www.webreview.com/universal/previous/usability/.*

Instone, Keith. "Usable Web: Guide to Web Usability Resources" (updated monthly). *http://usableweb.com/.*

Laurel, Brenda. *The Art of Human-Computer Interface Design.* Reading, MA: Addison-Wesley Publishing, 1990.

Miller, G. "The Magical Number Seven, Plus or Minus Two: Some Limits on Our Capacity for Processing Information." *Psychological Review* 63, no. 2. 1956: 81-97.

Nielsen, Jakob. *The Alertbox: Current Issues in Web Usability* (semi-monthly column). *http://www.useit.com/alertbox/*.

Nielsen, Jakob. *Usability Engineering*. Boston, MA: AP Professional, Academic Press, 1994.

Rubin, Jeffrey. *Handbook of Usability Testing: How to Plan, Design, and Conduct Effective Tests*. New York: Wiley, 1994.

Spool, Jared M. *Web Site Usability: A Designer's Guide*. North Andover, MA: User Interface Engineering, 1997.

General Design

Alexander, Christopher. *The Timeless Way of Building*. New York: Oxford University Press, 1979.

Brand, Stewart. *How Buildings Learn: What Happens After They're Built*. New York: Viking, 1994.

Franck, Karen A. and Lynda H. Schneekloth, eds. *Ordering Space: Types in Architecture and Design*. New York: Van Nostrand Reinhold, 1994.

Lynch, Patrick J. and Sarah Horton. "Yale C/AIM Web Style Guide." Yale University, 1997. *http://info.med.yale.edu/caim/manual/contents.html*.

Lyndon, Donlyn and Charles W. Moore. *Chambers for a Memory Palace*. Cambridge, MA: MIT Press, 1994.

Mok, Clement. *Designing Business: Multiple Media, Multiple Disciplines*. San Jose, CA: Adobe Press, 1996.

Nielsen, Jakob. *Multimedia and Hypertext: The Internet and Beyond*. Boston, MA: AP Professional, Academic Press, 1995.

Norman, Donald. *The Design of Everyday Things*. New York: Doubleday, 1990.

Norman, Donald. *Things That Make Us Smart: Defending Human Attributes in the Age of the Machine*. Reading, MA: Addison-Wesley Publishing, 1993.

Petroski, Henry. *The Evolution of Useful Things*. New York: Vintage Books, 1994.

Index

A

ad hoc navigation, 57–58
aesthetics, 7
alphabetical organization, 27, 115
ambiguity, 23, 29–31
architecture (see information architecture)
associative learning, 104
audiences
    attention span, 8–9, 73
    considering when indexing, 66–67
    database structure and, 41
    feedback from, 171–174
    getting label text from, 91–93
    how they search, 101–104
    indexing for, 128
    learning about, 139–141
    likes and dislikes of, 4–8
        critiquing sites, 134–136
        determining, 2–4
        labels and, 74
        measuring site's success, 138–139
    organization for specific, 32, 41, 128
    personalizing for, 8
    perspectives of, 12, 25
    search interface design and, 112, 120
    thinking like, 15
    usage tracking, 173–174

B

balancing perspectives, 18–19
blueprints, 154–156, 162–164, 170

C

bottom-up organization approach, 41–45
brainstorming site design, 148–150
breadth, hierarchy, 38–39
browser navigation features, 48–50
browsing (see navigation)

case study for architecture, 176–189
chronological organization, 28, 115, 129
chunks, content, 147, 162, 165–166
clickable image maps, 49
closed organization schemes, 32
collaboration, 19–21, 132–134
color as navigation feature, 48
comprehensive searching, 103, 122–124
computer science, importance of, 18
conceptual design, 148–160
    blueprints, 154–156, 162–164, 170
    brainstorming and exploring
        possibilities, 148–153
    metaphors for, 150–151
    page mockups, 156–157
    site prototypes, 160
    (see also graphic design and layout)
consumers (see audiences)
controlled vocabulary, 43–44
    taking label text from, 88–90, 94
critiquing
    information architecture, 136–137
    web sites, 134–136

About the Authors

Louis Rosenfeld is President of Argus Associates. A leading information architecture evangelist, Lou co-writes the regular "Web Architect" column for *Web Review* magazine, and has written and edited numerous other books, book chapters, and scholarly articles. Lou also regularly presents at such conferences as Web Design & Development, Internet World, and COMDEX.

Lou holds a Masters in Information and Library Studies and a B.A. in History, both from The University of Michigan. Luckily for him, the global Internet began to gain steam just after he completed his MILS degree in 1990, giving him a non-traditional setting to try out newly acquired skills in information science and librarianship. While at The University of Michigan, he did get some traditional library experience, and also worked as a researcher at the College of Engineering. In 1993, he founded a popular Internet research service, the Argus Clearinghouse (*http://www.clearinghouse.net*), based on the principles of librarianship. Before burning out as a doctoral student, Lou designed and co-taught what may have been the first academic courses that dealt specifically with the Internet (at The University of Michigan School of Information and Library Studies, 1993–1994).

Lou's favorite hobbies include getting injured while playing soccer, getting injured while playing racquetball, and gardening.

Peter Morville is Vice President of Argus Associates. Since 1993, he has provided project management and information architecture services to some of the world's largest companies. Prior to joining Argus, Peter worked as Manager of Online Services for Michigan Comnet, where he guided the creation and development of a highly successful online community for non-profit organizations.

Peter has written extensively on the topics of information architecture and information retrieval. Publications include the *Internet Searcher's Handbook* (Neal-Schuman, 1996) and the "Web Architect" column in *Web Review* magazine. He speaks frequently at national professional conferences such as Internet World, Web Design & Development, and COMDEX.

Peter holds a Masters in Information and Library Studies from The University of Michigan and a B.A. in English Literature from Tufts University. His current research interests include psycholinguistics, knowledge management, and the dynamics of polar bear society.

Founded in 1991, **Argus Associates** (*http://argus-inc.com*) specializes in information architecture design for large, complex intranets and web sites. Argus is somewhat unique in that it is staffed by entrepreneurial librarians who are interested in applying the principles of their profession in new venues where they're desperately needed, especially in the mammoth information systems that many large corporations are currently building. Argus helps its clients by creating organization, labeling, navigation, and indexing systems that help users find the information they need. Argus has provided consulting services to a diverse array of clients, including AT&T, *Barron's Magazine*, Borders Books & Music, Chrysler Corporation, Dow Chemical Company, *Encyclopaedia Britannica*, and SIGGRAPH.

Colophon

The animal featured on the cover of *Information Architecture* is a polar bear (*Ursus maritimus*). Polar bears live primarily on the icy shores of Greenland and northern North America and Asia. They are very strong swimmers, and rarely venture far from the water. The largest land carnivore, male polar bears weigh from 770 to 1400 pounds. Female polar bears are much smaller, weighing 330 to 550 pounds. The preferred meal of polar bears is ringed seals and bearded seals. When seals are unavailable they will eat fish, reindeer, birds, berries, and trash.

Polar bears are, of course, well adapted to living in the Arctic Circle. Their black skin is covered in thick, water-repellant, white fur. Adult polar bears are protected from the cold by a layer of blubber that is more than four inches thick. They are so well insulated, in fact, that overheating can be a problem. For this reason they move slowly on land, taking frequent breaks. Their large feet spread out their substantial weight, allowing them to walk on thin ice surfaces that animals weighing far less would break through. Because food is available year-round, most polar bears don't hibernate. Pregnant females are the exception, and the tiny 1 to $1^{1}/_{2}$ pound cubs are born during the hibernation period.

Polar bears have no natural enemies. Their greatest threat comes from hunting, but in the past 15 years most governments have placed strict limits on the hunting of polar bears. Their population has more than doubled in that time, and is now estimated to be between 21,000 and 28,000. They are not considered to be endangered. They are extremely aggressive and dangerous animals. While many bears actively avoid human contact, polar bears tend to view humans as prey. In encounters between humans and polar bears, the bear almost always wins.

Edie Freedman designed the cover of this book, using a 19th-century engraving from the Dover Pictorial Archive. The cover layout was produced with Quark XPress 3.3 using the ITC Garamond font. Whenever possible, our books use Rep-Kover™, a durable and flexible lay-flat binding. If the page count exceeds Rep-Kover's limit, perfect binding is used.

The inside layout was designed by Nancy Priest and implemented in FrameMaker 5.0 by Mike Sierra. The text and heading fonts are ITC Garamond Light and Garamond Book. The screen shots that appear in the book were created in Adobe Photoshop 4.0 and the illustrations were created in Macromedia Freehand 7.0 by Robert Romano. This colophon was written by Clairemarie Fisher O'Leary.

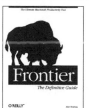

Developing Web Content

CGI Programming on the World Wide Web

By Shishir Gundavaram
1st Edition March 1996
450 pages, ISBN 1-56592-168-2

This book offers a comprehensive explanation of CGI and related techniques for people who hold on to the dream of providing their own information servers on the Web. It starts at the beginning, explaining the value of CGI and how it works, then moves swiftly into the subtle details of programming.

Information Architecture
for the World Wide Web

By Louis Rosenfeld & Peter Morville
1st Edition January 1998
226 pages, ISBN 1-56592-282-4

Learn how to merge aesthetics and mechanics to design web sites that "work." This book shows how to apply principles of architecture and library science to design cohesive web sites and intranets that are easy to use, manage, and expand. Covers building complex sites, hierarchy design and organization, and techniques to make your site easier to search. For webmasters, designers, and administrators.

Learning VBScript

By Paul Lomax
1st Edition July 1997
616 pages, includes CD-ROM
ISBN 1-56592-247-6

This definitive guide shows web developers how to take full advantage of client-side scripting with the VBScript language. In addition to basic language features, it covers the Internet Explorer object model and discusses techniques for client-side scripting, like adding ActiveX controls to a web page or validating data before sending it to the server. Includes CD-ROM with over 170 code samples.

Web Client Programming with Perl

By Clinton Wong
1st Edition March 1997
228 pages, ISBN 1-56592-214-X

Web Client Programming with Perl shows you how to extend scripting skills to the Web. This book teaches you the basics of how browsers communicate with servers and how to write your own customized web clients to automate common tasks. It is intended for those who are motivated to develop software that offers a more flexible and dynamic response than a standard web browser.

JavaScript: The Definitive Guide, 3rd Edition

By David Flanagan & Dan Shafer
3rd Edition June 1998 (est.)
800 pages (est.), ISBN 1-56592-392-8

This third edition of the definitive reference to JavaScript covers the latest version of the language, JavaScript 1.2, as supported by Netscape Navigator 4.0. JavaScript, which is being standardized under the name ECMAScript, is a scripting language that can be embedded directly in HTML to give web pages programming-language capabilities.

Designing Web Content

Designing with JavaScript

By Nick Heinle
1st Edition September 1997
256 pages, Includes CD-ROM
ISBN 1-56592-300-6

Written by the author of the "JavaScript Tip of the Week" web site, this new Web Review Studio book focuses on the most useful and applicable scripts for making truly interactive, engaging web sites. You'll not only have quick access to the scripts you need, you'll finally understand why the scripts work, how to alter the scripts to get the effects you want, and, ultimately, how to write your own groundbreaking scripts from scratch.

GIF Animation Studio

By Richard Koman
1st Edition October 1996
184 pages, Includes CD-ROM
ISBN 1-56592-230-1

GIF animation is bringing the Web to life—without plug-ins, Java programming, or expensive authoring tools. This book details the major GIF animation programs, profiles work by leading designers (including John Hersey, Razorfish, Henrik Drescher, and Erik Josowitz), and documents advanced animation techniques. A CD-ROM includes freeware and shareware authoring programs, demo versions of commercial software, and the actual animation files described in the book. *GIF Animation Studio* is the first release in the new Web Review Studio series.

Shockwave Studio

By Bob Schmitt
1st Edition March 1997
200 pages, Includes CD-ROM
ISBN 1-56592-231-X

This book, the second title in the new Web Review Studio series, shows how to create compelling and functional Shockwave movies for web sites. The author focuses on actual Shockwave movies, showing how the movies were created. The book takes users from creating simple time-based Shockwave animations through writing complex logical operations that take full advantage of Director's power. The CD-ROM includes a demo version of Director and other software sample files.

Photoshop for the Web

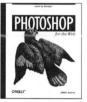

By Mikkel Aaland
1st Edition April 1998 (est.)
264 pages (est.), ISBN 1-56592-350-2

Photoshop for the Web shows you how to use the world's most popular imaging software to create Web graphics and images that look great and download blazingly fast. The book is crammed full of step-by-step examples and real-world solutions from some of the country's hottest Web producers, including *HotWired*, *c\net*, *Discovery Online*, *Second Story*, *SFGate*, and more than 20 others.

Designing with Animation

By J. Scott Hamlin
1st Edition June 1998 (est.)
250 pages (est.), ISBN 1-56592-441-X

Designing with Animation treats the subject of Web animation with a level of sophistication that both meets the needs of today's demanding professionals and pushes the envelope for amateur animators. Topics include GIF animation, advanced animation techniques, seamless integration of animation, creative interactive animation with Java, JavaScript, and Macromedia Flash, vector-based and 3D animation, adding sound to animation, and animation techniques with Photoshop.

Web Navigation: Designing the User Experience

By Jennifer Fleming
1st Edition March 1998 (est.)
250 pages (est.), Includes CD-ROM
ISBN 1-56592-351-0

Web Navigation: Designing the User Experience offers the first in-depth look at designing web site navigation. Through case studies and designer interviews, a variety of approaches to navigation issues are explored. The book focuses on designing by purpose, with chapters on entertainment, shopping, identity, learning, information, and community sites. The accompanying CD-ROM includes a tour of selected sites, a "netography," and trial versions of popular software tools.

O'REILLY™

TO ORDER: **800-998-9938** • *order@oreilly.com* • *http://www.oreilly.com/*
OUR PRODUCTS ARE AVAILABLE AT A BOOKSTORE OR SOFTWARE STORE NEAR YOU.
FOR INFORMATION: **800-998-9938** • **707-829-0515** • *info@oreilly.com*

How to stay in touch with O'Reilly

1. Visit Our Award-Winning Web Site

http://www.oreilly.com/

★ "Top 100 Sites on the Web" —*PC Magazine*
★ "Top 5% Web sites" —*Point Communications*
★ "3-Star site" —*The McKinley Group*

Our web site contains a library of comprehensiveproduct information (including book excerpts and tables of contents), downloadable software, background articles, interviews with technology leaders, links to relevant sites, book cover art, and more. File us in your Bookmarks or Hotlist!

2. Join Our Email Mailing Lists

New Product Releases

To receive automatic email with brief descriptions of all new O'Reilly products as they are released, send email to:
listproc@online.oreilly.com
Put the following information in the first line of your message (*not* in the Subject field):
subscribe oreilly-news

O'Reilly Events

If you'd also like us to send information about trade show events, special promotions, and other O'Reilly events, send email to:
listproc@online.oreilly.com
Put the following information in the first line of your message (*not* in the Subject field):
subscribe oreilly-events

3. Get Examples from Our Books via FTP

There are two ways to access an archive of example files from our books:

Regular FTP

- ftp to:
  ftp.oreilly.com
  (login: anonymous
  password: your email address)
- Point your web browser to:
  ftp://ftp.oreilly.com/

FTPMAIL

- Send an email message to:
  ftpmail@online.oreilly.com
  (Write "help" in the message body)

4. Contact Us via Email

order@oreilly.com
To place a book or software order online. Good for North American and international customers.

subscriptions@oreilly.com
To place an order for any of our newsletters or periodicals.

books@oreilly.com
General questions about any of our books.

software@oreilly.com
For general questions and product information about our software. Check out O'Reilly Software Online at **http://software.oreilly.com/** for software and technical support information. Registered O'Reilly software users send your questions to: **website-support@oreilly.com**

cs@oreilly.com
For answers to problems regarding your order or our products.

booktech@oreilly.com
For book content technical questions or corrections.

proposals@oreilly.com
To submit new book or software proposals to our editors and product managers.

international@oreilly.com
For information about our international distributors or translation queries. For a list of our distributors outside of North America check out:
http://www.oreilly.com/www/order/country.html

O'Reilly & Associates, Inc.
101 Morris Street, Sebastopol, CA 95472 USA
TEL   707-829-0515 or 800-998-9938
         (6am to 5pm PST)
FAX   707-829-0104

Titles from O'Reilly

Please note that upcoming titles are displayed in italic.

WEB PROGRAMMING
Apache: The Definitive Guide
Building Your Own Web Conferences
Building Your Own Website
CGI Programming for the World Wide Web
Designing for the Web
HTML: The Definitive Guide, 2nd Ed.
JavaScript: The Definitive Guide, 2nd Ed.
Learning Perl
Programming Perl, 2nd Ed.
Mastering Regular Expressions
WebMaster in a Nutshell
Web Security & Commerce
Web Client Programming with Perl
World Wide Web Journal

USING THE INTERNET
Smileys
The Future Does Not Compute
The Whole Internet User's Guide & Catalog
The Whole Internet for Win 95
Using Email Effectively
Bandits on the Information Superhighway

JAVA SERIES
Exploring Java
Java AWT Reference
Java Fundamental Classes Reference
Java in a Nutshell
Java Language Reference, 2nd Edition
Java Network Programming
Java Threads
Java Virtual Machine

SOFTWARE
WebSite™ 1.1
WebSite Professional™
Building Your Own Web Conferences
WebBoard™
PolyForm™
Statisphere™

SONGLINE GUIDES
NetActivism   NetResearch
Net Law   NetSuccess
NetLearning   NetTravel
Net Lessons

SYSTEM ADMINISTRATION
Building Internet Firewalls
Computer Crime: A Crimefighter's Handbook
Computer Security Basics
DNS and BIND, 2nd Ed.
Essential System Administration, 2nd Ed.
Getting Connected: The Internet at 56K and Up
Linux Network Administrator's Guide
Managing Internet Information Services
Managing NFS and NIS
Networking Personal Computers with TCP/IP
Practical UNIX & Internet Security, 2nd Ed.
PGP: Pretty Good Privacy
sendmail, 2nd Ed.
sendmail Desktop Reference
System Performance Tuning
TCP/IP Network Administration
termcap & terminfo
Using & Managing UUCP
Volume 8: X Window System Administrator's Guide
Web Security & Commerce

UNIX
Exploring Expect
Learning VBScript
Learning GNU Emacs, 2nd Ed.
Learning the bash Shell
Learning the Korn Shell
Learning the UNIX Operating System
Learning the vi Editor
Linux in a Nutshell
Making TeX Work
Linux Multimedia Guide
Running Linux, 2nd Ed.
SCO UNIX in a Nutshell
sed & awk, 2nd Edition
Tcl/Tk Tools
UNIX in a Nutshell: System V Edition
UNIX Power Tools
Using csh & tsch
When You Can't Find Your UNIX System Administrator
Writing GNU Emacs Extensions

WEB REVIEW STUDIO SERIES
Gif Animation Studio
Shockwave Studio

WINDOWS
Dictionary of PC Hardware and Data Communications Terms
Inside the Windows 95 Registry
Inside the Windows 95 File System
Windows Annoyances
Windows NT File System Internals
Windows NT in a Nutshell

PROGRAMMING
Advanced Oracle PL/SQL Programming
Applying RCS and SCCS
C++: The Core Language
Checking C Programs with lint
DCE Security Programming
Distributing Applications Across DCE & Windows NT
Encyclopedia of Graphics File Formats, 2nd Ed.
Guide to Writing DCE Applications
lex & yacc
Managing Projects with make
Mastering Oracle Power Objects
Oracle Design: The Definitive Guide
Oracle Performance Tuning, 2nd Ed.
Oracle PL/SQL Programming
Porting UNIX Software
POSIX Programmer's Guide
POSIX.4: Programming for the Real World
Power Programming with RPC
Practical C Programming
Practical C++ Programming
Programming Python
Programming with curses
Programming with GNU Software
Pthreads Programming
Software Portability with imake, 2nd Ed.
Understanding DCE
Understanding Japanese Information Processing
UNIX Systems Programming for SVR4

BERKELEY 4.4 SOFTWARE DISTRIBUTION
4.4BSD System Manager's Manual
4.4BSD User's Reference Manual
4.4BSD User's Supplementary Documents
4.4BSD Programmer's Reference Manual
4.4BSD Programmer's Supplementary Documents
X Programming
Vol. 0: X Protocol Reference Manual
Vol. 1: Xlib Programming Manual
Vol. 2: Xlib Reference Manual
Vol. 3M: X Window System User's Guide, Motif Edition
Vol. 4M: X Toolkit Intrinsics Programming Manual, Motif Edition
Vol. 5: X Toolkit Intrinsics Reference Manual
Vol. 6A: Motif Programming Manual
Vol. 6B: Motif Reference Manual
Vol. 6C: Motif Tools
Vol. 8 : X Window System Administrator's Guide
Programmer's Supplement for Release 6
X User Tools
The X Window System in a Nutshell

CAREER & BUSINESS
Building a Successful Software Business
The Computer User's Survival Guide
Love Your Job!
Electronic Publishing on CD-ROM

TRAVEL
Travelers' Tales: Brazil
Travelers' Tales: Food
Travelers' Tales: France
Travelers' Tales: Gutsy Women
Travelers' Tales: India
Travelers' Tales: Mexico
Travelers' Tales: Paris
Travelers' Tales: San Francisco
Travelers' Tales: Spain
Travelers' Tales: Thailand
Travelers' Tales: A Woman's World

O'REILLY™

International Distributors

UK, Europe, Middle East and Northern Africa (except France, Germany, Switzerland, & Austria)

INQUIRIES
International Thomson Publishing Europe
Berkshire House
168-173 High Holborn
London WC1V 7AA
United Kingdom
Telephone: 44-171-497-1422
Fax: 44-171-497-1426
Email: itpint@itps.co.uk

ORDERS
International Thomson Publishing Services, Ltd.
Cheriton House, North Way
Andover, Hampshire SP10 5BE
United Kingdom
Telephone: 44-264-342-832 (UK)
Telephone: 44-264-342-806 (outside UK)
Fax: 44-264-364418 (UK)
Fax: 44-264-342761 (outside UK)
UK & Eire orders: itpuk@itps.co.uk
International orders: itpint@itps.co.uk

France

Editions Eyrolles
61 bd Saint-Germain
75240 Paris Cedex 05
France
Fax: 33-01-44-41-11-44

FRENCH LANGUAGE BOOKS
All countries except Canada
Telephone: 33-01-44-41-46-16
Email: geodif@eyrolles.com
English language books
Telephone: 33-01-44-41-11-87
Email: distribution@eyrolles.com

Germany, Switzerland, and Austria

INQUIRIES
O'Reilly Verlag
Balthasarstr. 81
D-50670 Köln
Germany
Telephone: 49-221-97-31-60-0
Fax: 49-221-97-31-60-8
Email: anfragen@oreilly.de

ORDERS
International Thomson Publishing
Königswinterer Straße 418
53227 Bonn, Germany
Telephone: 49-228-97024 0
Fax: 49-228-441342
Email: order@oreilly.de

Japan

O'Reilly Japan, Inc.
Kiyoshige Building 2F
12-Banchi, Sanei-cho
Shinjuku-ku
Tokyo 160-0008 Japan
Telephone: 81-3-3356-5227
Fax: 81-3-3356-5261
Email: kenji@oreilly.com

India

Computer Bookshop (India) PVT. Ltd.
190 Dr. D.N. Road, Fort
Bombay 400 001 India
Telephone: 91-22-207-0989
Fax: 91-22-262-3551
Email: cbsbom@giasbm01.vsnl.net.in

Hong Kong

City Discount Subscription Service Ltd.
Unit D, 3rd Floor, Yan's Tower
27 Wong Chuk Hang Road
Aberdeen, Hong Kong
Telephone: 852-2580-3539
Fax: 852-2580-6463
Email: citydis@ppn.com.hk

Korea

Hanbit Media, Inc.
Sonyoung Bldg. 202
Yeksam-dong 736-36
Kangnam-ku
Seoul, Korea
Telephone: 822-554-9610
Fax: 822-556-0363
Email: hant93@chollian.dacom.co.kr

Singapore, Malaysia, and Thailand

Addison Wesley Longman Singapore PTE Ltd.
25 First Lok Yang Road
Singapore 629734
Telephone: 65-268-2666
Fax: 65-268-7023
Email: daniel@longman.com.sg

Philippines

Mutual Books, Inc.
429-D Shaw Boulevard
Mandaluyong City, Metro
Manila, Philippines
Telephone: 632-725-7538
Fax: 632-721-3056
Email: mbikikog@mnl.sequel.net

China

Ron's DataCom Co., Ltd.
79 Dongwu Avenue
Dongxihu District
Wuhan 430040
China
Telephone: 86-27-3892568
Fax: 86-27-3222108
Email: hongfeng@public.wh.hb.cn

All Other Asian Countries

O'Reilly & Associates, Inc.
101 Morris Street
Sebastopol, CA 95472 USA
Telephone: 707-829-0515
Fax: 707-829-0104
Email: order@oreilly.com

Australia

WoodsLane Pty. Ltd.
7/5 Vuko Place, Warriewood NSW 2102
P.O. Box 935
Mona Vale NSW 2103
Australia
Telephone: 61-2-9970-5111
Fax: 61-2-9970-5002
Email: info@woodslane.com.au

New Zealand

Woodslane New Zealand Ltd.
21 Cooks Street (P.O. Box 575)
Waganui, New Zealand
Telephone: 64-6-347-6543
Fax: 64-6-345-4840
Email: info@woodslane.com.au

The Americas

McGraw-Hill Interamericana Editores, S.A. de C.V.
Cedro No. 512
Col. Atlampa 06450
Mexico, D.F.
Telephone: 52-5-541-3155
Fax: 52-5-541-4913
Email: mcgraw-hill@infosel.net.mx

South Africa

International Thomson Publishing
South Africa
Building 18, Constantia Park
138 Sixteenth Road
P.O. Box 2459
Halfway House, 1685 South Africa
Telephone: 27-11-805-4819
Fax: 27-11-805-3648

O'REILLY™